Writing at the Limit

Frontiers of Narrative

SERIES EDITOR
David Herman *Ohio State University*

Writing at the Limit

The Novel in the New Media Ecology

DANIEL PUNDAY

University of Nebraska Press | Lincoln and London

Part of the introduction, "The Rhetorical Construction of Media Ecologies," originally appeared as "From Synesthesia to Multimedia: How to Talk about New Media Narrative" in *New Narratives: Stories and Storytelling in the Digital Age*, edited by Ruth Page and Bronwen Thomas, and is reprinted by permission of the University of Nebraska Press (2011). Part of chapter 5, "Negotiating Public and Private Spaces," was originally published in the *electronic book review*.

∞

Library of Congress Cataloging-in-Publication Data

Punday, Daniel.
Writing at the limit: the novel in the new media ecology / Daniel Punday.
p. cm. — (Frontiers of narrative)
Includes bibliographical references and index.
ISBN 978-0-8032-3646-2 (hardback: alk. paper)
1. American fiction—21st century—History and criticism—Theory, etc. 2. Narration (Rhetoric) 3. Mass media and literature—United States—History—21st century. I. Title.
PS374.N285P86 2012
813'.609—dc23 2011043319

Set in Minion Pro.

For Carol, who keeps asking about things

Contents

Illustrations

Acknowledgments

I began this book during a sabbatical in 2007. I would like to thank the School of Liberal Arts and Social Sciences at Purdue University Calumet for that invaluable support. I tried out many of the ideas that came to form this project at several conferences, including the Modern Language Association's 2007 meeting in Chicago and the Narrative conferences in Ottawa (2006), Washington DC (2007), and Austin (2008). This book is a product of the inspiring scholarly community that I found at those meetings.

I would like to thank the readers for the University of Nebraska Press for their careful attention to this manuscript, and for their excellent suggestions for improvement. I would particularly like to recognize David Herman for providing extensive and incisive comments about the project when I first contacted the Press.

I would like to thank Marjorie Luesebrink for permission to use two images from *Califia* and J. R. Carpenter for permission to use an image from "Entre Ville." Both have been generous in responding to my queries about their work and providing feedback about my project. Encyclopedia Britannica has generously allowed me to use two images from *Compton's Interactive Encyclopedia*. I would also like to thank Paul Auster for permission to use two images from *City of Glass*. Typographical details in chapter 4 are from *Gravity's Rainbow* by Thomas Pynchon, © 1973 by Thomas Pynchon. Used by permission of Viking Penguin, a division of Penguin Group (USA) Inc.

A part of the introduction to this book is reprinted from "From Synesthesia to Multimedia: How to Talk about New Media Narrative," in *New Narratives: Stories and Storytelling in the Digital Age*, edited by Ruth Page and Bronwen Thomas, by permission of the University of Nebraska Press, 2011. A portion of chapter 5 was published in an earlier form as part of a review for the *electronic book review*, "Middle Spaces: Media and the Ethics of *Infinitely Demanding*."

Introduction

The Rhetorical Construction of Media Ecologies

Media in the Contemporary Novel

Novels written today spill over with references to other media—television, film, music, the Internet. The presence of such alternate media in the novel can be seen as simply a natural reflection of contemporary life. During an average day, most of us spend some time watching television, sending e-mail, reading the newspaper, and listening to the radio. Is it any wonder that these media make their way into the contemporary novel?

It's hard to shake the impression, however, that contemporary writers are doing more than simply adding media to their stories as part of the narrative furniture of contemporary life. Indeed, everywhere we look we find examples of novels that use other media as models for their own narratives. We might think about that most canonical of contemporary American novels, Thomas Pynchon's *Gravity's Rainbow*, which not only includes copious references to music and comic books but also ends with the audience in a movie theater, blurring the line between film and novel. Or we might recall Toni Morrison's *Jazz*, a novel that uses the metaphor of being trapped in the track of a record to describe the destiny of the narrative as a whole. Or Sherman Alexie's *Reservation Blues*, a novel that is both a story about music and a kind of narrative lament about dead-end life on the Spokane Indian reservation. Or even more tellingly, we might think of contemporary authors who have referenced many different media. Paul Auster, for example, writes a novel called *The Music of Chance* but then in another, *The Book of Illusions*, turns to silent film as a metaphor for his story. Ronald Sukenick writes the novel *Long Talking Bad Conditions Blues* as a kind of musical improvisation but then shifts to the film industry in his next novel, *Blown Away*.

I will discuss many of these novels in more detail, but at the outset let me be explicit about my claim: in a significant portion of contemporary fiction, references to other media are more that just backdrop or theme;

these other media, paradoxically, provide writers with a way of talking about what it means to write and read a print novel.[1]

Although these references are important and more than just part of the furniture of contemporary life, we should avoid going to the other extreme and seeing the contemporary novel as trapped in a life-and-death struggle with alternative media. It may seem natural that authors would try to push back against the forms of contemporary entertainment that seduce the attention of readers away from the pleasures of reading. Alvin Kernan articulates this attitude quite clearly:

> The problem for literature in all this is not just that interest in reading great books is diminishing as television watching increases, or even that reading of all kinds is becoming a lost skill in a time when more and more information is available on the electronic screen. At the deepest level the worldview of television is fundamentally at odds with the worldview of a literature based on the printed book. As television watching increases, therefore, and more and more people derive, quite unconsciously, their sense of reality and their existential situation in it from television, the assumptions about the world that have been identified with literature will become less and less plausible, and in time will become downright incredible. (147–48)

Kernan's complaint is part of a popular genre of books bewailing the passing of literary reading and the lost pleasure of curling up with a good novel. Probably the best known of these is Sven Birkerts's *Gutenberg Elegies*, but this is a trend in publishing that can be traced from Allan Bloom's alarmist assault on popular culture in *The Closing of the American Mind*, through more recent books like Victor Nell's *Lost in a Book* and Alberto Manguel's *A History of Reading*.[2]

And yet this interpretation of media in the contemporary novel, too, seems off the mark. Jazz was hardly a main competitor when Morrison published her novel in 1992, and while film may indeed compete with reading for leisure time, Auster's focus on a silent film star in *The Book of Illusions* seems a wildly indirect way to convince readers to pass up a summer blockbuster to commit themselves to a year of reading Proust.[3] Indeed, authors appear to reference media out of intellectual curiosity more than competition. For this reason, the medium that the novel probably had most reason to fear in the twentieth century—television—has a relatively small footprint in contemporary fiction. A few novels come to mind that use television as a setting or theme—I will discuss Pynchon's *Vineland*, DeLillo's *White Noise*, and Coover's short story "The Babysitter"—but such references are less common than those to music, a medium than seems to pose less of a threat to reading.

In this book I will unpack how contemporary novelists use references to other media. Although the majority of my examples are novels, I occasionally draw on short fiction. Indeed, writers often find it easier to explore the relationship between writing and other media in short fiction because they can experiment with forms without committing to the novel's hundreds of pages of length. In fact, many of the novels that we discuss push the limits of what we would normally consider novel-length writing, like Gangemi's *The Interceptor Pilot* (127 whitespace-heavy pages) or Burroughs's *Blade Runner* (74 pages). Throughout, I refer to these narratives as "media novels" or "media stories." I recognize that this term is flawed. After all, every novel already is engaged in negotiating with the medium of print. From the very beginning, the novel has used elements of the medium beyond the words themselves, like illustrations and typographical ornamentation.[4] Although the term *media novel* suggests some kind of futuristic multimedia narrative that we view on a computer, I use this term in a rather limited and even bland way simply to describe novels in which media other than writing appear as a thematic or structural element. My references to the *media novel*, in other words, function as shorthand for the more precise but unwieldy *novels about media other than writing*. Analyzing these media novels is important not just because it helps us to understand writing's relationship to other media—certainly a fraught and anxious topic for novelists, even if that anxiety is not translated directly into narratives about evil television producers or manipulative video game designers. It is important because the fusion of media has been a promise frequently made by consumer electronics over the last twenty-five years. If the age of multimedia is upon us, then the way that these novelists handle references to multiple media in their own narratives will tell us something about the relevance of writing when so many new forms promise to supplement print with video, audio, and a variety of virtual experiences. Indeed, I suggest that contemporary novelists are searching for a model of writing's relationship to other media different from current technological dreams of endless media supplements: if a DVD containing a film is good, then a DVD containing a film and audio commentary is better, and adding production stills or an on-screen game is better still. Over the course of this book, I describe an aesthetics for the contemporary novel that embraces its media limits rather than seeking to supplement or escape them through appeals to other media.

In framing the contemporary novel's references to other media as part of a positive aesthetics and purpose for writing today, I depart from how critics usually discuss the novel's relationship to other media. Most work on the novel's relationship with other media has focused on those media with which it has an adversarial relationship. Kathleen Fitzpatrick's *The Anxiety of Obsolescence: The American Novel in the Age of Television* analyzes the representation of television and the imagery of the "crisis" of the novel. Although I discuss some novels concerned with television, I treat television here as simply one of many media that contemporary novelists use to define what it means to write a novel today. Television, in this regard, plays a role similar to music, film, and painting. Although I avoid implying a life-and-death battle between the novel and some other threatening medium, it is important to recognize that the media novels discussed in this book generally work by contrast—setting the novel against another medium and then exploring their differences. As a consequence, we avoid another trend within criticism on the novel's relationship to media: the claim that media differences have faded and that novels have become "media assemblages." In *Information Multiplicity: American Fiction in the Age of Media Saturation*, John Johnston offers this characterization, arguing that "instead of the separability of media, we now find a generalized 'culture medium'" (5). I argue quite strenuously against the idea that media differences are fading and that we are entering a period of generalized "multimedia." In fact, this understanding of the current moment as a period without media differences is the foil against which the media novels analyzed here will operate.

My approach to media in the contemporary novel requires, then, a flexible understanding of *medium* and the environment in which the novel is written, distributed, and read. The language of anxiety that Fitzpatrick is analyzing and critiquing defines the novel as a passive victim of an environment larger than itself. Instead, I treat the novel as an active agent within the media environment—not merely free to respond to its circumstances but able to help define the environment itself. Consequently, we need an understanding of the media environment that is flexible, open to change, and marked by the agency of its participants. Defining the media environment as open to change also works against the belief that there is any simple or objective basis on which media can be defined and differentiated from each other. We need a definition of a medium that can account for why, for example, the difference between *novel* and *news*, so obvious to us today, once seemed vague or nonexistent.[5] As the novel negotiates its place within the contemporary media environment with references to music, painting, and television, we are challenged to understand how media configurations can change over time. My approach below involves two crucial terms: the *media environment* and the nature of a *medium* itself.

System, Field, and Ecology

There are three principle metaphors for discussing the interaction between different media within any particular cultural moment. Many critics have referred to media as forming a *system*. As Bonnie Nardi and Vicki O'Day remark, at the heart of much interest today in media relations is a "broad scope of vision and a deep concern about large-scale social and technical systems" (33). Such systems seem to be first and foremost autonomous. Nardi and O'Day cite Jacques Ellul as an example of such an account of media and technology: Ellul claims that *technique*, as "a cultural mindset in which pure, unadulterated efficiency is the dominant human value, . . . has fashioned an omnivorous world which obeys its laws and which has renounced all tradition" (34, 35).

Theodor Adorno's *The Culture Industry* offers a particularly stark analysis of the American media system in the middle of the twentieth century. Adorno scathingly describes American popular music as distracting the masses from real art. For him, popular music mimics aesthetic experience without actually providing it: "In one of his essays, Aldous Huxley has raised the question of who, in a place of amusement, is really being amused. With the same justice, it can be asked whom music for entertainment still entertains. Rather, it seems to complement the reduction of people to silence, the dying out of speech as expression, the inability to communicate at all. It inhabits the pockets of silence that develop between people moulded by anxiety, work and undemanding docility" (30).

Popular amusement here is merely a simulacrum of pleasure, in which consumers participate, robotlike, because contemporary culture demands it. This amusement depends on misrecognition, the ability of consumers to deny what they are seeing and hearing and behave as if they were experiencing something quite different: "People have learned to deny their attention to what they are hearing even while listening to it" (30). Adorno concludes that the "passivity of the masses . . . makes the consumption of light music contradict the objective interest of those who consume it" (34).

Adorno's explanation of the cause of this change is quite direct: capitalism benefits by reducing freedom and transforming music from resistance to commodity: "In capitalist times, the traditional anti-mythological ferments of music conspire against freedom, as whose allies they were once proscribed. The representatives of the opposition to the authoritarian schema become witnesses to the authority of commercial success. The delight in the moment and the gay façade becomes an excuse for absolving the listener from thought of the whole, whose claim is comprised in proper listening. The listener is converted, along his line of least resistance, into the acquiescent purchaser" (32).

Consumers are forced to "capitulate before the superior power of the advertised stuff and purchase spiritual peace by making the imposed goods literally its own thing" (47–48). Adorno describes a heavily integrated system that transforms culture—it alters "the basic conditions of the relation between art and society" (39). Indeed, Adorno is even more direct in explaining this wholesale systematic transformation when he claims that "mass culture is an organized mania for connecting everything to everything else, a totality of public secrets" (83). The culture industry forms a whole system of "enforced solidarity" (84) that defines the nature of our participation in contemporary culture as a whole. Although the objects of Adorno's scorn are not the first that come to mind as examples of media hegemony today, it is difficult to deny that a "culture industry" operates within America. Indeed, corporations have pursued synergies between different media in marketing what once would have been simply called a *song* or a *story*. Few films with any appeal to children arrive in the movie theater without accompanying toys, books, and video games appearing in the store. It is a testament to the prevalence of the culture industry that the Harry Potter books, announced so often in the popular press as heralding the resurgence of reading, are routinely turned into movies, toys, and video games. What is especially relevant about Adorno's account is the image that he offers of an overarching and all-encompassing *system* according to which the media within a culture are organized.

The systemic view of media relations, then, locates agency elsewhere than in the creators or users of particular media. We have already seen that the audience for music is compelled to behave as consumers. Adorno is particularly eager to emphasize that the culture industry does not demand passivity but instead fosters a particular kind of vapid agency. Adorno describes commodified play as "duty" and explains that this economy "wipes out the trace of freedom in it" (57). It is this transformation of audience activity that seems to be particularly important to Adorno. He notes,

> Regressive listeners have key points in common with the man who must kill time because he has nothing else on which to vent his aggression, and with the casual labourer. To make oneself a jazz expert or hang over the radio all day, one must have much free time and little freedom. . . . The new listeners resemble the mechanics who are simultaneously specialized and capable of applying their special skills to unexpected places outside their skilled trades. But this despecialization only seems to help them out of the system. The more easily they meet the demands of the day, the more rigidly they are subordinated to that system. (55)

This passage encapsulates Adorno's critique, since it describes a particular form of activity without genuine agency. Adorno's own characterization of the culture industry is strangely vague about who, if anyone, is actually manipulating these media. For this reason, the systemic view of media relations is often coupled with a kind of technological determinism. In this way of thinking, new technology produces new ways of communicating, thus changing the gestalt of media at any one time. This account does not rely on some kind of corporate agency that manipulates consumers consciously, but instead implies that the whole process of technological change is beyond the control of anyone. This is what Ursula Heise means when she describes "the technological determinism that often surfaces when media are understood as an autonomously evolving system" (166). Such determinism was certainly an element of Marshall McLuhan's influential early attempts to describe the changing conditions of media in the twentieth century: "If a new technology extends one or more of our senses outside us into the social world, then new ratios among all of our senses will occur in that particular culture" (41). Among others, Raymond Williams has taken exception to the simplistic causality that McLuhan assumes in his description of media changes: "If the effect of the medium is the same, whoever controls or uses it, and whatever apparent content he may try to insert, then we can forget ordinary political and cultural argument and let the technology run itself" (*Television*, 131).

Neil Postman is a particularly clear spokesman for the technological determinism implicit in the systemic view of media relations. In *Technopoly*, Postman distinguishes tool-using cultures, technocracies, and technopolies (22). Of the first, Postman notes "the main characteristic of all tool-using cultures is that their tools were largely invented to do two things: to solve specific and urgent problems of physical life, such as in the use of waterpower, windmills, and the heavy-wheeled plow; or to serve the symbolic world of art, politics, myth, ritual, and religion, as in the construction of castles and cathedrals and the development of the mechanical clock" (23). According to Postman, what differentiates the tool-using culture from technocracy is the relation between technology and ideology: in the former, tools "are not intruders. They are integrated into the culture in ways that do not pose significant contradictions to its world-view," especially its spiritual beliefs (25). In technocracy, in contrast, "everything must give way, in some degree, to their [tools'] development. The social and symbolic worlds become increasingly subject to the requirements of that development. Tools are not integrated into culture; they attack the culture. They bid to *become* the culture" (28), in that technology promises to solve all human problems by removing questions of spirituality and belief (31). Technopoly is simply a way to describe what happens when this evolution is taken further, and the healthy if uneasy tension between technology and traditional culture is allowed to collapse. In contrast to the "two distinct thought-worlds" that "rubb[ed] against each other in nineteenth-century America," with the rise of Technopoly, one of those thought-worlds disappears. Technopoly eliminates alternatives to itself in precisely the way Aldous Huxley outlined in *Brave New World*. It does not make them illegal. It does not make them immoral. It does not even make them unpopular. It makes them invisible and therefore irrelevant. And it does so by redefining what we mean by religion, by art, by family, by politics, by history, by truth, by privacy, by intelligence, so that our definitions fit its new requirements. Technopoly, in other words, is totalitarian technocracy. (48)

Here is a particularly clear instance of the systemic view of media and its power to organize our lives and ways of thinking.

An alternative model of media relations, that of *field*, is provided by Pierre Bourdieu in his sociological work on the struggle between different groups to claim symbolic capital. In *The Rules of Art*, Bourdieu imagines contemporary culture as a kind of metaphorical field in which individuals take positions and struggle against each other to control power and legitimacy:

At each moment in time, in any field of struggle whatsoever (the whole social field, field of power, field of cultural production, literary field, etc.), agents and institutions engaged in the game are simultaneously contemporaries and temporally discordant. *The field of the present* is merely another name for the field of struggle (as shown by the fact that an author of the past is present to the exact extent that he is still at stake). Contemporaneity as presence in the same present only exists in practice *in the struggle* that *synchronizes* discordant times or, rather, agents and institutions separated by time and in relation to time. (158)

Here even temporal relationships—the "history of artistic movements since the end of the nineteenth century" (158)—are translated into a struggle within a synchronic "field" for cultural dominance. It is easy to understand how this model could be applied to media relations: watching television, reading fiction, and playing video games could be seen as struggling against each other to capture both cultural and economic capital. Although Bourdieu shares Adorno's materialist approach to culture and artistic production, it is clear that he has a fundamentally different understanding of the agency of participants. Indeed, Bourdieu imagines actors as highly aware and consciously participating in these symbolic struggles. Actors did not create the field itself, but they understand the field and behave in economically and culturally rational ways to make the best of the possibilities of that field. This is quite a contrast to Adorno's account of the culture industry, where the masses are literally tricked into thinking that "enjoyment" is enjoyable.

This account of culture as a symbolic field obviously produces a very different way of thinking about media relations. In *The Anxiety of Obsolescence*, Kathleen Fitzpatrick analyzes the rhetoric of the "death" of print: "What all these cultural critics have in common, by and large, is print, and the belief that Gutenberg's medium and the literature that it has made possible must be saved from twentieth-century technologies—among which they number television, of course, but also film and the Internet—that threaten to end more than five hundred years of print's dominance in Western culture and drive it into obsolescence" (1). Among the works that Fitzpatrick cites is Sven Birkerts's *The Gutenberg Elegies: The Fate of Reading in an Electronic Age*, a book whose subtitle nicely captures this sense of anxiety and change. In contrast to the system-based account of media relations, the field model describes a cultural space where media vie with each other. In the case of Birkerts's book, this conflict produces a story of loss: "As the world hurtles on toward its mysterious rendezvous, the old act of slowly reading a serious book becomes an elegiac exercise. As we ponder that act, profound questions must arise about our avowedly humanistic values, about spiritual verses material concerns, and about subjectivity itself" (6).

The field and the system models could not be less alike, but there is nonetheless enough overlap that some accounts of media relations manage to move between the two. Friedrich Kittler's influential theory of "discourse networks" implies that the ratio between media changes without any conscious choice or effort on the part of artists. And yet in other places Kittler recognizes that individual writers engage with different media with an understanding of a field of possibilities. He notes that to counter competition from film, literature has two options. First, it can accept that movies "took the place of the fantasy of the library" and produce screenplays. According to Kittler, literature's other option is to reject them, along with the imaginary and real aspects of discourse to which they cater, and which have become the province of popular writers. Because "kitsch will never be eliminated from humanity," one group of writers renounces it. After 1900 a high literature develops in which "the word" becomes something "too conspicuous," that is, it becomes a purely differential signifier. Once imaginary effects and real inscription have been renounced, what remains are the rituals of the symbolic. These rituals take into account neither the reaction thresholds of people nor the support of Nature. "Letters of the alphabet do not occur in nature." Words as literal anti-nature, literature as word art, the relation between both as material equality—this is their constellation in the purest art for art's sake and in the most daring games of the avant-garde. Since December 28, 1895, there has been one infallible criterion for high literature: it cannot be filmed. (*Discourse Networks*, 248)

In this regard, the movement toward the concrete word on the page is a straightforward attempt to embrace what other media cannot replicate. The reason why Kittler seems to be able to move between two antithetical accounts of contemporary media relations is because his understanding of the macro-conditions for media relations is systemic while his understanding of the local conditions in which individual writers operate is largely based on the field model. It may be that Kittler's work has been so influential in part because he has brought together these two seemingly competing models of media relations.

Out of this opposition between the system and field models of media relations has emerged a complex third model, the media *ecology*. It has been given so many definitions that it could be said to encompass both models already offered. Matthew Fuller notes that the term "is used and in circulation in a number of ways" and consequently defines it as a "crossroads" of multiple uses (2). Nardi and O'Day introduce the term *ecology* as a way to straddle the opposition between several competing metaphors: "We introduce the concept of the information ecology in order to focus attention on relationships involving tools and people and their practices. We want to travel beyond the dominant image of the tool metaphor, an image of a single person and his or her interactions with technology. And we want to capture a notion of locality that is missing from the system view" (50). The ecology model is frequently used to correct limitations in the previous metaphors. As Heise remarks, "The concept of 'media ecology' relies on a metaphorical transfer that media theorists took over from urban sociology, where 'human ecology' had in its turn developed out of translation of categories from biological ecology" (149). This highly indirect and metaphorical link means that the term is open to many different interpretations. Some use the term *media ecology* to refer simply to the field and system models that I have already discussed. Joseph Tabbi and Michael Wutz, for example, describe a struggle between media that will remind us a good deal of Bourdieu's field model: "Modern narratives . . . provide evidence of this changing media ecology, when writing and written narrative in general were displaced from their erstwhile centrality and forced to compete with gramophones, kinetoscopes and their technologically more sophisticated successors in the marketplace of inscription" (4). Other critics sometimes use the term as part of the system model of media relations; Fuller, for example, equates Postman's work with an "uncomplicated but rather more spiritually troubled technological determinism" that is one interpretation of media ecology (3).

Such uses of the term aside, referring to media relations as an ecology promises to overcome limitations of the system and field models in three important ways. First, the language of media ecologies emphasizes multiple relations among media at any one time. Often the system model can imply that a single force organizes the whole media landscape, while the field model can reduce all relations to a matter of simple competition. In contrast, as Heise notes, "ecology is associated with a mode of thinking that emphasizes multiple connections between simultaneously occurring phenomena and leads to a perception of cultural and social processes as a unified totality" (154). The ecology metaphor reflects the desire to find more sophisticated ways to talk about tensions between media: "We need more flexible *models* that allow us to investigate the interactions between different technologies and practices through time" (Winthrop-Young and Wutz, 6). Such multiple relations also produce an account of media changes that is considerably more complex than what we would expect from either the system or field model of media relations. In contrast to Birkerts's elegy for the falling fortunes of print, Tabbi and Wutz offer a more hopeful description of the place of print in what they call the "new media ecology": "Drawing on current research into the 'materiality' of literature and looking around at new forms of digital and electronic textuality, the contributors to this book seek to identify correspondent narrative forms and to reclaim a tradition of material self-awareness that has been a part of the novel all along. Their hopeful premise is that, as the scene of writing changes, the book will not be left behind—but neither will it be quite the same in its new context" (2). Tabbi and Wutz claim that shifts in the role of one medium within a whole cultural ecology do not just shuffle the prominence of different media; they also suppress or emphasize qualities that have always been implicit within those media. For example, the rise of online communication has made fan culture considerably easier to foster, thus making secondary, fan-created material more important to the original source. Thus fan sites can include fiction that extends the narratives in different ways. Many of these alternate narratives and games have long been part of our experience of the source material—the ability to imagine what happens after the end of a beloved book—but online communication has made these secondary uses more important.

Second, appeals to media ecologies frequently attempt to move away from high-level and very abstract explanations of the involvement of media in everyday life. The turn to an ecology is often an attempt to emphasize the particular locations in which these broad systematic tensions can be observed. Heise remarks, "Based on the assumption that media are not mere tools that humans use, but rather constitute environments within which they move and that shape the structure of their perceptions, their forms of discourse, and their social behavior patterns, ecology typically focuses on how these structures change with the introduction of new communication technologies" (151). Let us take the example of a particularly contemporary phenomenon that has redefined an earlier leisure activity: fantasy sports leagues. Such leagues emerged in the 1980s and involve players creating fictional teams by using real-life athletes (American football and baseball are especially popular); fictional games between players are won and lost based on the real-life accomplishments of these athletes. Approached from the perspective of the media ecology, we can say that people participate in fantasy sports leagues for a lot of reasons— some having to do directly with the instantaneous availability of statistics from the game, others with shifting social relationships as families and team loyalties are more geographically dispersed, and still others with the changing role of free agency in most professional sports—and we should not expect any one explanation to account for their popularity. In turn, the popularity of these leagues affects media: box scores in the daily newspaper become more important, but the delay between game and print is less tolerable in the age of electronic communication. The localism implicit in the concept of the media ecology is the reason why I have chosen to focus this book on the contemporary U.S. novel and forego the benefits of drawing on contemporary novels dealing with media written in other countries. Television, film, and music have different relations within the U.S. media ecology than they do in other countries because of their historical origins and cultural associations, and ultimately we will see a more coherent picture of the novel today if we remain focused on a single national literature.

Finally, the turn to the language of ecology also presents the agency of those operating within this environment in a more nuanced way. While the system model tends to dismiss any agency on the part of artists and consumers, the field model makes them unnaturally self-aware and locked in an existential struggle. The language of ecology, conversely, addresses all activities, both real and conditioned by circumstances. As Nardi and O'Day remark, "We define an information ecology to be a system of people, practices, values, and technologies in a particular local environment. In information ecologies, the spotlight is not on technology, but on human activities that are served by technology" (49). Heise agrees, praising "this tendency to envision ecology as a concept that makes room for theorizing human agency and values" (159). Although ecology seems to imply agency, it also recognizes that much of this activity happens without complete awareness on the part of the participants: "Such technologies form a cultural environment that most of its inhabitants take for granted, but that nevertheless shapes their cognitive possibilities and social behavior in significant ways" (157). For my own purposes, the ecology metaphor provides a nuanced image of novelists consciously engaged with media without fully controlling their circumstances.

The Rhetorical Organization of the Media Ecology

The concept of the media ecology offers us, then, a flexible understanding of the environment in which the novel functions today. As I noted earlier, in addition to this flexible understanding of the contemporary media environment, we also need a way to define *medium* itself that recognizes how incredibly fluid and complex the lines between media are.

Our characterization of the essential media qualities of any particular form of representation can be very subjective. At times, we seem to be willfully ignoring qualities of books, paintings, and songs. After all, printed texts have always had a visual quality, since they depend not just on the ideas conveyed by the words themselves, but on qualities of print, ink, typeface, and binding. Usually these aesthetic qualities are allowed to remain in the background, but some works shock us with their materiality—because of accidental damage to the text, because they obey a different aesthetic principle (like handwriting and illumination in manuscript copying), or because of self-conscious experimentation with the text that we see in modernist and postmodernist concrete poetry. We could say that the "stuff" necessary to articulate a sophisticated explanation of the visual elements of a book is already implicit in every book but generally ignored. And if the raw material for cross-media comparisons is already there in individual texts, so is it in our everyday language. John Gage notes,

> The experience of colour in the West has always been closely interwoven with the experience of music. In ancient Greece, one kind of musical scale (*genos*), introduced by Plato's friend Archytas of Tarentum in the fourth century BC, was named "chromatic." It was divided into semi-tones and was regarded as simply "colouring" its two neighbouring scales, the diatonic (divided into full tones) and the enharmonic (divided into quarter-tones). Some Greek theorists considered "colour" (*chrōia*) to be a quality of sound itself, together with pitch and duration; it may have been thought akin to what we now describe as timbre. (227)

Cross-media comparisons such as the "chromatic" quality of a scale are among the metaphors that we use in common language as well as in aesthetic analysis: we describe a painting as *dynamic*, a novel as *spatial*, or the themes of a song in *tension*. These analogies are part of art history. As Wendy Steiner remarks, "The fact that the analogy of painting to literature has a history at all is a function of the nature of analogies. Any similarity, as the theoreticians stress, depends on concurrent dissimilarities" (2). Steiner goes on to note that these metaphors can often play a role in creating (or responding to) the hierarchy of arts at any particular time: "Literature is so often compared to painting, I believe, because painting has stood as the paradigmatic 'mirror of reality'; the 'sister arts' analogy thus permits literature as well to be considered an icon of reality rather than a mere conventional means of referring to it. The need to discover the mimetic potential in literature has been the underlying motivation for the long history of critical comparisons of the two arts. When the motivation disappears, as it did largely during the romantic period, so does the comparison" (1–2). Steiner makes clear that no comparison between two media is natural or inevitable—not in everyday language, in a particular work, or in a whole cultural moment.

Thus far I have suggested that the ecology metaphor for describing media relations can be a powerful way to escape the problems with both the field and system accounts, but Steiner's observation also points out a problem with the ecology metaphor: it can seem natural and inevitable. This is certainly the case when McLuhan uses the term in *The Gutenberg Galaxy*: "My suggestion is that cultural ecology has a reasonably stable base in the human sensorium, and that any extension of the sensorium by technological dilation has a quite appreciable effect in setting up new ratios or proportions among all the senses" (35). The ecology metaphor's very physical and natural implications, coupled with its sources in scientific language, seem to imply that it is more than metaphorical. I suggest instead that a media ecology is always a rhetorical construction. There are, of course, material causes and practical relations that cannot be denied, but our sense that we are participating in an ecology is a way of giving imaginative meaning to these material causes. This is especially the case at the level of the individual work, which engages in the media ecology to the extent that it makes sense of these media relations and provides some aesthetic, political, or technological justification for them.

Let me provide an example, borrowed from another critic, of the sort of rhetorical shaping of material conditions that I am trying to describe. Lawrence Rainey has argued that modernist authors found that they could not support their writing through traditional publishing income and instead needed to generate other sources of support. For example: "Though he had generally received warm reviews of his early verse," Ezra Pound "soon learned that his writings could scarcely earn a sufficient income" (15) and instead found patronage support from Margaret Cravens.

The publication of James Joyce's *Ulysses* is an especially significant and well-known example of the economics that structured modernist literary production. Confronted by the legal difficulties that he faced from the putative obscenity of the work, Joyce recognized the possibilities of a different method of publication that limited the initial print run to one thousand copies, and made the book itself into an investment. In charging the equivalent of a week's salary for the book (64), Joyce was essentially fostering a more dispersed group of "patron-investors" drawn from the middle class instead of finding a single aristocratic patron (39). These material conditions obviously transform the nature of the book as an artistic and economic object, making the purchase of a first edition of *Ulysses* the equivalent of buying a painting whose value will increase as the artist's reputation grows. What seems to me especially important, however, is that this transformation of the material conditions of publishing Joyce's novel does not simply *cause* the novel to take on a different role within the media ecology. Instead, the initial pitch to the potential buyers of *Ulysses* is first and foremost a rhetorical act designed to *construct* the media ecology in a way that makes buying the novel at such a high price rational. The rhetorical construction of this media ecology is implicit within the conventional account of the publication of the novel as a heroic act: "Joyce and [publisher Sylvia] Beach are cast as heroic figures who have succeeded despite a benighted legal system, philistine publishers, and a hostile or indifferent public; and their efforts are readily appreciated by a small yet discerning circle of readers whose insight, in the course of many years, is gradually corroborated by critics and scholars, as the book achieves canonical status" (42–43). This story, told to potential buyers, essentially redefines the relationship between book and buyer, and transforms the place of the novel within the media ecology, associating it with visual art.[6] Thus, although the media ecology that arises around the novel at this time is no doubt in one sense a product of the changing material conditions in publication and readership, that ecology is also a rhetorical construction deployed for practical purposes by author and critic, publisher and buyer.

Aesthetic theories in part provide a rhetorical explanation for the material conditions of their texts; these theories, in turn, work to define the "field" in which various media will encounter each other as part of a particular culture's ecology. This way of thinking about the conceptual structures that help to organize a media ecology rhetorically is especially important as we return to our subject: references to other media within the contemporary novel. These novels are only loosely and occasionally bound by the material conditions that shape media relations in the culture in general. For example, the growing acceptance of digital photography is expected to have a profound influence on the ability of small-budget film-makers to shoot and edit their films; many have predicted a new golden age of independent film as digital cameras become less expensive. This material shift, however, is unlikely to have a direct influence on the way the novel can use films. Of course, this material shift *could* influence the use that novels make of film, but that influence will be mediated through the rhetorical meaning given to these material changes. For example, most uses of film in the contemporary novel tend to associate the me-dium with the studio system and to treat it as a highly compromised form of artistic expression. This is the case in Ronald Sukenick's *Blown Away* and Paul Auster's *The Book of Illusions*. In contrast, comic-book writing is often seen as underground and, because it is relatively low-tech, free from entanglements in the corporate publishing business. This is the case in Abraham Rodriguez's *The Buddha Book*, as well as Susan Daitch's *The Colorist* and Tom De Haven's *Dugan Under Ground*. If the material condi-tions for film production change, obviously we might see references to this medium as outsider art. But that shift will occur not because the material conditions themselves change but because the cultural understanding of the medium changes. More importantly, that shift in the cultural under-standing of the medium will change how media are differentiated from each other in the media ecology. Currently, comparisons between comic books and films tend to be organized conceptually on the basis of the technical sophistication of their production. If this difference disappears, the rhetorical interpretation of the ecology will have to develop some other conceptual basis for organizing these two media.

Contemporary novels work like aesthetic theories when they make references to other media. These references will be bound more by the conceptual terms that organize them and give meaning to material con-ditions, and less by the material conditions themselves, since—to state the obvious—its costs nothing to add an elaborate film production to a novel but quite a lot to create one in real life. The exception to this is, of course, contemporary novels that make use of actual elements drawn from other media. This would include inserted images and typographical manipulation.[7] These kinds of direct material influences are tangential to my project, because I want to focus on the way that *references* to other media (rather than the *use* of those media) engage in the conceptual structures that help to organize rhetorically the meaning of the contemporary media ecology. For that reason, the media novels that I discuss are usually *about* other media—as a plot or setting element, or even borrowing some structural elements from these other media—rather than actually including other media like photography, film, or sound.

Synesthesia, Intermedia, and Multimedia

The terms used to relate and compare media—both within a whole cultural ecology as well as in a particular novel—are constructed rhetorically. Attention to these terms has been sorely lacking in criticism on contemporary works that draw on several media. Indeed, the current celebration of "multimedia" as a category suggests why attention to the rhetorical framing of media relations is so important. Multimedia is as much an appeal to consumers as an aesthetic category. Writing in 1999, Frank Borchardt turned to the concept of multimedia essentially as a last resort: "Until such time as preconceptions from the antecedent technologies are abandoned, until such time as the Wagnerian or a comparable metaphor can address the complex interrelations of the constituent media, it will probably be necessary to investigate the components one at a time—e.g., video independent of audio" (26). Although other terms have recently emerged to characterize such digital works—including the terms *new media* and, especially, *multimodal representation*—the somewhat dated term *multimedia* reminds us of the historical origins and specific rhetorical work that any of these characterizations of media perform. The term multimedia is used far more often in advertising to pitch a new consumer electronic item (promising to combine music, film, television, and Internet material) or a package of media content, often a supplement updating a more traditional media product. Thus today a music CD or film DVD may include some "multimedia extras" such as interactive games, music videos (for audio CDs), production stills (for DVDs), and so on.

When the term multimedia is explored by critics, it is often structured rhetorically in terms of a shift toward digital culture. Peter Lunenfeld makes this point: "It is the capacity of the electronic computer to encode a vast variety of information digitally that has given it such a central place within contemporary culture. As all manner of representational systems are recast as digital information, then all can be stored, accessed, and controlled by the same equipment. This is the true basis of the 'multi-media' revolution" (xvi). Like many early accounts of new media, Lunenfeld overstates its revolutionary quality, but the dream of a complete transformation of the media ecology is alive and well. Friedrich Kittler opens *Gramophone, Film, Typewriter* with such a totalizing vision:

> *Optical fiber networks.* People will be hooked to an information channel that can be used for any medium—for the first time in history, or for its end. Once movies and music, phone calls and texts reach households via optical fiber cables, the formerly distinct media of television, radio, telephone, and mail converge, standardized by transmission frequencies and bit format. . . . Before the end, something is coming to an end. The generalized digitization of channels and information erases the differences among individual media. Sound and image, voice and text are reduced to surface effects, known to consumers as interface. (1)

Kittler here offers up multimedia as the end of media, a point at which a media ecology disappears into some new seamless space—what Rosalind Krauss calls "the post-medium condition." Even for those critics who have not imagined a future without media, most have seen multimedia less as a distinct organization of the media landscape, and more as a way of revealing the fundamental condition of all media landscapes. In fact, I will frequently return to Kittler's image of a future without media as an alternate understanding of the contemporary media ecology against which the novels that I discuss are working.

We need to consider, instead, how such multimedia works organize and justify the mixture of media rhetorically. The failure to do so is a key limitation of Jay David Bolter and Richard Grusin's influential book *Remediation*. Their definition of this central term is concise: "We call the representation of one medium in another *remediation*" (45). They contrast two ways of responding to previous media. *Hypermedia* is best exemplified by the windowed interface of personal computers, which "does not attempt to unify the space around any one point of view. Instead, each text window defines its own verbal, each graphic window its own visual, point of view" (33). This is not the only form that hypermediated space can take; Bolter and Grusin cite the mixture of images and text in the modern newspaper, as well as the "'multimediated' spaces of Dutch painting, medieval cathedrals, and illuminated manuscripts" (31). In contrast to works like this that create a mosaic of different media, Bolter and Grusin offer *immediacy*, "whose purpose is to disappear" (21). Their primary example is the interface-less structure of virtual reality games, but most photography and realistic painting also falls into this category. It would seem that hypermedia embraces remediation, while immediacy avoids engaging with previous media, but Bolter and Grusin disagree: "It is easy to see that hypermedia applications are always explicit acts of remediation: they import earlier media into digital space in order to critique and refashion them. However, digital media that strive for transparency and immediacy (such as immersive virtual reality and virtual games) also remediate. Hypermedia and transparent media are opposite manifestations of the same desire: the desire to get past the limits of representation and to achieve the real" (53).

The terms that Bolter and Grusin offer here have had a broad influence on new media theory, giving critics a powerful way to discuss the relationship between user interface and media ecology. The danger of this theory, however, is that it universalizes *one* way of imagining the media ecology. When Lessing opposes spatial and temporal forms of art, he is offering a universal statement that constructs a media ecology, but doing so for very specific historical reasons. The same is true of *Remediation*. Bolter and Grusin in fact flirt with the idea that this three-term theory is universal, before distancing themselves from that claim: "It would seem, then, that *all* mediation is remediation. We are not claiming this as an a priori truth, but rather arguing that at this extended historical moment, all current media function as remediators, and that remediation offers us a means of interpreting the work of earlier media as well. Our culture conceives of each medium or constellation of media as it responds to, redeploys, competes with, and reforms other media" (55). This passage limits the application of remediation to "our culture" but then also suggests that the tools provided by the term can be used as a way of "interpreting the work of earlier media as well." Indeed, Bolter and Grusin offer no alternative definition of media relations, leaving us with the impression that remediation is the only game in town. Remediation reflects an attempt to solve a problem that is particularly compelling in the contemporary media environment: how do we make sense of works (especially digital works) that mix together so many different, seemingly independent media? The limitation of this theory, like other aesthetic theories of the past, is that it offers a universal, trans-historical opposition as a way to explain that media relation.

Remediation's articulation of the media ecology is, of course, only one of many possible ways to frame media relations rhetorically. Let us consider two fairly recent and well-known cases: *synesthesia* and *intermedia*.

Synesthesia can refer to a psychological condition in which a person appears to "see" sound or "hear" color: "Synesthesia is an *involuntary* joining in which the real information of one sense is accompanied by a perception in another sense. In addition to being involuntary, this additional perception is regarded by the synesthete as real, often outside of the body, instead of imagined in the mind's eye" (Cytowic, 1). Synesthesia's role in literary and art history is, however, narrower. As an aesthetic principle, synesthesia is usually traced back to nineteenth-century French symbolist poets. Here is Charles Baudelaire's well-known poem "Correspondances," which articulates the poetic fusion of the senses:

> La Nature est un temple où de vivants piliers
> Laissent parfois sortir de confuses paroles;
> L'homme y passe à travers des forêts de symboles
> Qui l'observent avec des regards familiers
>
> Comme de longs échos qui de loin se confondent
> Dans une ténébreuse et profounde unité
> Vaste comme la nuit et comme la clarté
> Les parfums, les couleurs et les sons se répondent.

> [Nature is a temple of living pillars
> where often words emerge, confused and dim;
> and man goes through this forest, with familiar
> eyes of symbols always watching him.
>
> Like prolonged echoes mingling far away
> in a unity tenebrous and profound,
> vast as the night and as the limpid day,
> perfumes, sounds, and colors correspond.] (12–13)

Baudelaire is drawing broadly on the romantic tradition that celebrates the associative power of the mind. He praises Edgar Allan Poe's imagination for its ability to sense correspondences that cross the boundaries normally imposed by thought: "Imagination is an almost divine faculty which perceives immediately and without philosophical methods the inner and secret relations of things, the correspondences and analogies" ("New Notes," 127). Wassily Kandinsky picks up on this romantic tradition but makes his claim for the spiritual value of these inter-art correspondences even more strongly. "At different points along the road are the different arts," he writes in *Concerning the Spiritual in Art*, "saying what they are best able to say, and in the . . . language which is peculiarly their own." But, he notes, "there has never been a time when the arts approached each other more nearly than they do today" (40). For him, this search is spiritual: "In each manifestation is the seed of a striving towards the abstract, the non-material. Consciously or unconsciously they are obeying Socrates' command—Know thyself. Consciously or unconsciously artists are studying and proving their material, setting in the balance the spiritual value of those elements, with which it is their several privilege to work. And the natural result of this striving is that the various arts are drawing together" (40–41).

Kandinsky uses the romantic notion of the correspondences between the senses to define the very nature of the spiritual within art. For him, this spirituality involves breaking down conventional distinctions between the arts, which he sees as particularly strong in the modern period: "Perhaps with envy and with a mournful sympathy we listen to the music of Mozart. It acts as a welcome pause in the turmoil of our inner life, as a consolation and as a hope, but we hear it as the echo of something from another age long past and fundamentally strange to us. The strife of colours, the sense of balance we have lost, tottering principles, unexpected assaults, great questions, apparently useless striving, storm and tempest, broken chains, antitheses and contradictions, these make up our harmony" (86).[8] This image of an art beyond media differences echoes Richard Wagner's description of the artwork of the future: "Not one rich faculty of the separate arts will remain unused in the United Artwork of the Future; in *it* will each attain its first complete appraisement" (190).

The rhetorical construction of the category of *intermedia* is quite different. Although the term is used by a number of different critics to mean different things,[9] I focus on the particular way it is framed by Dick Higgins in his influential 1965 essay, "Intermedia." His example is the "Happening," which "developed as an intermedium, an uncharted land that lies between collage, music and the theater. It is not governed by rules; each work determines its own medium and form according to its needs" (16). Higgins is responding to a tradition in art and literary criticism in the first half of the twentieth century in the United States emphasizing that each medium had its own unique qualities that needed to be exploited. Clement Greenberg argued in the 1930s that "the poet or artist turns [his attention] in upon the medium of his own craft" (6): "Picasso, Braque, Mondrian, Miró, Kandinsky, Brancusi, even Klee, Matisse, and Cézanne derive their chief inspiration from the medium they work in. The excitement of their art seems to lie most of all in its pure preoccupation with the invention and arrangement of spaces, surfaces, shapes, colors, etc., to the exclusion of whatever is not necessarily implicated in these factors" (7). In literary criticism, this emphasis on the unique qualities of the written medium is embodied in New Criticism's exploration of the aesthetic qualities of the poetic word. Here is W. K. Wimsatt: "Poetry achieves concreteness, particularity, and something like sensuous shape not by irrelevance of local texture . . . but by extra relevance or hyperrelevance, the interrelational density of words taken in their fullest, most inclusive and symbolic character. A verbal composition through being supercharged with significance, takes on something like the character of a stone statue or a porcelain vase. Through its meaning or meanings the poem *is*" (231). This passage exemplifies the rhetorical construction of media relations and is clearly offered with an eye toward institutional as well as theoretical effects. For my purposes, however, it is more important as a foil against which we read Higgins's call for intermedia. Higgins's focus on the theatrical "happening" is typical of the 1960s' reaction to the aesthetic separation called for by Greenberg and by Wimsatt. Michael Fried makes this point in *Art and Objecthood*: "Theatre and theatricality are at war today, not simply with modernist painting (or modernist painting and sculpture), but with art as such—and to the extent that the different arts can be described as modernist, with modernist sensibility as such" (163).

It is clear that Higgins's term *intermedia* is designed to intervene rhetorically into these debates, and to define a ground on which media relations can be understood. Specifically, Higgins sees art forms as independent of institutions and aesthetic categories. According to his account, institutions try to pigeonhole such works, but we need merely to recognize the limitations of these categories in order to escape their influence. Such an aesthetic claim clearly arises from Higgins's own outsider position relative to more established publishing houses. More importantly for my purposes, *intermedia* defines a different theoretical framework according to which different media can meet. In contrast to Baudelaire's synesthesia in which the mixture of media reflects the way that the human mind combines its faculties, Higgins defines the mixture of media as evidence of the failures of categories. For him, intermedia is not an attempt to define how the mind works but a way to combat institutional pressures on artists to conform.

The "ecology" of these media relations clearly reflects the material changes that critics like Fuller emphasize. Among these is certainly the increasing availability of inexpensive forms of reproduction—both in print (mimeograph, Xerox copying, and cheaper offset printing) as well as audiotape and film, both of which became accessible to a much greater portion of the population during the 1950s and '60s. It is also clear that media are not merely products of a technical and economic environment but also a means for imagining this environment. In this I am following Raymond Williams in his definition of the relationship between historical events and our ideas of culture: "The history of the idea of culture is a record of our reactions, in thought and feeling, to the changed conditions of our common life. Our meaning of culture is a response to the events which our meanings of industry and democracy most definitely define. But the conditions were created and have been modified by men. . . . The history of the idea of culture is a record of our meanings and our definitions, but these, in turn, are only to be understood within the context of our actions" (*Culture*, 295).

The idea of the media ecology is in part an attempt to avoid the danger of technological determinism, to see the workings of human agency through and in response to media. But we need to recognize that a fundamental part of that response involves defining the ground or field upon which these various media meet. That definition is rhetorical and is the very thing that the media novels examined in this book strive to accomplish. Similar exercises are at work throughout contemporary culture, from the changing ways that films are packaged and distributed to the ongoing arguments about the relationship between video games and their source material in narrative media like novels and films. We live in a period of aesthetic flux prompted by the expanding possibility of linking together many different media that initially seem to be separate. Whether doing so is necessary for future art, merely one possibility among others, or a diluting of various media is a question being asked throughout contemporary artistic practice. In this book, I analyze what I see as a consistent focus on *media limits* in the contemporary U.S. novel, and I suggest in the end that embracing such limits is a direct rejection of the fantasy of unlimited media fullness implied by advocates of "multimedia" technology.

When Does One Medium Become Another?

At the outset I noted that we need a particularly flexible and sophisticated definition of *medium* if it is to account for the way that the configuration of various media can shift from period to period, or even from work to work. Having defined the rhetorical construction of media relations, we now have just such a definition.

How we distinguish between media depends on the framework we bring to the term. Marie-Laure Ryan notes the way that different fields use the term *media*: "If we ask specialists of different disciplines to propose a list of media, we will receive a bewildering variety of answers. A sociologist or cultural critic will answer TV, radio, cinema, the Internet. An art critic may list music, painting, sculpture, literature, drama, the opera, photography, architecture. An artist's list would begin with clay, bronze, oil, watercolor, fabrics, and it may end with exotic items used in so-called mixed-media works, such as grasses, feathers, and beer can tabs" (*Avatars*, 16). As Ryan's list demonstrates, any definition of a medium depends on a range of possible forms; indeed, the very nature of a medium implies that it is one form among a limited range of others. What is also clear from Ryan's list is that any account of multimedia or mixed media depends on an understanding of the conventional boundaries that define the normal use of the medium. Why is gluing a beer-can tab to a canvas more "mixed media" than applying several different colors of paint? Paint is defined as a single medium so long as we ignore the fact that any particular paint is made up of many different substances. Likewise, we are more likely to understand music that involves accidental sound or found speech recordings as mixed media even though, of course, the "song" that results is made up of a single medium—sound waves recorded on CD or tape. And, to move to the other extreme, even works that embrace a single medium in the most traditional way have qualities that *could* make them multimedia. A painting has a tactile and gustatory quality (even though we're not supposed to touch or lick it) and no doubt could be forced to produce sound in any number of ways. But we are supposed to ignore these "multimedia" qualities when viewing most paintings.

The same is true of popular media. Is digital cable or high-definition television the same medium as older analog broadcasts delivered over the air? Or take the case of printing. Is a book that has been offset printed the same as a book that has been printed using movable type? How about a book printed on rag paper in comparison to wood-pulp paper? Likewise, is a song recorded digitally on a CD the same as a song recorded on an LP? How about when it is turned into an MP3 file? Usually we say that these media have remained the same despite some technical changes: television is television, a book is a book, and a song is a song. But clearly there are limits. Even if a book has been offset printed from a PDF file, if we are asked to read the PDF file on a computer screen instead of on paper, we usually feel that we are now encountering a new medium. Likewise, once television shows can be purchased on a show-by-show basis (as they can be through iTunes), the nature of the medium seems to be undergoing a shift as the idea of "owning" a show is introduced into the broadcast relationship and connected to different systems of distribution, storage, and viewing. In each of these cases there is no one technological addition or change that suddenly turns one medium into another. The shift is partially rhetorical (with advertisers trying to convince consumers that a product is either a new thing or the same product they know and love), partially perceptual (as we may be unaware that a particular media product has been produced differently than in the past), and partially a matter of the work's place within a whole ecology. One reason why buying a television show through iTunes seems more like the birth of a new medium than does buying an offset-printed book is that in the former case we have a choice of how to acquire this product, while in the latter we (usually) do not.

I am suggesting, then, that the differences between media are always rhetorically constructed, although that rhetorical work obviously also reflects the material conditions at the time. This is especially important for the novels discussed in this book, because other media are invoked by these authors for very specific theoretical and practical purposes, and thus it is often hard to predict how the lines between media will be drawn before we understand the work as a whole. For example, in Ronald Sukenick's short story "Duck Tape," audio recording of voices is treated as the opposite to writing because he focuses on the way that information gets into the story (through dialogue rather than narration). In Marianne Hauser's *The Talking Room*, the transmission of voices by radio is largely associated with writing, and is contrasted to music recordings, because she thinks about radio as a matter of bringing in information from the outside world in contrast to the repetition of the record played again and again. Likewise, Kurt Vonnegut lumps together various kinds of images in *Breakfast of Champions* (including signs seen by characters and his own drawings) as examples of the cultural detritus that fills the author's mind, but in *The Colorist* Susan Daitch is very careful to distinguish photography from drawn comics in terms of how they represent historical specificity. In each of these cases, it is impossible to know beforehand whether differences in transmission or production technology, or in visual or auditory appeals, will make one medium different from another in the context of the novel. Because the construction of these relationships is essential to the way that these novels comment on the media ecology, the definition of medium will be contingent on the nature of the individual novel.

In defining media as a matter of rhetorically deployed differences, I am drawing on but also extending the writing of several critics working on narrative's ability to travel through different media.[10] In particular, Ryan argues that different narrative modes have "strong affinities for certain media, while others can appear in several physical supports" (*Avatars*, 16). She goes on to distinguish "three broad media families: verbal, visual, and aural" (18) and then describes what each "can easily do," "cannot do," "can do only with difficulty," "[can make] up for its limitations through [certain] strategies," and so on (19–20). Ryan is less concerned with absolute rules regarding a medium, and instead focuses on the relative strengths and weaknesses of each. Ryan's emphasis on the *affordances* and *affinities* of various media is a powerful and refreshing contrast to the absolute definitions of media, like Lessing's distinction between the spatiality of painting and the temporality of poetry. Equally important, however, is her insistence that much of what we understand about what one medium offers is culturally constructed. Ryan gives the example of the commonly accepted difference between novel and newspaper: "Newspapers, for instance, rely on the same semiotic channels and printing technologies as books, but 'the press' is widely regarded by sociologists as a medium in its own right, on par with the other so-called mass media of TV, film, radio, and the Internet" (24). Not only do different media have different affordances that we can accept or supplement, but even our perception of a medium's affordances is shaped by its place within a larger culture. It may be, for example, that a graphic narrative like *Maus* can manipulate the shading in the representation of prisoners to "mak[e] their faces impossible to differentiate . . . suggesting powerfully and graphically their psychic need to blend into a crowd in moments of danger" (Ewert, 184), but it is very unlikely that the *New York Times* would choose to use this medium in a front-page news story about prisons. The affinities and affordances of a medium are defined not just by its semiotic qualities but also by its place within a particular culture's media ecology. At least at the moment, graphic narrative is not considered an appropriate medium for the front page of a daily newspaper.

Although it seems that my qualifications have made hopeless any attempt to define one medium against another—mediated, as that definition is, by the relativism of affordances, supplements, and cultural definitions—I suggest on the contrary that these qualifications ultimately work together to give each medium its precise place within the culture. As I will show, the place of one medium within the whole contemporary ecology is defined by a network of actors and the circulation of that medium's artifacts throughout the culture.

The Media Supermarket

Both synesthesia and intermedia imply aesthetic theories, and both articulate goals for this mixture of existing media. What goals do contemporary novelists have when they make references to media other than writing? If these writers approach media from a rhetorical and theoretical perspective, as I suggest, they seem to lack any engagement in a specific practical goal. If media ecologies can be constructed in different ways by different writers and in different texts, the converse is also true: we live in a time when the purpose of writing itself is very much up for grabs, and writers are burdened with the task of defining a media ecology for themselves.

The writers discussed here are remarkably free to pick and choose the media to which they refer, since (as novelists) they are independent of the need to use any of these media. Although their imagining of these media is not free from material constraints—as my comparison between comic books and film earlier suggested—these writers clearly can move between and combine media within a single narrative in a way that would be very difficult if they had actually to produce the media objects that appear in their stories. In this regard, they seem to have a remarkable degree of choice; they exist in a veritable supermarket of media options. Adorno has already suggested that such freedom of choice unrestricted by aesthetic goals is the hallmark of the contemporary hobbylike pseudo-activity that he associates with the jazz expert. Indeed, the supermarket is an unlikely but appropriate metaphor for the situation of contemporary novelists, since they appear to have a nearly unlimited choice of options, but those options are possible in part because none of them really matter—they are disconnected from any specific aesthetic requirement or expectation on the novelist today.

We might frame this by turning to the distinction between medium and genre. Ryan notes that the line between medium and genre is not absolute:

> Both medium and genre exercise constraints on what kinds of stories can be told, but while genre is defined by more or less freely adopted conventions chosen for both personal and cultural reasons, medium imposes its possibilities and limitations on the user. It is true that we choose both the genre and the medium we work in. But we select media for their affordances, and we work around their limitations, trying to overcome them or to make them irrelevant. For instance, painters introduced perspective to add a third dimension to the flat canvas. Genre by contrast deliberately uses limitations to optimize expression, to channel expectations, and to facilitate communication: for instance, tragedy *must* be about the downfall of a hero and use the mimetic mode of narrativity; sonnets *must* consist of fourteen lines, organized in two quatrains and two tercets with a certain rhyming pattern. (*Avatars*, 27)

We might quibble with this distinction, which certainly is less than absolute: there are times when we use the conditions of a medium to channel expectations, and certainly others when we might feel constrained by the genre expectations that shunt plots to acceptable endings. But Ryan's point seems broadly valid for traditional writing and art, and it helps to define the background against which the media references that are common in the contemporary novel must be understood. These novels are clearly using the conditions of media like film, music, and painting in a way that exaggerates the constraints under which they are telling their stories. In the context of these media references, then, medium begins to behave much more like a genre. This should not be surprising, since these media function in the novel not as means of contact with the reader, but rather as an *idea* or set of conditions to be explored. As a theme, these media exert a very different kind of limitation on writer and reader. There is a long tradition of seeing media like painting and music as simple *others* to writing. Françoise Meltzer opens her study of portraiture in the novel by offering a sweeping claim about writing and its others: "The portrait, because it is 'other' to the verbal economy of the text, functions as a good barometer for literature's views on itself, on representation, and on the power of writing. The choice of the portrait is essentially arbitrary on my part; I could as well have considered music, landscapes, tactile expressions, and so on" (1).

The problem of agency in the contemporary media novel reflects a larger tension that has been implicit in the study of the novel and narrative for more than forty years. In 1960 Mary McCarthy answered the question "Is it still possible to write novels?" in the negative: "Almost no writer in the West of any consequence, let us say since the death of Thomas Mann, has been able to write a true novel" (439). Specifically, McCarthy focuses on the fundamental importance of fact to the novel, so that "even when it is most serious, the novel's characteristic tone is one of gossip and tittle-tattle" (453). Such gossip reinforces commitment to fact and defines the novel as a means of getting to truths that might nonetheless be scandalous. In the world of 1960, however, McCarthy argues that horrors like Hiroshima and Auschwitz have made such human facts obsolete:

And here is the dilemma of the novelist, which is only a kind of professional sub-case of the dilemma of everyone: if he writes about his province, he feels its inversimilitude; if he tries, on the other hand, to write about people who make lampshades of human skin, like the infamous Ilse Koch, he feels still more the inversimilitude of what he is asserting. His love of truth revolts. And yet this love of truth, ordinary common truth recognizable to everyone, is the ruling passion of the novel. Putting two and two together, then, it would seem that the novel, with its common sense, is of all forms the least adapted to encompass the modern world, whose leading characteristic is irreality. (455–56)

McCarthy's "death of the novel" essay is, of course, only one of many that I might have cited—indeed, it became a bit of a genre itself. Some of the best known of these, in an American context, are John Barth's "The Literature of Exhaustion" essay or Louis Rubin's *The Curious Death of the Novel*. What is interesting to me is that McCarthy defines the death of the novel not as a problem of exhaustion (nothing new to write about) or changing economic conditions (no one reads anymore) but about vocation: we have lost our sense of why we need novelists. This is an idea seconded by Tom Wolfe in his description of the "new journalism." For Wolfe, the new journalism's attempt to marry investigative reporting to a literary style and narrative structure reflects the novel's loss of vocation: "In 1948 Lionel Trilling presented the theory that the novel of social realism (which had flourished in America throughout the 1930's) was finished because the freight train of history had passed it by. The argument was that such novels were the product of the rise of the bourgeoisie in the nineteenth century at the height of capitalism. But now bourgeois society was breaking up, fragmenting. A novelist could no longer portray a part of that society and hope to capture the Zeitgeist; all he would be left with was one of the broken pieces" (28–29). Like McCarthy, Wolfe sees the novel as bereft of its original motivation and purpose, and points to the early 1960s as the period when this loss became obvious.

Just a year after McCarthy's essay, in 1961, Wayne Booth published an influential book of literary criticism, *The Rhetoric of Fiction*, which at first blush seems to have little to do with McCarthy's essay. Booth saw himself as countering the modernist insistence on the inherent value of impersonality in narrative; as he says, these specific goals have evolved "from justified revolt to crippling dogma" (23). Booth's method is to avoid claiming that any one narrative device is better, and instead, to analyze how each device contributes to the storytelling goal that it is intended to achieve. Doing so involves accepting the artificiality of any form of storytelling: the novelist "signs an agreement with me *not* to know every-thing. He reminds me from time to time that he cannot, in this particular instance, 'go behind' because of the convention he has adopted. I accept this, provided it serves larger ends that I can also accept. But in no case do I pretend that I am not reading a novel" (53). It is hard not to sympathize with Booth's overall theoretical claim that there are a lot of different ways to tell stories, and that no one method is inherently better than another. But his rhetorical approach to the novel is also in some sense the result of the cultural condition that McCarthy describes—a world in which the novel has lost a specific vocation.[11] It is that vocation that would allow a critic to say definitely that one way of storytelling is right and another is wrong. Without such a vocation, the novel can be anything. We might recall the quip of Ishmael Reed's surrogate, Loop Garoo, in *Yellow Back Radio Broke-Down*: "No one says a novel has to be one thing. It can be anything it wants to be, a vaudeville show, the six o'clock news, the mum-blings of wild men saddled by demons" (36). For all we might cheer Loop's revolutionary verve, the reason why we would want the novel to be any-thing in particular is left unexplained in this passage. In the decades that followed, critics have offered many different definitions of what the novel really is about. Just in the last couple of years, James Phelan has used this rhetorical approach to character narration to account for "the multilayered communications that authors of narrative offer their audiences, commu-nications that invite or even require their audiences to engage with them cognitively, psychically, emotionally, and ethically" (*Living*, 5). Conversely, Lisa Zunshine answers the question "Why do we read fiction?" this way: "The cognitive rewards of reading fiction might thus be aligned with the cognitive rewards of pretend play through a shared capacity to stimulate and develop the imagination. It may mean that our enjoyment of fiction is predicated—at least in part—upon our *awareness* of our "trying on" mental states potentially available to us but at a given moment *differing* from our own" (*Why We Read*, 17).

But all these suggestions operate in the post-1960 world—to give it a specific date—in which there is no clearly accepted purpose for writing or reading a novel. One only needs to review the titles of books published in the last few decades to see the variety of definitions of narrative that are being offered: *Narrative as Communication*, *Narrative Ethics* (the first chapter of which is "Narrative as Ethics"), *Narrative as Rhetoric*, *Narrative as Virtual Reality.*[12] It is not hard to hear, too, an echo of the same open-endedness in the way that contemporary novels use references to other media. If there is no commitment to synesthesia or intermedia, then the use of these references threatens to be just one choice among many in the media supermarket.

The study of the novel in the wake of Booth's book goes in two seemingly opposite directions. One follows Booth's lead and develops a rhetorical approach to the novel (often extended to film and, more recently, to graphic novels) that tries to categorize choices and devices such narrative works can use. This has produced a lively if somewhat technical debate about the validity of specific terms like "implied author" and "point of view." Seymour Chatman summarizes these debates and introduces his own contribution in these terms: "Clearly the house of narratology, like the house of fiction itself, has many mansions. Different formulas have different strengths, some of which a partisan account always risks neglecting or even misrepresenting. I present mine for the sake of continuing a debate that has kept narratology one of the livelier topics on the academic scene" (*Coming to Terms*, 5). The other direction narratology can take is quite the opposite, and involves a shift from the very local, theoretically agnostic perspective that Booth uses, toward sweeping universality. Here is Roland Barthes in 1966 in his well-known essay "Introduction to the Structural Analysis of Narratives":

> The narratives of the world are numberless. Narrative is first and foremost a prodigious variety of genres, themselves distributed amongst different substances—as though any material were fit to receive man's stories. Able to be carried by articulated language, spoken or written, fixed or moving images, gestures, and the ordered mixture of all these substances; narrative is present in myth, legend, fable, tale, novella, epic, history, tragedy, drama, comedy, mime, painting (think of Carpaccio's *Saint Ursula*), stained-glass windows, cinema, comics, news item, conversation. Moreover, under this almost infinite diversity of forms, narrative is present in every age, in every place, in every society; it begins with the very history of mankind and there nowhere is nor has been a people without narrative. (251)

This urge to universality in some ways runs directly counter to Booth's attempt to make storytelling decisions local and determined by the particular ends that a novelist has chosen. However, it is also clear that this universality is possible only because the category of *narrative* has been separated off from the particular genre of *novel*, freeing it up to be "present in every age, in every place, in every society."[13] Indeed, by generalizing the novel's techniques into a set of tools for achieving various goals, Booth pulls the novel out of history and into the realm of the use of language in general. Once that has been done, we can begin to see these techniques in places that are clearly outside the novel itself. In 1986 Wallace Martin summarized this shift: "During the past fifteen years, the theory of narrative has displaced the theory of the novel as a topic of central concern in literary study. The difference between the two is not simply one of generality—as if, having analyzed one species of narration, we went on to study others and then described the genus. By changing the definition of what is being studied, we change what we see; and when different definitions are used to chart the same territory, the results will differ, as do typographical, political, and demographic maps, each revealing one aspect of reality by virtue of disregarding all others" (15). Martin is especially helpful in reminding us that the shift from novel to narrative is not inherently good but rather is a response to changing ideas of what critics hope to accomplish.

Thus, the rise of the study of narrative in the 1960s—what is often referred to now as narratology—is of a piece with the vanishing vocation of the writer, to which McCarthy and Booth both testify in different ways. In fact, we could say that an exploration of the theoretical possibilities and conditions of narrative is precisely the search for a vocation that the novelist appears to have lost. This is also why these writers are so eager to exaggerate the media constraints under which they operate. The danger for the novelist of having been freed from any of the rules that restricted writing in the past—be it the demand that the novel tattletale on private lives or that it be objective and impersonal—is that he or she is left with nothing to write precisely because *anything* can be written. John Barth makes this point quite directly in "The Literature of Exhaustion," while reviewing intermedia literary works published by Dick Higgins's Something Else Press: "One conspicuous thing, for example, about the 'intermedia' arts is their tendency to eliminate not only the traditional audience . . . but also the most traditional notion of the artist: the Aristotelian conscious agent who achieves with technique and cunning the artistic effect" (65). This anxiety can help to explain the appeal to the physical form of the book in Birkerts's *Gutenberg Elegies*: unable to define the function of the novel in broad theoretical or social terms, critics turn back to stories of their own childhood encounter with the physical medium of the book to explain why we write and read novels. Ironically, though, this fascination with the physical form of the book reminds us just how much the printed novel is one medium among others—an irony that I will explore in the last chapter. Emphasis on the physical form of the book can easily become a critique of normative ideas about reading—as, for example, the contemporary "artist book" movement that creates works that simply cannot be read in conventional ways. Johanna Drucker describes works that often involve blank, defaced, or otherwise inaccessible pages: "The books don't function in their current form. Limited, suspended, static, they serve as icons, images of what books are known to be—but they are no longer accessible as dense repositories of human thought, reflection and revelry. Nor is the familiar function of the book duplicated by the monitors [that make up one particular book installation]—watching and displaying, they refuse interaction while the pages of a book are available to be flipped back and forth at the whim and random interest of the reader" (169).

The novelists we are concerned with in this book take quite the opposite approach, and consider novels not as one-of-a-kind physical artifacts but instead as instances of narrative articulated through print. The transformation of the novel into a species of narrative and the exploration of writing's relationship with other media can be seen as a way to find theoretical constraints that help to give shape and meaning to the vocation of being a novelist. We can see this in Barthes's essay. After his very general opening definition, in which narrative is everywhere, Barthes turns to implicit rules that help to define narrative. He states the problem in direct terms that should remind us of the situation of the novelist after 1960: early formalist theories of narrative "have taught us to recognize the following dilemma: either a narrative is merely a rambling collection of events, in which case nothing can be said about it other than referring back to the storyteller's (the author's) art, talent, or genius—all mythical forms of chance—or else it shares with other narratives a common structure which is open to analysis, no matter how much patience its formulation requires" (252–53).

Contemporary novelists find themselves in something of the same ambiguous situation in relation to other media. Given the fact that no one medium has a fundamental role in relation to the novel, and given that there is no broadly accepted definition of the natural place of the novel in relation to these media, novelists have done just what Wayne Booth and Roland Barthes have done—turn to theoretical tensions and conditions that promise to provide a set of conditions according to which the novel should be written. For Patrick O'Neill, this is what narrative has always done: "There is clearly a sense in which all narratives are a form of semiotic game, presenting particular and particularly effective arrangements and interrelationships of real or invented events for reception and interpretation by known and/or unknown audiences" (26). Novelists, in other words, have become narratologists. This is true not only of writer-critics like Umberto Eco and Christine Brooke-Rose but even of those writers like Toni Morrison or Kurt Vonnegut who rarely address theoretical concerns or offer grand claims about narrative outside their fictional practice.

We could argue, of course, that *all* novels are in some way or another about the process of storytelling. Gerald Prince notes that, while it may be difficult to argue that every "narrative . . . takes narrative as a theme, it is not easy to prove the contrary" (17). In fact, he argues, "the realist novel, which claims to avoid any self-examination the better to reach reality, represents not the apex to which an entire tradition led from its very birth on but—quite to the contrary—an aberration, a monstrosity. Doesn't the first novel, *Don Quijote,* offer a long meditation on itself in order to overcome the paradox of the feigned and the true? and isn't auto-meditation the only way, for any novelistic expression, to escape both naiveté and bad faith?" (17–18). Thematizing narrative, Prince argues, is a well-established way that allows "texts better to define themselves, to specify and emphasize the meanings they wish to communicate, and to designate the values they develop and aspire to" (38). What is different about the contemporary media novel is that it articulates this theme of narrative in terms of the defining characteristics of *written* narrative. Here, then, is the thesis that I develop in this book: novelists today use other media not as contemporary furniture but as a way to explore the nature of writing as a form for storytelling, and thus to position themselves within the contemporary media ecology.

Plan of the Book

Contemporary writers are redefining the vocation of the novel today by exploring the limits of the novel as a medium. To do so, they invoke media like film, music, and comics as "others" against which the limits and strengths of writing can be understood. The central paradox that emerges in this study is that an emphasis on media limits turns out to connect the novel and its readers to a larger social space. The novel becomes, I argue in the last chapter, a "middle space" poised between the traditional privacy of reading and the larger world to which writing is connected by its very limits.

I begin by delineating the contemporary media novel from the way that earlier novels used other media. Media play many practical and aesthetic roles within traditional narratives. We draw on the familiar distinction between the "story" of the novel's plot, characters, and events, and the "discourse" of its telling. At the story level, media objects provide the occasion for action, can be an object of action, an actor itself, or an opportunity to provide story exposition. At the discourse level, appealing to other media can help to explain and justify the novel's aesthetics; drawing on the language of the theater, for example, can lend the story grandeur—or make the characters seem small and petty by comparison. While the story-level effects of media objects are the most inherently connected to the task of storytelling, discourse-level appeals to other media provide the simpler means of making claims about the place of writing in a media ecology. Having described general possibilities, we examine a variety of contemporary media novels. Some, like Raymond Federman's *Take It or Leave It* and Maxine Hong Kingston's *Tripmaster Monkey*, take the relatively simple approach of referring to other media primarily at the discourse level. Others, like Toni Cade Bambara's *The Salt Eaters*, Ronald Sukenick's "Duck Tape," and Thomas Pynchon's *Vineland*, invoke other media at the story level in a way that shows their effects on the tales being told. These latter, more complex cases exemplify the media novels that appear in this book. Such novels integrate media into the plot level of the narrative in order to explore the nature and limitations of writing as a medium. This emphasis on media limitations, I suggest, is what sets the contemporary novel apart from its modernist antecedents.

Having described the unique emphasis on media limits in the contemporary novel, we turn in chapter 2 to the cultural uses of writing as a way to define its vocation. Earlier I cited Ryan's observation that the nature of a medium depends in large part on the way that a particular culture understands it, rather than exclusively on qualities that are formally inherent to it. In chapter 1, we note that the novel is a particularly important means of thinking about media relations because of the ease with which it represents the circulation of stories as concrete objects told, written down, and passed from person to person. This circulation of stories makes it especially easy to see how writing can take on a role within a larger media ecology. In chapter 2 we see that contemporary media novels are particularly aware of the importance of cultural use in defining media, and I suggest that they frequently describe the circulation of media objects within a community in order to discuss the nature of writing and other media. Contemporary culture seems to be suspicious of a simple distinction between experience and its narrative representation, and in this chapter I link an interest in the circulation of media objects through cultural use to a broad critique of contemporary experience. I describe the circulation of media objects within three novels—Oscar Hijuelos's *The Mambo Kings Play Songs of Love*, Tom Robbins's *Still Life with Woodpecker*, and Toni Morrison's *Jazz*—and show that in each case this circulation leads to an examination of the nature of a medium's potentials and limits. Other examples of media circulation such as the rewriting of stories in fan communities suggest that this interest in the cultural use of media is part of a broad trend within contemporary culture.

The contemporary media novel seeks to rediscover a vocation by exploring the limits of the medium. What do writers discover when they do so, and how does this help to give impetus for their writing? In chapter 3 we turn to a variety of novels that challenge some conventional justification for fiction—from the description of realistic possible worlds to the provoking of reader reactions—to which writers might appeal in order to explain what it means to write and read a novel. After rejecting such conventional qualities of the novel, each story turns to one particular narrative element to find what is distinctive about writing. This chapter is organized around five novels or short stories: Kenneth Gangemi's *The*

Interceptor Pilot, Robert Coover's "The Babysitter," Susan Daitch's *The Colorist*, Kurt Vonnegut's *Breakfast of Champions*, and Don DeLillo's *White Noise*. In rejecting some common justification of the novel, each of these works turns to one general narrative element and considers what is unique about its role in the medium of writing: description, setting, world, character, and plot. Exploring the nature of writing allows these novelists to rethink the vocation of the novel today. The way that writers characterize other media like music, film, and comics can vary greatly—often because these writers are more interested in what these media can contribute to their specific storytelling goals than in making a general claim about these other media. There is considerably more agreement among these writers, however, in their characterization of the novel itself. Each of these novelists ends up emphasizing writing's ability to describe what is absent in one way or another: the potential, the possible but unrealized, or the merely missing. This emphasis on the absent naturally dovetails with the aesthetics of limits that the contemporary novel embraces. Indeed, for these writers, the novel is particularly capable of pointing to what is beyond itself, and thus is particularly good at connecting to other media.

Although the writers we discuss may explore the limits of writing from within the traditional boundaries of the novel, many new electronic forms of textuality promise to place writing into an entirely different context. Specifically, "new media" extends writing into a multimedia, networked, or virtual environment and seems to have the potential to escape the limits of writing by supplementing the text with images, sounds, or video. In doing so, these works embrace Kittler's image of a future without specific media limits. In chapter 4 we explore the way that new media's promises of encyclopedism, network integration, and transparency encounter limits. I turn to three media stories that help to show why the limits of writing will continue into these new media forms. We examine Thomas Pynchon's encyclopedic *Gravity's Rainbow* in order to analyze media in the electronic encyclopedia, Walter Abish's story of the California media landscape, "Ardor/Awe/Atrocity," to discuss the nature of networked space, and Paul Auster's novel about a disappearing silent film star, *The Book of Illusions*, to understand the nature of character transparency in video games. In each of these cases, the dream of a future without media boundaries turns out to be unrealistic, and the media novel's exploration of the specific uses and limits of various media helps to explain the contradictions in these postmedia dreams.

In the final chapter we return to the issue introduced in chapter 2: the way that an emphasis on limits can work, paradoxically, to connect the novel to it larger social environment. Recalling the complaints of those critics who see print culture today as fading, we see that these critics evoke the novel's traditional association with privacy and solitary thoughts, against which new electronic technologies seem to be pressing so aggressively. But even these appeals to traditional reading are ways of connecting the novel to its media environment; much the same emphasis on limits and social connections can be found in the debate over the role of the novel today. To explore this debate, we turn to a series of novels that meditate on the place of the novel within a larger community context: Sherman Alexie's *Reservation Blues*, Abraham Rodriguez's *The Buddha Book*, Marianne Hauser's *The Talking Room*, and Jonathan Lethem's *The Fortress of Solitude*. Each of these novels sees an encounter with the limits of the medium as a point at which the novel is connected to the larger world.

In the concluding coda of the book, we contrast the model of media limits to the competing idea of multimedia. Multimedia promises a kind of fullness by supplementing the limits of one medium with others. The media novels explored in this book take a decidedly different and more complex route, revealing that an emphasis on the limits of the medium of writing can be a way of rejuvenating the novel and defining its place within the contemporary media ecology.

1   Multimedia Moments Old and New

Doing Things with Media in the Novel

Media other than writing have always had a place in the novel, whose history is full of stolen paintings, romances developed during a piano duet, and social faux pas at gala theatrical performances. In the introduction we have already considered (and dismissed) the idea that media appear in the contemporary novel simply as part of the "furniture" of everyday life. It is an inadequate explanation, but it does touch on a truth that we will explore in this chapter: the novel seems to use other media as a tool for storytelling in a pragmatic way that is independent of whatever it may also be accomplishing in commenting on media ecologies. Furthermore, if the contemporary novel seems more engaged with competing media today—the somewhat arbitrary date I offered was since 1960—we need to distinguish these recent novels from their immediate predecessors. Indeed, the modernist narratives of Joyce, Woolf, and Mann draw heavily on media like painting and music. What is different about the contemporary media novel?

Before we can begin to define ways that the contemporary novel can place itself within media ecologies, then, we need to unpack the more pragmatic functions that these media references perform. Because narratives move through time and space, telling a story of any complexity involves orchestrating event and setting—getting characters to the right place at the right time so that they can meet or avoid each other, and so on.[1] The need to orchestrate so many pragmatic concerns is the reason we so often use mechanical language to describe narratives that fail, as when we call a poor plot resolution a *deus ex machina*. Media inserted into the story can help to accomplish some of these pragmatic, mechanical tasks of moving characters around the fictional world, bringing them into contact, and conveying information from character to character and from character to reader.

This emphasis on the mechanical role of media in the novel depends on but also complicates the "mediacy" that many narratologists say is essential to narrative. Defining mediacy as the way that news is conveyed by a "mediator," F. K. Stanzel offers it as "the generic characteristic which distinguishes narration from other forms of literary art" (4). Narrating involves presenting information to a reader, and as readers we usually strive to understand the way that this information has been shaped and filtered by the method of narration.[2] Stanzel distinguishes three such forms of mediacy: the voice of a first-person narrator, the account of an external author, and the perspective of a reflector character "who thinks, feels and perceives, but does not speak to the reader like a narrator" (5). This focus on mediacy underlies the convenient and well-known distinction between story and discourse levels in the text. Seymour Chatman summarizes this distinction concisely: "Structuralist theory argues that each narrative has two parts: a story (*histoire*), the content or chain of events (actions, happenings), plus what may be called the existents (characters, items of a setting); and a discourse (*discours*), that is, the expression, the means by which the content is communicated. In simple terms, the story is the *what* in a narrative that is depicted, a discourse the *how*" (*Story*, 19). Distinguishing story and discourse is another way that narratology emphasizes mediacy, how information is being conveyed to the reader. Although this distinction continues to play a part in most narrative analysis, there are a number of ways in which it is problematic. The story level of the text is ultimately inaccessible, since, as Patrick O'Neill remarks, "it quickly becomes clear that we can only ever reach that (fictional) story through the medium of its discursive presentation" (35). This distinction has remained a fundamental element of most narrative analysis in part because of its pragmatic value; as Phelan suggests, "the story-discourse distinction is better seen as a heuristic than as an absolute" (*Narrative as Rhetoric*, 103).

We will use this story/discourse distinction to organize the discussion of the way that media can appear within the novel, recognizing, however, that the cultural *use* of a medium, discussed in the introduction, is at odds with a focus on mediation. Stanzel's description of forms of mediation is essentially formalist, implying that different ways of conveying information shape the story differently. Ryan's emphasis on the meaning of a medium within a culture suggests something rather different: the medium is defined not just by its form (how it turns story into discourse) but also by its role within a community. In this regard, a full discussion of media in the novel will have to account for their role not just in mediating knowledge but also in how they function as cultural objects. In particular, we will discuss the way that media novels describe the *circulation* of media within a community as a step beyond the classic distinction between story and discourse.

This element of mediacy in the novel has been given relatively little attention by critics working in the light of Stanzel's approach. Recent criticism on mediacy, inspired by cognitive approaches to narrative, has emphasized the continuities between novels and our everyday ways of observing, experiencing, and telling. In a recent overview of the "newer developments" on the topic of mediacy, Jan Alber and Monika Fludernik describe a shift toward "natural narratology," which "moves away from the idea of the narrator or the illusion of narration to a wider spectrum of cognitive frames and processes on different levels which feed into the constitution of narrative and its reception" (182). This recognition of the porosity of literary and everyday language has brought a welcome new perspective on narrative, but it also neglects an important element of novelistic writing. The history of the novel is full of stories claiming to be found documents. Michael McKeon calls this the "discovered manuscript topos" (56) and associates it with the transition from romance to novel. Although treating the raw material of the novel as assembled from discovered documents is part of mediacy in general, it is also a very particular way of emphasizing the life that a story takes on as an artifact in the world. Although not all novels claim to be found documents, novels are especially good at emphasizing the life of documents and the circulation of stories within a community. This is true not only of explicit claims about how the manuscript of the story came to be published, which we see in many early novels like *Moll Flanders*, but also the fascination with lost or discovered documents in Poe's short stories, or even the emphasis on the transmission of narration as a physical artifact that is central to the epistolary novel. This focus on the embodiment of the story in an artifact that then circulates through a community is related to the broader issue of mediacy, but is a particular tradition within the novel. This tradition of describing the circulation of a story within a community, in turn, provides the basis on which the contemporary media novel discusses the role of the novel within the media ecology.

In focusing on the particular way that the novel handles the broader issue of narrative mediacy, we move away from abstract definitions of media like the opposition between temporal and spatial arts, between writing and image, or even between print and screen. Theorists of the media ecology like Fuller and Heise insist that relations between particular actors are very local and specific. Although the novel obviously shares many qualities with other forms of written communication, its traditions and the material conditions of those who produce, distribute, and consume it have very particular contours. For this reason, although I frequently refer to the qualities of *writing*, I insist that those more general qualities are always mediated by the specific context of the novel. This contrast will become increasingly important in our discussion, and it provides the central point of debate in the new media's promise to fundamentally change the role of writing in culture, which I discuss in chapter 4.

I will treat the circulation of media within culture in more detail in the next chapter. We must first define the more general spectrum of uses of media in the novel, however, so that we can identify what is unique about the contemporary media novel.

Media at the Story Level

In her book on pictorialism in the novel, Marianna Torgovnick suggests five ways that modern novels can use the visual arts. The first is the *decorative* use: "Passages of description frequently stand out as influenced by the visual arts and suggest a particular movement or an actual work. Sometimes the historical work or artist is actually named" (14). Such a decorative use of the visual arts is largely a matter of allusion or metaphor. More significant for Torgovnick is the use of works of visual art that are *biographically motivated*, which "send us back to the author's *life* and not more deeply into the author's *work*" (18). Next, Torgovnick describes the *ideological* use of the visual arts: "An ideological use of the visual arts embodies major themes of the fiction—especially its views of politics, history, society or, more generally, of 'reality'—in descriptions, objects, metaphors, artist figures, or scenes based upon the historical visual arts or in the same aspects of fiction conceived and experienced pictorially" (19).

The final two terms in Torgovnick's typology are related. The *interpretive* use of the decorative arts "refers to the ways in which *characters* experience art objects or pictorial objects and scenes in a way that provokes their conscious or unconscious minds" (22), while the *hermeneutic* use of these arts "stimulate the interpretive processes of the *reader's* mind and cause him to arrive at an understanding of the novel's methods and meanings" (23).

Torgovnick deserves a great deal of credit for offering a theory that covers so many different uses of the arts in the novel, and hers is one of the few that address the effects of story-level media objects in the novel. But despite this strength, Torgovnick's five-part model also reveals the dangers of focusing too much on biographical or even interpretive uses of media, since there are many practical roles that media can play in the novel that are poorly categorized as "decoration." Critics have naturally gravitated toward broad interpretive issues (the items that come later in Torgovnick's list); however, these lower-level, seemingly decorative elements are often crucial to the mechanical tasks of organizing narrative. I propose five practical uses of media at the story level.

Media as an Object of Narrative Action

One of the simplest and most common uses of media within the novel is as an object of pursuit or desire. A painting may be stolen and the thieves pursued. This can be handled narratively in a relatively mundane way, where the media piece is simply one of many possible "MacGuffin" objects of value fought over by characters, such as the Maltese falcon statue. But it can also be the subject of considerable psychological and social subtlety, as when M. de Nemours steals the portrait of Madame de Clèves: "Madame de Clèves was not a little embarrassed. It would have been reasonable to ask to have her portrait back again, but if she did so out loud it would proclaim to everybody there his feelings for her, while to do so when alone with him would have looked like an invitation for him to speak of his love" (de Lafayette, 97). Likewise, a particular artwork may prompt questions and puzzles, which characters in the novel then try to unravel. A recent example of this use of media is Dan Brown's popular *The Da Vinci Code*, which uses *The Last Supper* as a prompt for inquiry by the novel's detective and scholar. In this case, *The Last Supper* is not itself an object to be pursued, because the ownership and location of the painting is never in doubt. Instead, the painting prompts characters to seek out answers regarding its formal qualities and the narrative context of the represented scene, culminating in a lecture by scholar Leigh Teabing midway through the novel, which provides an explanation for the mysterious events of the novel to this point and defines the object to be pursued for the remainder of the narrative—the hiding place of the "Sangreal" documents that will explain the marriage of Jesus and his subsequent lineage (256).

The pursuit of such media objects need not, of course, be the center of the narrative action. A collection of media can be used, for example, as an element of characterization—as, for example, the way his collection of photographs of automobile accidents and celebrities described at the beginning of J. G. Ballard's *Crash* immediately helps us to understand the novel's central character, Robert Vaughn. Likewise, giving a particular character the *job* of being a writer or artist can perform practical narrative work by freeing up that character from the need to be "at work" all day or justifying the isolation of a character from the outside world—as, for example, when Stephen King provides plot justification for the isolation of Jack Torrance and his family in the haunted resort hotel of *The Shining* by making Jack a writer eager for a quiet environment.

Media as the Occasion for Narrative Action

Although media itself can prompt character action, it can also simply provide the setting for actions otherwise independent of that medium. In *Angelic Airs, Subversive Songs*, Alisa Clapp-Itnyre notes that the domestic scene of performance at the piano is especially important in the Victorian novel: "It would not be an overstatement to say that authors were utterly *fascinated* with romance at the piano. The literature of the nineteenth century repeatedly cloaks romantic encounters in the guise of domestic music concerts: what begins as a pure display of music ends as a display of physical attractiveness or verbal wit" (36). Character actions in response to media objects need not have a direct or literal plot significance in the story. In Raymond Carver's short story "Cathedral," the principal characters—a blind man visiting an old friend and that friend's resentful husband—end up watching television together. Confronted by the problem of describing the visual elements of the documentary being broadcast, the narrator admits his inability to describe the cathedral: "I can't tell you what a cathedral looks like. It just isn't in me to do it" (277). The story ends with the husband drawing a cathedral while the blind man holds his hand and feels the lines of the paper. The television documentary and its transfer to the drawing paper are obviously included for thematic purposes, and it seems clear that the narrator is recognizing something larger than himself: "The men who began their life's work on them, they never lived to see the completion of their work. In that wise, bub, they're no different from the rest of us, right?" (276). The media object here—mostly the television but in a secondary way the drawing paper—functions less as an element of important narrative action and more as an occasion to stage the psychological transformation of the narrator.

Similar uses of media as the occasion for action abound. One common way that eighteenth-century novels signal the lack of refinement and taste in characters is by introducing them to the theater and allowing them to respond crassly. In Fanny Burney's *Evelina* we know all we need to about the differences between the heroine and her superficial cousins simply because of how they behave at the opera: "This song, which was slow and pathetic, caught all my attention, and I leaned my head forward to avoid hearing their observations, that I might listen without interruption: but, upon turning round, when the song was over, I found that I was the object of general diversion to the whole party; for the Miss Branghtons were tittering, and the two gentlemen making faces at me, implying their contempt of my affectation" (81–82). Such public media events can enable characters of different social spheres to meet—allowing, among other things, Evelina to be pursued by the predatory Sir Clement Willoughby while also furthering her romantic attachment to the admirable Lord Orville. Likewise, the theatrical performance that ends *A Midsummer Night's Dream* connects the largely independent story lines of the lower-class "mechanical" characters like Bottom and Quince with the noble audience of Theseus and Hippolyta, which had only been thematically parallel for most of the story.

Media as the Occasion for Narrative Exposition

Media can prompt or provide exposition. This is the role of the painting in Robert Browning's "My Last Duchess," which provides the occasion for the duke to explain his previous marriage and implicitly to warn the intermediary arranging his next: "Sir, 't was not / Her husband's presence only, called that spot / Of joy into the Duchess' cheek." Browning's duke goes on to mix such character analysis ("She had / A heart—how shall I say?—too easily made glad") with narration: "This grew; I gave commands; / Then all smiles stopped together" (252). As this example suggests, such exposition can itself be an inciting element within the story. This is certainly the case in Balzac's "Sarrasine," where Madame de Rochefide's questions about a painting prompt the telling of the story of Sarrasine and La Zambinella, and according to Barthes's analysis in *S/Z*, repeats themes of sexuality and narrative exchange. Another famous example of such exposition is the mural that Aeneas encounters shortly after arriving in Carthage:

> For while he waited for the queen, he studied
> everything in that huge sanctuary,
> marveling at a city rich enough
> for such a temple, at the handiwork
> of rival artists, at their skillful tasks.
> He sees the wars of Troy set out in order:
> the battles famous now through all the world,
> the sons of Atreus and of Priam, and
> Achilles, savage enemy to both. (p. 17; Book I, ll. 642–50)

This image clearly gives Virgil an opportunity to summarize the siege of Troy and to explain Aeneas's relation to those events.[3]

Exposition is often, of course, an element of the *discourse* level of a narrative. In each of these cases, however, exposition is prompted by a narrative event and articulated through a *character's* voice or vision rather than being offered directly by the narrator. Obviously, the line between these two can be quite blurry. When Melville's Ishmael describes the paintings that line the walls of the Spouter-Inn at the outset of *Moby-Dick*, they become an occasion to launch into a whole theory of the meaning of whaling in this community: "On the one side hung a very large oil-painting so thoroughly be-smoked, and every way defaced, that in the unequal cross-lights by which you viewed it, it was only by diligent study and a series of systematic visits to it, and careful inquiry of the neighbors, that you could any way arrive at an understanding of its purpose" (103). There is a great deal of continuity between descriptions prompted by objects and seen by characters, and extradiegetic commentary provided by the narrator focused on a hypothetical "you."

Media as the Object of Interpretation

As Phelan notes, "because characters' actions include their judgments, readers often judge characters' judgments" (*Experiencing*, 9). Media can function as foils through which we evaluate characters and their interpretations of the world. We can reach such judgments in several ways. First, as Tamar Yacobi notes, often "we find the viewpoint on or through the art form mediated, split, problematized" by seeing the artwork "through the perspective of fictional observers, dramatized and less than reliable." In this case, "we must . . . distinguish between two typically narrative and often incompatible viewpoints on the relevant model: from within the fictive world and, simultaneously and more intricately, from without, where the storyteller communicates with the reader alone" (635). Emma Kafalenos provides the example of Poe's "The Oval Portrait," in which readers need to evaluate the narrator's claim that the lifelikeness of the painting is "appalling": "Because the painting is represented in the story only through ekphrasis, which makes it impossible for readers to envision it except through the double lens of the narrator's perceptions and the narrator's words that describe his perceptions, some readers may question whether visual representation can ever be sufficiently lifelike to be considered appalling. For these skeptical readers, the narrator's finding the 'life-likeliness' of expression appalling may corroborate and extend their earlier worry that the narrator is delirious and that his perceptions—and now his conceptions also—cannot be trusted" ("Effects of Sequence," 261).

More recently, Kafalenos has complicated this account by noting that our experience of an artwork to which characters respond changes dramatically if that work is available to us in the real world. Kafalenos notes that there are, in fact, three possible configurations of the artwork in the real and fictional world: "In a first category, the visual representation embedded in a narrative exists only in the fictional world; it can be seen by members of the fictional world but not by readers of the fiction. In a second category, the embedded visual representation exists both in the fictional world and in our world; thus it can be seen both by members of the fictional world and by readers. In a third category, the embedded visual representation exists only in our world; it can be seen by readers but not by members of the fictional world" ("Embedded Artworks," 1). Artworks that exist in both worlds allow authors to signal unreliability easily, simply by giving the characters interpretations that depart significantly from the way that the work is usually understood. When we do not have access to the artwork in the real world, Kafalenos notes, "our inability to see the embedded artwork is a source of ambiguity" (6).

Media as Actors

Although it is a much less common function, a medium can be used at the story level as itself an agent or actor. We might take as an example the mysterious bowl that is the subject matter of Ann Beattie's short story "Janus." Beattie tells the story of Andrea, a real estate agent who owes her success in some mysterious way to a decorative bowl that she places in each home that she is trying to sell. At times the bowl is described merely as having "brought her luck" (107), but in other places Andrea clearly invests the bowl with more agency: "She had the foolish thought that if only the bowl were an animate object she could thank it" (108). She goes on to wonder about the bowl in a way that clearly reflects on the nature of her problematic relationship with the men in her life: "Could it be that she had some deeper connection with the bowl—a relationship of some kind. She corrected her thinking: how could she imagine such a thing, when she was a human being and it was a bowl? It was ridiculous. Just think of how people lived together and loved each other . . . But was that always so clear, always a relationship?" (109). It seems obvious that Andrea's relationship with the bowl reveals the way that people treat each other as objects, and that their cohabitation is sometimes not so different from a collection of decorations in a room.

This example makes clear that when media objects become actors, there is usually some ambiguity about how seriously we should take this agency. The bowl of Beattie's story is as much a symbol of her interpersonal problems as a genuine actor in its own right; in a way, we are encouraged to "judge characters' judgments" when a character sees a bowl as an actor. In the case of Beattie's story, it seems clear that the bowl's agency is explained by a mixture of authorial-level symbolism and character-level psychology, where the bowl is an object onto which the narrator projects her feelings about her past. Examples of narratives in which media act in a more literal way are almost exclusively contemporary; in fact, I will discuss several of these over the course of this book. Toni Morrison's assertion that characters are controlled by music in *Jazz* might come to mind: "Alice Manfred had worked hard to privatize her niece, but she was no match for a City seeping music that begged and challenged each and every day. 'Come,' it said. 'Come and do wrong'" (67). We see media as agents in those contemporary narratives that, like *The Matrix*, describe future dystopias where media have converged into a self-perpetuating system. We also see media acting in theoretical inquiries into the forces that shape human creativity—in fact, much of the writing on media ecologies we discussed in the introduction could be seen as this kind of narrative. T. S. Eliot's "Tradition and the Individual Talent" is a kind of story in which the medium of art itself acts, using individual artists as passive tools: the mind of the poet "may partly or exclusively operate upon the experience of the man himself; but, the more perfect the artist, the more completely separate in him will be the man who suffers and the mind which creates; the more perfectly will the mind digest and transmute the passions which are its material" (54). In each of these cases, allowing the artwork or medium to become an actor drives the narratives toward a literal articulation of the media ecology. However, it should also be clear that this way of using media essentially stacks the deck in favor of one model of media relations, the account of media as a system. I have suggested that media *ecology* is a more powerful model for thinking about these relations than media *system*. Thus, although it may seem to be a natural way that contemporary fiction might articulate the relationship between writing and other media, in fact this form of media embedding makes only rare appearances in this fiction. Its absence suggests that contemporary authors are seeking a more nuanced understanding of the contemporary media ecology.

Media as Mise en Abyme

When Torgovnick defines the *hermeneutic* use of the visual arts in the modernist novel, she identifies what is the most direct and familiar way that narratives can position themselves within a media ecology through story-level objects. By concluding *To the Lighthouse* with the completion of Lily Briscoe's painting, Virginia Woolf is implying some similarity between the novel and the painting, and that the flash of insight that allows Lily to complete her painting applies to our reading of these characters and their relationships within the novel: "With a sudden intensity, as if she saw it clear for a second, she drew a line there, in the centre. It was done; it was finished. Yes, she thought, laying down her brush in extreme fatigue, I have had my vision" (209). With this closing line, the reader can also now see the novel as a whole and should be able to share Lily's epiphany. The painting essentially tells us how to read the novel; as Paul Goring says, "The reader is positioned to conceive of the novel in terms of the painting, and thus to 'see' its elements functioning in the same formal way as those in the painting" (222). Such *en abyme* figures involve a kind of metalepsis, in which the author uses an object at the storytelling level to make a commentary on the narrative at the level of the reader's interaction with the text.

Although metalepsis is often used to disrupt narrative,[4] in the case of media placed *en abyme* the effect is usually to emphasize the coherence of the work rather than to disorient the reader. Brian McHale notes that such *mise en abyme* figures can be particularly helpful in providing a whole image of the text when the work is complex or difficult to grasp. Taking the instance of Gilbert Sorrentino's *Mulligan Stew*, McHale describes the function of a masque within the novel: "The heterogeneity—disorienting shifts of style and mode, abrupt changes of level, and collision of planes that make the form of *Mulligan Stew* so hard to grasp—is captured in miniature in the masque" ("En Abyme," 194). Related to this use of *mise en abyme* is a second function: to provide a "model of the reader's relation to the novel's world" (198). This seems to be what Woolf is hoping to accomplish with Lily's painting, and we can hypothesize that models like this will be particularly common when authors worry that their readers may not know how to make sense of the novel. In a novel with so little plot resolution, and where the deaths of major characters take place in brackets in the novel's middle "Time Passes" section, Woolf clearly felt that she needed to nudge readers into recognizing that they are being offered a pleasure in reading *To the Lighthouse* that is different from what they would get from a traditional novel.

This kind of modeling is at work in the *Künstlerroman* tradition of novels about the development of an artist. As Maurice Beebe notes, "a portrait of the artist helps us to understand the novelist who wrote it. The novel can be seen in much the same manner as the writer's letters, diaries, notebooks, prefaces, or memoirs" (4). Jerome Hamilton Buckley notes that even though writers frequently treat their artist figures with some irony, this irony is generally defensive. For example, *Portrait of the Artist as a Young Man* "remains to a degree a self-apology; like most Bildungsromane, it demands a considerable sympathy for the hero, who is at least a partial portrait of the author as he was in his immaturity and early promise" (244). The aesthetic claims made by the artist-hero and the artworks described generally give us clues about the nature of the work that we are reading in much the same way as *en abyme* artworks might— although, as Buckley suggests, these works may be filtered through irony designed at least to suggest distance between the hero and the author.

Media at the Discourse Level

As we might expect, it is easier to understand the use of other media at the discourse level than at the story level. Appeals to media at this level seem to be relatively simple and involve the narrator adopting the style of one medium to convey the events of the novel. We might think, for example, about how Melville's narrator picks up language from drama when introducing Ahab into *Moby-Dick*, beginning with the chapter title "Enter Ahab; To Him, Stubb" and then continuing through the use of scene descriptions in "The Quarter-Deck": "*(Enter Ahab: Then, all)*" (257). Such scene descriptions become more common as the novel goes on, and eventually form the basis for the polyphonic dialogue of the "Midnight, Forecastle" chapter.

As this example makes clear, such uses of a style associated with another medium are usually limited to small sections in a larger work. Good examples of this are the "Camera Eye" and "Newsreel" sections of John Dos Passos's *U.S.A.* trilogy. In contrast to the theatrically inspired scene description that Melville works into his novel in several different ways, Dos Passos isolates these media imitations in specific (but recurring) sections. The "Newsreel" sections are fundamentally collage in nature, which creates strange and ironic combinations of information by juxtaposing stories and headlines: "Whites in Congo Lose Moral Sense" and "Woman Held a Captive by Ambulance Chasers" (79). Conversely, the "Camera Eye" sections strive for a direct presentation of subjective perception: "When you walk along the street you have to step carefully always on the cobbles so as not to step on the bright anxious grassblades easier if you hold Mother's hand and hang on it that way you can pick up your toes but walking fast you have to tread on too many grassblades the poor hurt green tongues shrink under your feet" (13). Joyce's *Ulysses* is, of course, an encyclopedia of discourse-level stylistic effects. In the Aeolus section, Joyce includes newspaperlike headlines between miniature sections of the chapter: "WITH UNFEIGNED REGRET IT IS WE ANNOUNCE THE DISSOLUTION OF A MOST RESPECTED DUBLIN BURGESS" (98). In the Circe section, Joyce adopts the form of a playscript, including separated scene descriptions and dialogue attribution.

These discourse-level uses of media directly position writing within a media ecology. Where story-level media objects frequently serve narrative mechanically, at the discourse level rhetorical goals are naturally more easily emphasized. Indeed, we see time and again that discourse-level uses of media are not just a way of telling a story but are also commentary on how stories *should* be told, and thus on writing's place within the media landscape. This use of media at the discourse level is a natural supplement to the *mise en abyme*, and like that device is often best at redirecting readers' expectations. This is why such devices are particularly common in difficult, modernist narrative. But novels from earlier periods also borrow the style of other media at the discourse level, especially for comic effect. A good example of this kind of borrowing is Thackeray's use of theatrical metaphors to frame *Vanity Fair*. He opens his novel "As the Manager of the Performance sits before the curtain on the boards, and, looks into the Fair, a feeling of profound melancholy comes over him in his survey of the bustling place" and ends his introduction by withdrawing to allow the novel to start: "And with this, and a profound bow to his patrons, the Manager retires, and the curtain rises" (5–6). In his novel, Thackeray does not imitate the style of drama so much as allude to it, but the effect is much the same in that both are ways of defining the novel by reference to some other medium.

Putting Aside Influence

In emphasizing the narrative role of media objects in these novels, I have consciously avoided instances where media could be described as merely influencing the narrative—what Torgovnick calls biographically motivated elements that direct us to the author's life more than into the work itself. Such influences are, of course, pervasive and important. Consider, for example, Alan Spiegel's influential *Fiction and the Camera Eye*, which describes the way that the visual thinking inherited from film influenced the novel: "By the time Joyce was writing *Ulysses*, a novelist need never have gone to a movie to know what was meant by one. The film 'idea' had become so much a part of a general cultural style that one could catch the tone and rhythm of what Arnold Hauser called 'the Film Age' in the ordinary events of one's daily life." Spiegel describes a particularly indirect form of influence, in which film's "visual consciousness" is manifested in media like billboards and magazines. As he writes, "Any artist could be influenced by film and know all about it simply by being alive and visually alert in the modern world" (xii–xiii).

The relation between literature and visual culture is an especially important instance of influence studies. In *The Emergence of Cinematic Time*, Mary Ann Doane examines the shifts in modern culture to which cinema and other forms of representation responded. She notes, for example, the challenge of accepting shock and chance:

> Nevertheless, shock is not to be avoided or rejected in a historically regressive nostalgia for the auratic. Instead, it must be *worked through*. Benjamin refers to Baudelaire—who in his estimation is the literary figure most sensitive to the phenomenological and epistemological crises of modernity—as a "traumatophile type," actively searching out the shocks of an urban milieu. Similarly, photography and film have a special relation to shock and, in the case of film, a potentially redemptive one. The snapping of the camera shares with other modern technologies the drive to condense time, the aspiration for instantaneity. But photography's impact upon the perception of the "moment" is historically decisive. (14)

Doane's suggestion that these media are trying to "work through" the challenges of modern culture nicely captures the basic assumptions of influence-based studies of media. Likewise, Nancy Armstrong's analysis of the influence of photography on the realist novel, *Fiction in the Age of Photography*, argues that the rising prominence of the photographic image in Victorian culture provided "the social classifications that novelists had to confirm, adjust, criticize, or update if they wished to hold the readership's attention" (3). She goes on to argue that literary realism itself is fundamentally dependent on this visual vocabulary. She gives the following example: "When a novel such as *Bleak House* refers to the street people and dilapidated tenements of nineteenth-century London, that novel is actually referring to what either was or would become a photographical commonplace" (5). Armstrong is not suggesting that the relationship is entirely one-sided; she explains that the novel and photography have a "mutually authorizing relationship" (5), but she is primarily concerned with those ways that this set of "visual codes" (11) was introduced into the novel and helped to shape the novel's vocation of "offering them [readers] mastery of the world of objects" (27).

I have intentionally avoided discussing borrowings like these and the narrative effects they produce because it seems to me that they address novels on a fundamentally different level—what we might refer to not as story or discourse but authorial-level perspective. The influences that critics like Armstrong and Spiegel describe manifest themselves in a variety of ways, some of which are subtle; such works may never mention films or photographs directly. The novels we are focusing on insert media in a much more direct way: locating explicit references to film or theater at the level of discourse, or inserting paintings or songs into the narrative at the level of story. Although works with such embedded media are usually easier to identify, the implications for the narrative itself can often be considerably more complex. In the works that we will discuss, media emerge as narrative objects that position writing in relation to other media. By including these media within the story, novelists are able to explore how each makes storytelling possible and to describe the limitations and predispositions imposed by those media. In contrast to the subtle, background, and frequently unconscious influence described by critics like Armstrong, the works discussed here are quite explicit in this rhetorical work.

Two Preliminary Examples

Media references made at the story and discourse levels have very different effects. Story-level uses of media often work to further the story, provide exposition, and join together narrative strands without necessarily making any comment on the media ecology. Conversely, media references at the discourse level have a considerably easier time making a comment on the relationship between writing and other media. However, such discourse-level references to media seem less engaged in specific narrative concerns about storytelling, character, and plot. That is, writers rarely seem to be compelled to direct the story in a particular way because of discourse-level media references. In contrast, if you make a main character a film director (for example), some settings and events become more or less natural additions to the story. The exception to this generalization is *mise en abyme*, and it should be no surprise that the most familiar novels about writing's relation to other media employ either an artist or an artwork that comments on this media ecology. This is a dominant strategy in the contemporary novel's immediate predecessor—the modernist narratives of Woolf, Joyce, and Mann. Indeed, writing in 1964 Maurice Beebe saw an explosion in the *Künstlerroman* tradition: "The tradition of artist fiction, which had developed steadily for more than a century, reached a crest in the first two decades of the twentieth century" (4).

Mise en abyme modeling has a significant limitation, however. In general, such *mise en abyme* figures function most naturally to show that two media can accomplish much the same thing. It should be no surprise, as a result, that this *en abyme* use of other media in the novel becomes especially common during the period when there is widespread interest in synesthesia and the unification of different artistic media articulated by Baudelaire and Kandinsky. Contemporary novels, as we will see, are more interested in the tensions between writing and other media, and usually explore the limitations of storytelling in different media instead of seeking out commonalities or analogues between those media. As a result, media appear in a much more complex position within the contemporary novel. And, because these writers are interested in the storytelling *effects* of these media, they tend to insert these media into the story level—all the while trying to explore this medium's relation to writing and the way that writing itself shapes the stories that can be told. To describe this general strategy in contemporary fiction, we will look at a series of increasingly sophisticated uses of other media in the contemporary novel.

In *Take It or Leave It*, Raymond Federman's invocation of jazz improvisation is a discourse-level commentary on the structure of his own narrative. Federman's picaresque story claims to be "an exaggerated second-hand tale," the story of a young Frenchman drafted into the U.S. Army, trained to be a paratrooper, who ends up traveling cross-country to San Francisco to depart overseas. Federman's narrative joyfully exploits the conventions of page and typography—inserting images, manipulating type for effect (for example, to suggest the confused motion of the troops as they charge), and even shaping the text block (for example, to form an image of paratrooper wings). Federman's playful narrative reflects his narrator's worries about whether the digressive story that he is telling is worthwhile. At one point a "Gentleman" intrudes to question the story: "In fact I find it rather incoherent rather styleless and even . . . no my little man don't try to hide in the crowd. . . . And even if he invents well even if he tells a good story it's not really literature it has no plot no dramatic development" (n.p.). In response, Federman offers a radically open-ended definition of literature as (in part) "a simple question of copying adding multiplying cutting folding correcting quoting transforming." The model for this style of writing is music. Looking back on the young man who told him the story that is being retold in this novel, the narrator remarks about its disjointed style:

> And his words, his pieces of sentences, his fucked up syntax,
>   began to articulate themselves into an incredible discourse!
> It quickly degenerated into a preposterous verbal mess
> a torrent of exclamations
> which I can only compare to a long uninterrupted tenor saxo-
>   phone solo and indeed it was pure improvisation
> without shape
> without form
> without order
> and to tell the truth without meaning

This description obviously matches the style of the novel as a whole and functions as a justification for its departure from convention.

Federman's use of another medium is quite straightforward, since it offers up jazz as a model for the novel. He is able to do this because he evidently believes that jazz embraces personal performance without regard to convention and that his readers will be able to accept this principle in music in a way that they might be unwilling to in literature. Federman's appeal to music as an aesthetic justification for his novel seems to be loosely equivalent to what Melville accomplishes with the use of theater in *Moby-Dick* or Joyce with the use of newspaper headlines in *Ulysses*. Indeed, Federman emphasizes that music is part of the *discourse* of the story, and what is at the center of this novel is the voice of the storyteller rather than the events that it relates; after all, Federman promises us "an incredible discourse."⁵ Such commentary clearly functions above the level of the story itself, is addressed directly to the reader, and works to position literature within a whole media ecology by claiming an entirely different vocation for the novel. Federman's fiction can be "pure improvisation" despite appearing to be "a preposterous verbal mess" according to traditional standards of good writing. Perhaps because of this, Federman also ends up using music as a simple analogue for writing, rather than exploring its similarities and differences from the novel. In other words, in asserting that his novel is like music, Federman simply provides a model for reading that to a large extent conforms to modernist practices.

As a novel that weaves another medium into its plot in a somewhat more complex way, consider Maxine Hong Kingston's use of theater in *Tripmaster Monkey: His Fake Book*. Kingston's novel tells the story of Wittman Ah Sing, a Chinese American poet and playwright who has recently graduated from college and now rambles around 1960s San Francisco. Much of the focus in the novel is on writing as the primary medium of creative expression; early in the novel, riding around on a city bus, Wittman thinks, "Will one of these listening passengers please write to the City Council and suggest that there always be a reader on this route? Wittman has begun a someday tradition that may lead to a job as a reader riding the railroads throughout the West" (9). Kingston's story, however, soon places the novel into a larger media context. Wittman's girlfriend, Taña, describes attending "America Needs Indians," which is glossed as "the first multi-media event in the world. There had been movies and slides, color, and black and white, projected against these four walls, the sky with moon and clouds overhead, and music and wise Indian voices chanting like Gregorian, like Sanskrit Buddhist" (152). Kingston focuses on how this event encourages audience participation and involvement: "The crowds turned around and around to see everything, and their juxtapositions" (152). This involvement is linked eventually to community theater. Kingston and Wittman express regret at the disappearance of the Chinese theater in San Francisco: "That friendship ritual was one thousand six hundred and twenty-nine years old when the Forty-Niners, our great-great-grandfathers, brought it to the Gold Rush. Every matinee or evening for a hundred years, somewhere in America, some acting company was performing *The Oath in the Peach Orchard*, then it disappeared, I don't know why. The theater has died" (141). Wittman decides to recreate this community theater to tell Chinese stories and myths, and particularly to involve the audience. He gives his actors—drawn from the many people he has met through the course of the novel because "everyone really does want to get into the act"—only a loose script, full of gaps "soon to be completed by improv and workshop" (276). The productions that occur change every night, and depend on contradiction and overlap to create a sense of energy and involvement: "This was not the end, only the end of a night's performance. Just because they all die, it isn't the end. Gwan's grandchildren were gathered to find out: Then what?" (284).

Kingston's vision of community theater at the end of *Tripmaster Monkey* depends, then, on breaking down traditional barriers between audience and actors, between history and invention, and between plot and spontaneous event. In this regard, Kingston's novel is much like Federman's (and Woolf's for that matter) in that it appeals to another medium to model what literary writing can and should do, to redefine the place of writing in the contemporary media ecology. It seems clear that for her the participation and multiplicity of story lines implicit in this community theater is simply inherently more realistic: "As in real life, things are happening all over the place. The audience looked left, right, up and down, in and about the round, everywhere, the flies, the wings, all the while hearing reports from off stage. Too much goings-on, they miss some, okay, like life" (298). Wittman clearly sees this community theater as the solution to the problem of isolation in America. In telling the history of the Chinese theater in America, Kingston remarks, "Anybody American who really imagines Asia feels the loneliness of the U.S.A. and suffers from the distances human beings are apart. Not because lonesome Wittman was such a persuader but because they had need to do something communal against isolation, the group of laststayers, which included two professional actors, organized themselves into a play" (141). The community theater works against this kind of isolation. At the end of the novel, Wittman gives an extended "combination revue-lecture" (288) that explains this link. Through the show "he was defining a community, which will meet every night for a season. Community is not built once-and-for-all; people have to imagine, practice, and re-create it" (306).

Like Federman's use of jazz, Kingston's appeal to community theater in this regard is quite straightforward: she holds up theater as a model that solves many problems implicit in the traditional novel. And just as Federman's novel seems improvised like jazz, Kingston has integrated her model (theater) in her own discourse-level style of telling in small ways; in particular, Kingston adopts a narrative voice that imitates an oral style and makes explicit reference to audience responses and expectations. The first chapter closes, "Our Wittman is going to work on his play for the rest of the night. If you want to see whether he will get that play up, and how a poor monkey makes a living so he can afford to spend the weekday afternoon drinking coffee and hanging out, go on to the next chapter" (35). Clearly, this voice is designed to replicate the style of address that Wittman strives for in the community theater. Kingston moves beyond Federman in integrating theater into the story itself, making the construction of theater part of the novel and consequently offering a more thorough articulation of the value of this other medium in story-level events. But that integration seems limited and ultimately only articulated clearly in the narrator's voice. In this regard, it is significant that Kingston ends the novel with Wittman's "revue-lecture" that makes his claims about isolation directly. Mita Banerjee has described this as the novel's primary formal novelty, "that it *explains* the quality of cultural open-endedness inscribed by its narrative style" (65), but in light of our discussion of story- and discourse-level uses of media, it is easy to see this as a kind of compromise formation. Here Kingston's novel blurs the line between story and argument and allows narrative *use* of another medium to be subordinated to making a comment about the relation between different media, about the media ecology. In this sense, although Kingston's novel clearly integrates media more thoroughly into the story-level characters and events than does *Take It or Leave It*, because she simply equates theater and the novel, her analysis of media relations remains relatively limited. It is only when writers are able to demonstrate the effects of media on the stories they tell—on the characters we encounter, the settings we visit, the plots that develop—that we really see novelists exploring the nature and limits of the novel.

Ambiguity and Metafiction in the Media Novel

A novel that takes media even further into the story level is Toni Cade Bambara's *The Salt Eaters*. In this novel, Velma Henry is undergoing a spiritual healing led by Minnie Ransom in a community infirmary in the town of Claybourne. She is struggling to overcome the grievances that she holds against friends and relatives within the community. At times the story moves out from Velma's mind through flashback or shifts to the perceptions of others in the room during the healing. But a great deal of the novel occurs with a much looser connection to this central scene, including characters with whom Velma apparently has no direct contact. There are times when Bambara suggests that the whole novel occurs in the time that Velma remains in the infirmary being healed (106), but other events muddy or complicate any clear temporal structure, including a musical performance that is apparently going on independently at the long-closed Regal Theater and an arts festival that is rained out by a thunderstorm.

Bambara obviously wants to challenge our traditional understanding of narrative time and place. In fact the novel ends with Ransom speaking to her spiritual guide, who comforts her, "Everything in time," to which Ransom replies, "Mmm. None of this ain't happened yet? Some of this is happening now? All of this is going on, but I ain't here? All of the above? None of the above? Will you at least tell me, is it raining or not?" (295). This exchange, on the last page of the novel, unravels the story and suggests that the narrative itself might be merely hypothetical or imagined. In her discussion of the novel, Eleanor Traylor suggests that its organization is "subjunctive" in the sense that events are offered as possible rather than definite: "The novel, which is less novel than rite, begins with a question. It moves around the central word, *if*. *If* we wish to live, *if* we wish to be healthy, then we must *will* it so. *If* we *will* it so, then we must be willing to endure the act of transformation. *The Salt Eaters* is a rite of transformation quite like a jam session" (69). Bambara's innovative organization arises from a spiritual model in which the everyday world is marked by interaction with loa and ghosts, or "haints." Again, Ransom's exchange with her guide helps to explain. Ransom asks of her, "You dead ain't you?" to which her guide replies, "There is no death in spirit, Min. I keep telling you. Why you so hard head? You and the gal on the stool cut from the same cloth" (62). Bambara's narrative, then, mixes the present, past, future, and possible not only because of the workings of particular characters' perceptions—Velma's thinking about her past or dreaming of others—but also because her narrative world itself blurs the line between the real and the possible, the living and dead.

One of the means by which Bambara accomplishes this complex and challenging form of narrative organization is by invoking music. The novel ends with a concert at the Regal, which itself is a sign of rebirth: "This was great, live music again at the Regal after all these years" (157). The thunderstorm that ends the novel and washes out the arts festival is also musical. Characters struggle to distinguish thunder from drums, and the rain itself is rhythmic: "The rain's music more insistent than the drumming sounding from across the way" (287). Even more direct, however, is the link that Ransom makes between Velma's healing and music. The healing itself is conducted to Ransom's singing: "Velma caught up, caught up, in the weave of the song Minnie was humming, of the shawl, of the threads, of the silvery tendrils that extended from the healer's neck and hands and disappeared into the sheen of the sunlight" (4). As the healing develops, Ransom specifically describes the visions Velma will experience and the movement between past and present that will constitute the novel as music: "We can't stay long now. The loa are setting up to make music for Velma to dance by" (62). Throughout the novel we are reminded of Ransom's presence by her humming (103, 106). The novel describes the healing as a "jam session" (114), and Minnie's job as a healer is to "put this music on" (262). At the end of the novel Ransom is reminded, "Dancing is her [Velma's] way to learn now" (264).

In *The Salt Eaters*, music is defined by rhythm and movement. It is for this reason that Bambara's main discussion of music in the novel refers to dancing: "And she'd have to travel the streets in six-eighth time cause Dizzy said righteous experience could not be rendered in three-quarter time" (264). Music does not offer an alternative principle for organization so much as a way of invoking rhythm in general. Rhythm, in turn, stands for experience and learning to understand the world differently. Indeed, throughout the novel Ransom is urging Velma to reexperience her past as she sends her off into memories and visions through her humming and touch:

A barrier falling away between adulthood and child. Like the barrier that dropped away for the passengers on the highway silent and still in the hum of the wheels over asphalt, silent and still in the sonic boom echoing back from a blasting event to occur several years hence, and to occur with so powerful an impact, its aftereffect ripples backward and spreads over their moment now, giving them a glimpse of their scripts which they can acknowledge and use, or ignore and have to reexperience as new. Always the choice. But with attention able to change directions as sharply and as matter-of-factly as the birds winging toward Claybourne. (104–5)

The choice here between ignoring an effect and being willing to "reexperience [it] as new" seems to be one faced directly by Velma. The description of this choice echoes the visual language used to describe habits throughout the novel. Bambara refers to "habits of illusion" that people live by (147) and links visibility to what people expect: "Invisible is being not visible . . . not looking like the something or someone a cop is after or a trickster is expecting" (158). This passage goes on to invoke Ralph Ellison's novel, specifically suggesting about "the Black man": "Our natures are unknowable, unseeable to them" (158–59). The visual stands for our knowledge, which is structured by expectations. For this reason, one of the goals of Velma's healing through dance is to get her to pay attention to "the eye of the heart. The eye of the head. The eye of the mind. All seeing differently" (7). Although it may at first seem like a mixed metaphor, Bambara's point seems to be that our understanding is all part of a larger way of moving through the world that fuses all of our senses in an experience of the body. This way of thinking about health as a way of experiencing the world is central to Velma's healing: "The rest of the old-timers, though, remained in deep concentration, matching the prayer group in silence and patience. For sometimes a person held on to sickness with a fiercesomeness that took twenty hard-praying folk to loosen. So used to being unwhole and unwell, one forgot what it was to walk upright and see clearly, breathe easily, think better than was taught, be better than one was programmed to believe—so concentration was necessary to help a neighbor experience the best of herself or himself" (107). Bambara links understanding of the world with a certain way of moving and experiencing the body, which is exemplified in dance. So it is that Ransom's song hummed to Velma during her healing feels like "notes pressing against her skin" (4–5)—hearing and seeing mix with other senses like touch to describe a whole manner of being in the world.

Bambara, then, wants us to think about memory and narrative as a matter of rhythm. In this, she is like Federman and Kingston because she models her novel on another medium. What makes *The Salt Eaters* different, however, is that Bambara seems as fascinated by the slipperiness of the novel-music connections as by their power. Indeed, one of the most striking parts of the novel is the ambiguity of some of the musical language. Critics have noted that one of the central problems in reading this novel is the difficulty of finding "a single, coherent voice" (Butler-Evans, 174). In part this can mean that we have difficulty in locating a single view of gender relations, but I want to emphasize that these problems carry over to the traditional task of representing characters' thoughts. Typical of the novel's style is the following passage from early in the story, when we are still clearly in Velma's consciousness:

All Velma could summon now before her eyes were the things of her kitchen, those things she'd sought while hunting for the end. Leaves, grasses, buds dry but alive and still in jars stuffed with cork, alive but inert on the shelf of oak, alive but arrested over the stove next to the matchbox she'd reached toward out of habit, forgetting she did not want the fire, she only wanted the gas. Leaning against the stove then as the performer leaned now, looking at the glass jars thinking who-knew-what then, her mind taken over, thinking, now, that in the jars was no air, therefore no sound, for sound waves weren't all that self-sufficient, needed a material medium to transmit. (19)

This much of the passage seems to be loosely a kind of stream of consciousness. But as it develops, the voice becomes more complex: "And she'd be still in the globes, in the glass jars, sealed from time and life. All that was so indelible on her retina that the treatment room and all its clutter and mutterings were cancelled out. Her kitchen, that woman moving about in obsessive repetition, the things on the shelf, the search, the demand would not let her eyes, let her, come back to the healer's hands that were on her now" (20). The voice in this passage drifts between Velma's mind and Ransom's way of explaining her mind, between imagery and analysis. When the passage begins, it seems clear that we are following the stream of Velma's thoughts; by the time it ends, it seems clear that we are hearing Ransom's analysis of Velma. This blurring of voice is typical of Ransom's role within the novel, which initially seems like a recorder but in other places seems to manipulate the story. As Traylor remarks about these kinds of slippages, "Suspended between sub- and midconsciousness, Velma half hears" these voices, including "Minnie's persistent hum" (63). Ransom reveals the ambiguity of imagery in the novel in general—which so often shuttles between character and author, between a representation of a mind and a use of that mind for literary purposes.

The complexity of reported thought has been debated by narrative theorists for decades. The central problem in analyzing narration that delves into a character's mind is being able to tease apart those elements that reflect the character's own thinking and those that reflect the analysis by the narrator. Alan Palmer has noted that much of the early work on the reporting of character thought privileged moments of "self-communing," where narrators are essentially able to record the characters as they speak to themselves mentally: "Self-communings lend themselves to the highly verbalized self-conscious form of thought that is known as *inner speech*, and the theoretical predilection for fictional introspection is accompanied by a decided preference for this form of thought" (9). Palmer goes on to note that "most of our lives are not spent in thoughtful self-communings" (53) and particularly urges attention to "the thought that takes place . . . in purposeful, engaged, social interaction" (59). Palmer's recent critique is a particularly clear articulation of a problem that has confounded critics since the beginning of modern narratology. In particular, Stanzel's "reflector characters," through whose eyes we see the events of the novel, reveal that the narrator's way of dipping into the minds of characters is more than simply representing a "stream of thoughts." Stanzel notes that even stories with a first-person narrator shuffle between character and authorial personality: "If we tried to assimilate the individual personality of a fictional narrator to the personality of the author for the sake of the clarity and reliability of the narrative, we would relinquish the most important use which the mediacy of narration has: to reveal the biased nature of our experience of reality" (11). Monika Fludernik has summarized this mediacy as the "dual voice" problem implicit in nearly all fictional representation of minds, as even the most traditional novels mix the representation of character thoughts with opinions and observations that can only be attributed to the narrator, "a contest, between figural and narratorial idiom, a merging or juxtaposition of voices, of the narrator and the character respectively" (323). This duality seems to be one of the ambiguities "afforded" (to borrow Ryan's term) by the medium of writing, since Fludernik and others have noted that such a dual voice is "first and foremost a linguistic concept" (322).

It is clear that Bambara is evoking exactly this traditional, theoretical problem in written narrative. Describing Velma as "dancing" manages to capture the ambiguity of the novel's description of character minds, since the characters must recognize rhythm themselves, and yet can only be "seen" dancing from the outside. The dance in which Velma participates in is poised between inside and outside worlds, a position that even the most traditional novel straddles as well. Bambara, we can say, has embraced the nature of writing and integrated its limits directly into the events of the story. Velma is healed in part because of ambiguities built into the nature of narrator voice. Music is not just a part of the discourse-level telling, as it is in Federman, and unlike Kingston, there is no simple equation of the novel and another medium offered. Instead, Bambara uses music as a way to reveal qualities that are especially important to writing. This is the reason that Bambara does not need a "revue lecture" at the end of the novel: she is not offering a simple claim about music's relation to the novel that can be lifted out of her performance as a writer. In other words, what is most important about Bambara's appeal to another medium is how it affects her telling of the story and how it helps to reveal some of the ambiguities of writing in general and the novel in particular.

Another narrative, Ronald Sukenick's short story "Duck Tape," similarly uses another medium, audio recording, to disrupt the distinction between teller and subject, and thus to investigate writing and the novel. Sukenick's story is written as if it were a transcription of a casual conversation between the male writer and his sometime girlfriend. The story initially is offered as a more or less factual account of what the writer knows about a past girlfriend and where he met her, but at the outset the writer is trying to decide how to reshape this material: "Maybe this is a story about coincidence," the man muses (70). As the writer's account develops over the next several pages, it becomes clear that he is inventing some details about this woman from his past, using his interlocutor as a sounding board. The interlocutor asks questions and helps the writer to develop and extend his story by offering possible explanations to cover gaps or vague spots in the woman's background. After explaining generally that "apparently as a freshman [she] got mixed up with some junky freak in New Haven" (77) the writer has to admit that it's surprising that she never got hurt while experimenting with the city's drug culture. "[S]he's lucky," the writer offers, but the interlocutor corrects him: "I'll bet it's not lucky, I'll bet it has something to do with the kind of vibes she puts out" (77). This in turn prompts a series of hypothetical scenes that the writer imagines: "Yeah imagine her going up to Harlem alone in the middle of the night for cocaine" (77). As the account winds down the writer fills in gaps and offers possible solutions to create resolution, all the while editing and revising his account.

Sukenick's use of audio recording focuses on what it means for something to be "in" the story. Initially this begins as a practical precaution of leaving names and details out of the story; the writer remarks about "this well known poet, whose name I'm leaving out of the story" (71). Later the dialogue turns to a mutual friend who is supposed to have eaten monkey brains in China, and the writer worries about "put[ting] him in the story": "I'm just worried about being sued. After all he's a famous lawyer" (80). Eventually the couple decides that they can't "be sued for anything so far" because "we didn't say anything about him why don't we drop it" (80). The issue in this exchange is whether this famous lawyer is now "in" the story, or by leaving out a name or keeping the details vague they have managed to keep him out of the account. Being in the story is even more complex in other places, and makes particularly rich use of the tension between the recorded and the transcribed dialogue. An exchange earlier in the story is particularly worth noting:

"You know nobody knows that you're a girl, I mean woman. Nobody knows that because this is being written down. I mean they can't see us. We're being written down now. We are written down in effect."

"Oh no, they know I'm a woman because I was talking about writing my name down on dollar bills for men and things."

"That's true."

"In fact I'm sitting here with my shirt off, can't they tell?"

"No that's what they can't tell. They would be very surprised. It's a topless duck dinner story." (74)

This passage plays on the gap between the tape recording—which presumably would make clear that the interlocutor is a woman by the quality of her voice—and the loss of that information as it is transcribed. Likewise, events and qualities become part of the account here only when they are mentioned in dialogue. The woman in the story becomes topless only when it comes up in conversation. Although in some ways innocuous, this gap between taped and written information clearly resonates with the issue of including real-life friends in the story and the kinds of legal problems that may ensue.

As the story goes on, tape recording becomes a means of describing the power of the novel. The change in the story begins shortly after the writer becomes nervous about being sued by the lawyer. The writer asks the woman, "Don't you think it's time to make it clear to everybody that this is a story I'm making up and not a tape recording?"

> "How do we do that?"
> "Easy. Just add 'he said, she said' to everything we say. Then we become characters who are being narrated."
> "'Okay.' She said.
> 'See, it's not hard at all.' He said. (81)

The story progresses from this point as a more conventional narrative, dutifully employing "he said" and "she said" throughout. With this transition into conventional writing comes power for the writer. In this passage, that power provides a certain protection from lawsuits, as the novelistic form marks the narrative as fictional. This is not, however, the only benefit of the written form of the dialogue. Shortly after the writer begins to use these conventions, descriptions of the characters' actions begin to crop up in the dialogue: "he said thoughtfully, crushing out his cigarette" (82). The woman responds to this description:

> "I didn't know you smoked."
> "Well I stopped, but I still like it, and in stories I can smoke without it being harmful to my health."
> "In that case, can I have one?"
> "Sure. In the story."
> "'What happened next,' she asked. Taking a deep drag on her cigarette. (82)

The introduction of description into the story finally moves it away from the transcription of a tape recording. In fact, early in the story Sukenick has to go out of his way to get events and characters into the story in dialogue, often unrealistically describing events or objects unnecessarily: "And here's the other cat. The other cat is walking through the room sneezing like a locomotive" (68). By this late point in the story, when the novelistic conventions of writing have been fully adopted, objects can get into the story without dialogue.

Acceptance of the conventions of the short story, then, provides the author with more control over the story. At the beginning of the narrative, the writer has ceded some control over his account of the woman to his interlocutor. In fact, early in the story the writer announces his plans: "But you have to remember this is my story so I can do what I like in it. You just happen to be in it. But I guess you have certain rights as a character. Since I let you loose" (69). His anxiety about the appearance of the lawyer in the story seems to confirm this lack of control. Adopting novelistic conventions allows the writer to assert more control and to limit characters' rights. This becomes especially evident at the end, when the writer removes himself from the story. He claims, "I don't have any sexual fantasies. I guess I just lack imagination. So my thing is I sort of hitch hike on other people's fantasies" (86). Initially this seems to be a humble admission of limitations, but it soon becomes apparent that by denying his own act of creativity the writer is working to control the story situation. He claims a few paragraphs later, "I don't make up stories, *he said*, I'm a lawyer. I deal in facts. The fact is that Pamela here has nothing but fantasies. If you took away her fantasies she'd evaporate like a ghost at dawn" (86). In contrast to the good-natured exchange that characterizes the earlier parts of the story, the interlocutor is limited now simply to resisting and rejecting the writer's story: "You're just projecting your fantasy life onto me. As usual" and "You're such a liar. He's psychopathic" (86). By the end of the story the writer has claimed authority and control over his story by adopting narrative conventions.

Read next to *The Salt Eaters*, Sukenick's use of another medium to reveal the nature of written narration is obvious. In both cases, other media do not simply provide a model for how the story is told (imitating a jazz solo, to use Federman's example) but also question the nature of narrative categories. In both cases, the outcome of the story depends on the presence of this other medium. Both use this medium to resolve plot lines and to achieve narrative goals—the healing of Velma Henry and the writing of the story in "Duck Tape," respectively. In these two cases, it is easy to see why having media occur at the story level of the narrative is so crucial: the presence of these media within the narrative allows us to see their influence on the way the story develops, rather than isolating the media at the discourse level of the description of the story. Somewhat more explicitly than Bambara, Sukenick uses these media objects to comment about the nature, power, and limitations of writing. "Duck Tape" confirms a quality that we observed in *The Salt Eaters*—that contemporary novels are more concerned with exploring the tensions between media than with asserting similarities between the novel and other media.

Media Objects beyond Metafiction

My thesis, then, is that contemporary novels use other media to explore the nature of novelistic writing, not as a simple aesthetic parallel (as the *mise en abyme* use of media does), but instead to provide an occasion for comparison and contrast, through which the qualities of the novel emerge. Because of this interest in tensions between writing and other media, these contemporary novels frequently feel like experiments in which the author and reader observe the way that other media affect the direction of the written narrative. Both Bambara and Sukenick have produced novels that emphasize the ambiguities and limitations of the medium: the duality of narrator voice in *The Salt Eaters* and the conflicting ways that people become part of the recorded and then written story in "Duck Tape." This emphasis on the contours and limitations of the medium of writing contrasts sharply to the tendency within modernist narrative to use other media *en abyme* to stretch the range of writing to include qualities that initially seem to belong to some other medium. There is, of course, no rule that all modernist texts must use *en abyme* structures, or that contemporary novels may never use them; after all, one of the examples of *mise en abyme* that I have cited from McHale is drawn from *Mulligan Stew*, a postmodernist novel by Gilbert Sorrentino. And it is not difficult to think of many modernist and contemporary novels that use media objects in even more traditional ways, from the theatrical setting as a site for character meetings in E. M. Forster's modernist *Howards End*, to the stolen film that becomes a plot object in Joseph McElroy's contemporary *Lookout Cartridge*. When I associate *mise en abyme* with the modernist novel and exploration of writing's limits with the contemporary novel, I am describing instead a broad aesthetic approach to the relationship between media that informs writings of these two periods. In many ways, this contrast is already well established through modernism's embrace of synesthesia and the interest among many contemporary writers in what the *Electronic Book Review* recently called "writing under constraint." From Oulipo through Jackson Mac Low and Walter Abish, contemporary writers have been fascinated by artificially imposed restrictions. The exploration of the limits imposed on a story by the medium of writing among contemporary media novels is simply one element of this broad trend.[6]

I want to correct one possible misunderstanding about contemporary media novels and their concern with limits. It may seem natural that such works gravitate toward ambiguity, incompleteness, and metafiction; in many ways, both *The Salt Eaters* and "Duck Tape" move in this direction. It is important to recognize, however, that an interest in the limits of writing does not necessarily entail a commitment to frustrating the reader or confusing narrative levels. Indeed, most of the novels concerned with other media that we discuss are not primarily metafictional or especially ambiguous. Thomas Pynchon's *Vineland*, a novel that accomplishes some of the same things that "Duck Tape" does, does so in a way that tells a somewhat more traditional story. What strikes me as especially interesting is that *Vineland* lacks the metafictional disruption of "Duck Tape" or even the earlier *Gravity's Rainbow*. Looking at *Vineland* helps us to broaden our understanding of the possible ways in which contemporary novels can make use of other media.

In many ways Pynchon's use of television in this novel is straightforward. *Vineland* is set in 1980s Reagan America and concerns Zoyd Wheeler, his ex-wife, Frenesi Gates, and their daughter, Prairie, whose lives in the novel's present resulted in part from Frenesi's radical political filmmaking in the 1960s. In contrasting the radical activities of the 1960s and the reduced lives of the 1980s, the political filmmaking of the 1960s and the consumerist television viewing of the 1980s, Pynchon seems to tell the story of a society that has simply become numbed by the contemporary media landscape. This is the accusation made by Prairie's boyfriend, Isaiah: "Whole problem 'th you folks's generation . . . nothing personal, is you believed in your Revolution, put your lives right out there for it—but you sure didn't understand much about the Tube. Minute the Tube got hold of you folks that was it, that whole alternative America, el deado meato, just like th' Indians, sold it all to your real enemies, and even in 1970s dollars—it was way too cheap" (373). Isaiah's critique certainly seems on the mark, since throughout the novel characters define their lives through television. Zoyd is approached by Hector Zuñiga, a DEA agent from his past, and Zoyd imagines his danger in terms of a television game show: "It was like being on 'Wheel of Fortune,' only here there were no genial vibes from any Pat Sajak to find comfort in, no tanned and beautiful Vanna White at the corner of his vision to cheer on the Wheel, to wish him well, to flip over one by one letters of a message he knew he didn't want to read anyway" (12–13). Such references occur throughout the novel: Pynchon invokes the Gidget movies (17), the Sylvester and Tweety cartoons (22), and *Star Trek* (285). Although some of these references occur in dialogue, the example of *Wheel of Fortune* suggests that Pynchon himself uses these references unironically as part of his narrator's voice. Particularly striking is Pynchon's citation of specific years for relatively trivial pop-culture artifacts: "They were talking about *Return of the Jedi* (1983), parts of which had been filmed in the area and in Buster's view changed life there forever" (7). This kind of specific date can only come from the narrator's own voice and certainly suggests a storyteller just as involved with popular media as his characters are.

Vineland is populated by a number of characters who are particularly obsessed with television. Shortly after his encounter with Hector, Zoyd meets up with "Dr. Dennis Deeply, M.S.W., Ph.D. / National Endowment for Video Education and Rehabilitation," who explains that Hector has escaped from a facility that treats "tubal abuse and other video-related disorders": "One of the most intractable cases any of us has seen. He's already in the literature. Known in our field as the Brady Buncher, after his deep although not exclusive attachment to that series" (33). Hector has apparently lost his grip on reality and has become obsessed with the idea of making a big-budget film about drug abuse: "Even with a 1% penetration we're oll gonna be rich forever off of this, man!" (51). Even more striking is the case of the Thanatoids, who are spirits kept from "advancing further into the condition of death" (171) by resentment and "karmic imbalances—unanswered blows, unredeemed suffering, escapes by the guilty" (173). "Thanatoids spent at least part of every waking hour with an eye on the Tube. 'There'll never be a Thanatoid sitcom . . . 'cause all they could show'd be scenes of Thanatoids watchin' the Tube!'" (170–71).

Like Hector, the Thanatoids seem to be part of a contemporary culture that has been completely warped by the omnipresence of television.

We make a mistake, however, if we conclude that Pynchon is simply calling for a return to a simpler time and a rejection of mass media. After all, the climactic moment in the novel occurs when Prairie finally meets her mother, from whom she was separated as an infant. They overcome their awkward first meeting by recalling that as a baby Prairie was happiest when watching *Gilligan's Island*: "Whenever the show came on, you'd smile and gurgle and rock back and forth, so cute, like you wanted to climb inside the television set, and right onto that *Island*—" (368). The reference breaks the ice, and Prairie and her mother are able to go off and "sit and hang out for hours, spinning and catching strands of memory, perilously reconnecting" (368). Television here clearly isn't just a matter of the decline and decadence of the 1980s, nor does television deaden or dull all human interaction. Likewise, late in the novel, Zoyd is comforted by a glance from Prairie that is described in television terms: "This look from brand-new Prairie—oh, you, huh?—would be there for Zoyd more than once in years to come, to help him through those times when the Klingons are closing, and the helm won't answer, and the warp engine's out of control" (285).

Television, then, has a much more complicated role in *Vineland* than Hector's comic "tubal abuse" suggests. We should note that the complaint that Isaiah makes is not simply that Zoyd's generation watches television but that it "sure didn't understand much about the Tube." This implies that television is less an unmitigated problem than something that can be easily misused, especially when it is taken as a source for plot models. The benign references to *Star Trek* or *Gilligan's Island* work by providing a way to understand the events that occur in life, but characters disabled by television seem to have internalized its narrative models in a more problematic way. Pynchon observes about Hector, perhaps mimicking Frenesi's point of view: "It was disheartening to see how much he depended on these Tubal fantasies about his profession, relentlessly pushing their propaganda message of cops-are-only-human-got-to-do-their-job, turning agents of government repression into sympathetic heroes" (345). Here television seems to disable critical thought by providing a narrative model that hides political repression.

Clearly Pynchon has integrated media objects into the most basic components of the story level of his novel. This is perhaps most fully (and playfully) brought home when we are told about Hector's wife, who in divorce proceedings "had named the television set, a 19-inch French Provincial floor model, as correspondent, arguing that the Tube was a member of the household, enjoying its own space, fed out of the house budget with all the electricity it needed, addressed and indeed chatted with at length by other family members, certainly as able to steal affection as any cheap floozy Hector might have met on the job" (348). But even beyond this instance where the medium becomes a character, it is clear that media objects influence the narrative itself, pushing characters into certain roles (Hector's tubal abuse) and making connections between characters possible (Prairie's bonding with her mother). Pynchon links these practical narrative uses of media to larger concerns about American culture, in part through characters who comment on the media ecology—like Isaiah's reference to the influence of television on Zoyd's generation—and also through media references in the narrator's voice. But like Sukenick and Bambara, Pynchon uses this medium ultimately to explore the nature of writing—and its most important suggestions about the media ecology appear not in a revue lecture or direct claim by the author's voice, but instead through the construction of the novel as a written document.

In *Vineland*, this exploration concerns the way that media can serve to produce an alternative reality. As Brian McHale notes, television in the novel is an "ontological pluralizer" (*Constructing*, 128). At the very beginning of the novel Zoyd stages a publicity stunt of diving through a plate-glass window before assembled reporters. After the stunt, Zoyd watches his performance replayed on television: "Over on one of the San Francisco channels, the videotape was being repeated in slow motion, the million crystal trajectories smooth as fountain-drops, Zoyd in midair with time to rotate into a number of positions he didn't remember being in, many of which, freeze-framed, could have won photo awards someplace" (15). Pynchon sees these media accounts as pointing to a ghostlike alternative narrative that stands alongside the main story. In fact, Pynchon invokes the ghost comparison when Prairie first has the chance to learn about her mother through a computer database: "So into it and then on Prairie followed, a girl in a haunted mansion, led room to room, sheet to sheet, by the peripheral whiteness, the earnest whisper, of her mother's ghost"

(114). The same comparison is evoked many times as a way to describe an alternative narrative: Prairie remarks, "Sometimes . . . when I get very weird, I go into this alternative-universe idea, and wonder if there isn't a parallel world where she decided to have the abortion, get rid of me, and what's really happening is is that I'm looking for her so I can haunt her like a ghost" (334). Frenesi has the same sort of feeling when she decides to turn against campus revolutionary Weed Atman back in the 1960s: "Frenesi understood that she had taken at least one irreversible step to the side of her life, and that now, as if on some unfamiliar drug, she was walking around next to herself, haunting herself, attending a movie of it all. If the step was irreversible, then she ought to be all right now, safe in a world-next-to-the-world that not many would know how to get to" (237). In the novel, television and film are associated with invoking these other worlds. This is most clear in the flashback story of Frenesi's 1960s filmmaking. The political activity of the group is described as "a doomed attempt to live out the metaphor of movie camera as weapon" (197). This metaphor is certainly a cliché, but it is animated and renewed by Pynchon's interest in alternative and parallel worlds opened up my media. As the Kollective's manifesto says, "A camera is a gun. An image taken is a death performed. Images put together are the substructure of an afterlife and a Judgment" (197).

Pynchon's narrative, then, is woven of these other possible stories, which remain shadowy presences within his novel—what McHale calls "a world next door" (*Postmodernist Fiction*). Although Pynchon uses film and television to invoke these alternatives, he sees the novel as particularly good at organizing them. In fact, the main challenge Pynchon's characters face—what Isaiah claims Zoyd's generation does not understand—is keeping these pluralities in context. The failure of television addicts like Hector is the inability to sort actual from alternative narratives. If another medium is able to cover reality completely and to provide a totalizing template, then these alternative narratives lose their "shadowy" quality and become real—in the process, making the characters involved passive. Over and over again, Pynchon associates this inability to separate possibility from actuality with television. In fact, there are good reasons to think that written narrative is particularly able to represent and sort these incomplete, alternative narratives that spring up around the novel's main plot line. In her discussion of fictional worlds and narrative theory, Marie-

Laure Ryan offers a complex, modal structure of the narrative universe in which the "textual actual world" of the story is surrounded by a halo of other worlds: obligation worlds that describe "a system of commitments and prohibitions defined by social rules and moral principles" (*Possible Worlds*, 116); wish worlds that are defined by "propositions involving the axiological predicates good, bad, and neutral" (117); pretended worlds created "in order to deceive another" (118), and so on. Ryan notes that visual narratives can sometimes replicate these functions by describing nonactual states (95–101); dream sequences are common in film, and thought bubbles are a standard element of graphic narratives. But Ryan's account of modality arises first and foremost out of an understanding of verbal reference and the kinds of linguistic modal operators that make possible references to nonactual states: "I wish I'd brought an umbrella." Language gives us an especially sophisticated framework for contextualizing these imagined possibilities. In writing we can easily distinguish between many different modalized worlds in a way that would be more difficult in visual narrative: "I wish I'd brought an umbrella," "I'm glad I didn't bring an umbrella," "I was afraid to bring an umbrella," "I didn't know that I was expected to bring an umbrella," and so on. I discuss this quality of writing in more detail in chapter 3, but it seems that one of the "affordances" of verbal language exploited by the novel is facility at organizing nonactual states into a complex network of nested worlds.

Like Bambara and Sukenick, Pynchon uses another medium in order to discover the particular strengths of writing. What seems especially important in the context of this chapter is that Pynchon gets to this particular quality of written narrative by integrating a media object (television) into the basic story level of his novel and then by exploring its effects on the action. Where *Vineland* departs from *The Salt Eaters*, and especially from "Duck Tape," is by creating the tension between writing and this other medium (television) without relying on the metafictional breakdown between character and author. Instead, the "ontological plurality" made possible by television is encountered and explored by the characters themselves, and we discover the power of writing by understanding how it differs from television and film. Integrating this medium into the world of the narrative is one of the reasons that *Vineland* is perhaps the most accessible of all of Pynchon's novels. All the stories discussed in this chapter can be considered variations of the contemporary use of media to position writing within an ecology, but in many ways Pynchon's strategy of creating a media object (television) which then circulates through the novel—encountered by character and author alike, reflecting the challenges of storytelling but also making some kinds of stories possible—represents a particularly clear break from the modernist use of media as *en abyme* representatives of the novel. In the next chapter, we will focus on the circulation of these media objects through the story world.

2 : Story, Discourse, and Circulation

The contemporary novel uses media other than writing as a way to investigate the strengths and ambiguities that writing provides to the novel. Already we have seen some of the ways that media stories like "Duck Tape," *The Salt Eaters,* and *Vineland* investigate some of the basic elements of narrative as they appear in writing. In the next chapter we will discuss this in a systematic way and come to some tentative conclusions about what contemporary authors find to be unique about the novel as a written medium. This investigation into the qualities of writing is fundamentally rooted in an understanding of the uses to which media are put. Following Marie-Laure Ryan we have located the differences between media primarily in their cultural uses. To return to an example discussed earlier, the difference between newspaper and novel is not based so much in their inherent physical qualities as in the role they play in our lives. The contemporary media novel is particularly concerned with precisely this issue—the way that media objects *circulate* within a community and achieve their significance though their role in our lives. We have already seen this in *Vineland*'s use of television, where that medium becomes an object to which characters react within the story itself.

Ultimately, how media objects circulate within a community gives them their meaning. In turn, recognizing the importance of circulation leads us to appreciate the power and necessity of media limits. Once we understand that media objects are put to use within a cultural context, the limits of a medium are less a restriction than an opportunity to *move across* boundaries, groups, and uses by handing the story off to other media. This link between media limits and what I call the "middle spaces" between author and public is gradually unpacked over the course of this book.

Story/Discourse/Circulation

I have invoked the standard distinction between story and discourse, but I suggested that the representation of media within the story world as an object that circulates within a community complicates narratology's traditional focus on mediacy. Returning to this distinction between story and discourse helps us to see how introducing the issue of the uses to which a story (or, for that matter, any media object) is put complicates but also resolves some problems inherent in narrative in general. Patrick O'Neill clearly articulates one of the central problems of the story/discourse distinction: "The more closely we examine the notion of story, the apparently most basic and most solid level of narrative, in fact, the more clearly it reveals itself as a readerly construct, a putative back-formation from what is really the most basic level, namely, the narrative text itself, the words upon the page, the *account* of what happened. Story, as Rimmon-Kenan observes, is ultimately merely an abstraction from the narrative text" (40).

O'Neill describes the myth on which the story/discourse distinction depends: that there is some preexisting "story" that is then articulated through the "discourse." Especially in the case of fictional narratives, this account of the movement from story to discourse is obviously untrue. Even in apparently nonfictional narratives, the story that we discover in the process of reading cannot be understood to preexist its telling in any simple way. A historian may frequently piece together the real story only in the process of writing about it. Likewise, few of us would argue that the story we choose to tell often reflects what we think will be effective in its presentation. The story, in other words, is an effect of discourse as well—in fact, it is an effect that is even more complex because it presents itself not in the discourse directly, but at a doubly constructed distance once removed from the actual account of the writer. This is what O'Neill calls a back-formation. Jonathan Culler suggests that this means that the interpretation of any narrative will have to be a "double reading" (176). Taking as his example the way that Oedipus uses prior events to define his guilt, Culler explains:

> This logic by which event is the product of discursive forces rather than a given reported by discourse is essential to the force of the narrative, but in describing the play in this way we have certainly not replaced a deluded or incorrect model of narrative by a correct one. On the contrary, it is obvious that much of the play's power depends on the narratological assumption that Oedipus's guilt or innocence has already been determined by a past event that has not yet been

revealed or reported. Yet the contrary logic in which Oedipus posits an act in response to demands of signification is essential to the tragic force of the ending. These two logics cannot be brought together in harmonious synthesis; each works by the exclusion of the other; each depends on a hierarchical relation between story and discourse which the other inverts. (175)

The distinction between story and discourse, which is fundamental to traditional narratology, in this regard depends on a misdirection in our understanding of what a story is "about."

The problems with the traditional narratological distinction between story and discourse has no doubt been heightened by the feeling that postmodern culture has eroded the nature of firsthand experience. Indeed, the somewhat technical debate that Culler and O'Neill engage in can be seen as a corollary to the postmodern expansion of simulation, which Jean Baudrillard famously articulated: "The age of simulation thus begins with a liquidation of all referentials—worse: by their artificial resurrection in systems of signs, which are a more ductile material than meaning, in that they lend themselves to all systems of equivalence, all binary oppositions and all combinatory algebra. It is no longer a question of imitation, nor of reduplication, nor even of parody. It is rather a question of substituting signs of the real for the real itself" (167). Baudrillard describes here a kind of nonexperience engineered through a system of representations that refer only to themselves. There are many different (but interrelated) reasons why we feel that experience has been suppressed or problematized by simulation. One is what John Johnson refers to as "the fundamental incompatibility between experience and information" (37), the feeling that the abstract information that floods our daily life isolates us from direct experience. This flood of information results from the increased role of media in our everyday lives. Andy Warhol summarizes the way that media transforms personal experience in *The Philosophy of Andy Warhol*. He explains,

The acquisition of my tape recorder really finished whatever emotional life I might have had, but I was glad to see it go. Nothing was ever a problem again, because a problem just meant a good tape, and when a problem transforms itself into a good tape it's not a problem

any more. An interesting problem was an interesting tape. Every-body knew that and performed for the tape. You couldn't tell which problems were real and which problems were exaggerated for the tape. Better yet, the people telling you the problems couldn't decide any more if they were really having the problems or if they were just performing. (26–27)

Warhol's style depends on exaggeration, and in some ways he is offering a caricature of contemporary media culture. Nonetheless, the transformation that he is describing is similar to Baudrillard's. Warhol is less interested in the experience (problems) and more in the representation and circulation of that experience on tape.

The effects of embedding a different medium within written narrative, which I described in the previous chapter, can be seen as a reflection of these problems of experience. Indeed, the breakdown of the line between narrator and tale that is evident in "Duck Tape" and *The Salt Eaters* means that there is no story that the narrator is simply relating; instead, the narration itself becomes an element of our experience of the work. In other words, this narrative has at its heart the disappearance of the prior experience that a story is traditionally supposed to be conveying. Although early accounts of postmodernism tended to describe breakdowns like this as a feature of contemporary life, the shock of nonexperience has been implicit in media since the advent of early devices for mechanical recording like photography and the phonograph. Friedrich Kittler notes that, unlike painting or writing, "the phonograph permitted for the first time the recording of vibrations that the human ears could not count, human eyes could not see, and writing hands could not catch up with" (*Gramophone*, 118). These include events that we can see only when they are recorded and slowed down—for example, the beating of the hummingbird's wings. Likewise, Kittler notes that the phonograph makes possible "generating acoustic phenomena without any previous acoustic existence by scratching the necessary marks on the record" (46). Nonexperience, then, is made possible by mechanical recording already evident in the nineteenth century. Pynchon probes this kind of nonexperience in *Vineland* in the already-quoted passage in which Zoyd watches his performance of crashing through a window replayed on television: "Over on one of the San Francisco channels, the videotape was being repeated in slow motion, the million crystal trajectories smooth as fountain-drops, Zoyd in midair with time to rotate into a number of positions he didn't remember being in, many of which, freeze-framed, could have won photo awards someplace" (15). In some ways, all fictional narrative exploits nonexperience while denying it, since fiction implicitly promises to give the reader an experience of something that never happened.

What makes the contemporary media novel different, however, is that this quirk of narrative becomes the ground upon which these novels build a structure capable of analyzing the particular limitations of writing. These media novels add to the story/discourse distinction an additional layer focusing on the circulation of those stories within a community. Such circulation then provides the means to analyze the cultural definitions of writing as a medium, and thus the place of writing within the current media ecology.

Complicating Experience as the Basis of the Media Novel

We begin with a novel that is about the attempt to reclaim experience from the conventional literary forms that try to limit it. This attempt to validate experience leads in an unlikely direction to an interest in how narratives and other media circulate within a community.

Ishmael Reed's *Yellow Back Radio Broke-Down* tells the story of Loop Garoo, who was (as the opening paragraph of the novel explains) "a cowboy so bad he made a working posse of spells phone in sick. A bullwhacker so unfeeling he left the print of winged mice on hides of crawling women. A desperado so ornery he made the Pope cry and the most powerful of cattlemen shed his head to the Executioner's swine" (9). This opening exemplifies the tone of the novel, which imitates the tall-tale Western style but mixes in references to the supernatural ("a posse of spells") and anachronistic contemporary life ("phone in sick") in a way that creates a strange layering of traditionally separate frames of reference. Loop plays the role of a Western outlaw who uses "hoodoo" magic to work against the interests of established government, religion, and business. Loop's antagonist is Drag Gibson, the "most powerful of cattlemen," who hopes to drive Loop from the town of Yellow Back Radio. This town has been taken over by children, and their parents have sought out Drag for help. Loop uses magic to call down a "wangol" on Drag: "It will be the strongest malice ever. Never again will they burn carnivals and murder children" (62). The curse that Loop puts on Drag seems to be working; in fact, it is so effective that the latter has to seek out the help of the Pope himself, who tells Drag, "It's important that we wipe it [Loop's hoodoo religion] out because it can always become a revolutionary force" (154). In the end, we discover that Loop is less concerned with defeating Drag himself than with becoming a martyr to help to start the practice of hoodoo in America. Asked by the Pope what his point is, Loop explains:

> Horse opera. Clever, don't you think? And the Hoo-Doo cult of North America. A much richer art form than preaching to fishermen and riding into a town on the back of an ass. And that apotheosis. How disgusting. He had such an ego. "I'm the Son of God." Publicity hound, he had to prolong it for three hours, just because the press turned out to witness. And his method had no style at all. Compare his cheap performance at the gravesight of Lot—sickening—and that parable of our friend Buddha and the mustard seed. One, just a grandstand exhibition, and the other, beautiful, artistic, and profound. (163)

In the end, however, Loop is rescued when the children of the town return; the children, in turn, are distracted a moment later: "Come on, let's go, the late late late show is about to begin on the boob toob and we can watch eating Pooped Out Soggies" (173). Loop eventually sails off with the Pope, having been "left standing on the scaffold and cheated out of his martyrdom" (174).

Loop describes a kind of artistic practice that departs from our traditional ideas about serious art and writing. Although Loop associates himself with the avant-garde (164–65), he also works against attempts to limit art to narrow institutional roles. The hoodoo spell that he casts ends by calling for a more inclusive definition of cultural experience and art: "O Black Hawk American Indian houngan of Hoo-Doo please do open up some of these prissy orthodox minds so that they will no longer call Black People's American experience 'corrupt' 'perverse' and 'decadent.' Please show them that Booker T and the MG's, Etta James, Johnny Ace and Bojangle tapdancing is just as beautiful as anything that happened anywhere else in the world. Teach them that anywhere people go they have experience and that all experience is art" (64). Later, Loop's spells are specifically associated with jazz performance; he is described as "scatting arbitrarily, using forms of this and adding his own. He's blowing like that celebrated musician Charles Yardbird Parker—improvising as he goes along" (154). In both of these passages, music stands in for those artistic practices that depart from narrow ways of thinking about creativity. For Reed, redefining what counts as a valid form of artistic activity is inherently connected to changing cultural experience.[1] For this reason Reed includes his famous satire of Bo Shmo in this novel, the leader of the "neo-social realist gang" who criticizes Loop for obscurity and being "given to fantasy and . . . off in matters of detail. Far out esoteric bullshit is where you're at" instead of using realism to liberate the masses (35–36). For Reed, conversely, liberation begins first and foremost by validating forms of cultural experience and expression that have been neglected or denied both by mainstream and politically revolutionary forces: "No one says a novel has to be one thing. It can be anything it wants to be, a vaudeville show, the six o'clock news, the mumblings of wild men saddled by demons" (36).

It is into this complex dynamic, then, that Reed's use of mass media like radio and television comes. When the adults turn to Drag for help, they give him control of the town as if it were a media device; they promise to "give you the hand over of Yellow Back Radio, so that you could adjust all the knobs and turn to whatever station you wished" (22). Nearby is another town, Video Junction, which becomes part of Drag's plan: "Now get busy and before you know it Drag Gibson will be the big name in Yellow Back Radio and then Video Junction then va-va-voom on to the East, heh heh heh" (23). The fight over Yellow Back Radio, then, is an allegory for the control of mass media; Loop struggles to keep these media from being taken over by the large businesses that Drag embodies, and instead to use them for revolutionary purposes. His magic involves being in two places at once, and this is possible apparently because Loop is able to take over the control room of a television station: "All the engineers were in the control room, transfixed. She [a woman from a talk show] said that the Loop Garoo Kid come in there and put some bad waves into her transmitter. She said the 'demons of the old religion are becoming the Gods of the new,' cause he put something on her that had her squawking like a chicken" (83). In this sense, Loop's struggle with Drag is an attempt to wrest control of media from him.

But Reed's novel is not quite so simple. What is most important about

Loop's fight to represent experience is that his stories get away from him and are swept up into another level of narrative entirely. We will recall that at the end the children go off and ignore Loop, seduced by the promise of the "late late late show." Likewise, it is not clear that the children's rejection of adults at the beginning of the novel is an entirely good thing. They complain that they chased the adults out of town in part because "we went to school to hear teachers praise the old. Made us learn facts by rote. Lies really bent upon making us behave. We decided to create our own fiction" (16). Although the creative energy of the children seems positive, Loop himself is steeped in tradition and earns mockery even from his helpers because of his attachment to hoodoo rituals (60). The children are also drawn to the promise of a technical paradise where everyone is freed from work, which seems to foreshadow their fondness for television at the end: "Inanimate things, computers do the work, feed the fowl, and programmed cows give cartons of milkshakes in 26 flavors" (17). When they leave Loop behind, it is specifically because they found this "really garish smaltzy super technological anarchoparadise" that is "as far as you can see from where you're standing now" (170). In this sense, technology itself seems to be a dangerous and seductive undercurrent in the use of mass media. This is why Loop is shown throughout the later part of the novel to be working against Yellow Back Radio as a vehicle for transmission. The town is described as "falling apart, its batteries were going on the bum, and soon the whole kit and kaboodle would blow a fuse" (134), and instead of helping to repair it, Loop is described as "riding back to the cave to get on with the serious business of closing every conceivable repair shop available to Yellow Back Radio, whose signals were needless to say becoming very very faint. In fact, it seemed that the whole valley would soon be off the air" (118). It would seem, then, that while Reed finds some elements of mass media attractive, he sees in this technology more danger than promise.

Early accounts of Reed's novel naturally emphasized the way that he plays on literary forms, but this interest in literary forms and styles is supplemented by the larger and more problematic issue of media transmission. This is obviously the case when Reed describes the control of radio and television signals. But it seems to me that this issue of transmission is also evident in the way that the story is received by the children that Loop is trying to save, since those children turn around and neglect the story because they are blinded by the possibility of the technological future. In other words, a fundamental mistake on Loop's part is to assume that the challenge of being a writer is to find forms appropriate for the representation of experience. Loop's fight with Bo Shmo—which critics love to quote—assumes that telling stories about experience is a matter of unpacking the baggage in our discourse-level styles and freeing up the writer to tell stories in whichever way he or she sees fit. But in the end, although Loop wins his battle with Bo decisively, he loses the war with Drag because he does not solve the larger issue of the dissemination of these resulting narratives: how they are packaged and distributed to the audience. The stories that Loop tells—for all that they are revolutionary and powerfully attuned to the lives of the children—get caught up within the network of transmission, and it is here that Loop loses control over them. The desire to control every aspect of transmission is associated in the novel with Drag, and so it should probably be no surprise that such control escapes Loop. It is a sign of the children's freedom in the end that they can choose to ignore Loop.

Reed's novel, then, stages a transformation of traditional narrative but not quite in the way critics have previously imagined. Initially, the novel distinguishes experience and its forms of articulation, which are embodied in the contrast between story and discourse. Loop is, in other words, a more skillful narrator than Bo Shmo. But implicit within Reed's novel is a third element—the transmission or circulation of that articulation within the larger world. This third dimension for storytelling moves beyond the issue of the story and how it is told and instead emphasizes the life that this story takes on after its articulation. We have, then, three elements: a story that is told, a particular way that story is presented to the reader by the narrator, and an account of the way that presentation is transmitted to and circulates among the audience. Of course, this concern with the circulation of the story cannot be called another layer of the narrative in the literal sense that (for example) a framing device like the "General Prologue" of *The Canterbury Tales* adds another layer to the individual stories told by the travelers. There are, of course, ways that we might genu-inely add another layer to the text. This can involve additional elements of editorial commentary that describe the life the story takes on after its composition. Mark Danielewski does this in *House of Leaves*, where the story of the film *The Navidson Record* produces a heterogeneous and disorganized manuscript that is then framed by an editor's notes and commentary. Most of the novels discussed in this book address this issue of transmission not by treating it as a separate level of the work, but instead by integrating the issue into the thematic structure and plot of the novel. In some ways, this makes the issue of circulation somewhat less challenging to narrative structure than the metafiction of a story like "Duck Tape." However, because circulation can manifest itself in a wide variety of ways through plot and theme, it is also more flexible and capable of contributing in a greater number of ways to the storytelling goals of the novel.

Narratives of Media Circulation

We opened with Reed's *Yellow Back Radio* because this novel addresses the changing place of experience within novels focused on media, and because it beautifully captures the way that contemporary fiction is moving beyond the story/discourse structure for its narratives. Reed's novel does not, however, articulate much of a story about the circulation of media objects after their moment of telling. Instead, circulation emerges mostly as a forgotten element that ruins Loop's plans. Two novels that do depend on the extensive circulation of media objects are Oscar Hijuelos's *The Mambo Kings Play Songs of Love* and Tom Robbins's *Still Life with Woodpecker*.

Hijuelos's novel opens with two Cuban musicians appearing on *I Love Lucy* where they are cast as Ricky Ricardo's friends scheduled to play his nightclub, the Tropicana. In fact, the novel does not even open with the two brothers, Cesar and Nestor Castillo, actually playing on the show, but instead with Nestor's young son excitedly watching a rerun of the episode long after his father had died and Cesar had degenerated into alcoholism. This captures the peculiar way that media other than writing is handled in this novel. *Mambo Kings* is less concerned with music itself—indeed, we see relatively few performances—and more interested in the afterlife of music and its recordings in records and television shows. After this initial encounter with the rerun, the novel shifts back twenty-five years to narrate the two brothers' immigration to the United States, their one genuine musical hit, and the circumstances of their appearance on *I Love Lucy*. Their hit song is the same one that attracts Desi Arnaz's attention and earns them the invitation to perform on his show: "Beautiful María of My Soul." Although written before he meets her, the song becomes associated with Nestor's frustrated romance with a woman (María) with whom he falls in love but who leaves him to return to her abusive husband in Cuba. The loss of María haunts Nestor for the rest of his life and makes his early death in a car crash seem more self-inflicted than accidental. Indeed, both brothers are haunted by the past. Nestor's son, Eugenio, notes this as he narrates his excitement about seeing *I Love Lucy* at the outset of the novel, as Cesar is sleeping on the couch:

> Between the delicate-looking index and middle fingers of his right hand, a Chesterfield cigarette burning down to the filter, that hand still holding a half-glass of rye whiskey, which he used to drink like crazy because in recent years he had been suffering from bad dreams, saw apparitions, felt cursed, and, despite all the women he took to bed, found his life of bachelorhood solitary and wearisome. But I didn't know this at the time, I thought he was sleeping because he had worked so hard the night before, singing and playing the trumpet for seven or eight hours. (4–5)

The novel fundamentally changes after Nestor's death, when Cesar enters a kind of afterlife. Hijuelos embodies this shift in time in the structure of the novel by moving away from linear narrative in the second half of the novel. The first part of the novel is subtitled "Side A: In the Hotel Splendour 1980" while the second is called "Side B: Sometime later in the night in the Hotel Splendour." This shift from a definite (but retrospective) narrative reference of the hotel to the vague sense of "sometime later" captures the way that Cesar's life falls apart after Nestor's death. Although Hijuelos narrates Cesar's alcoholism and gradual self-destruction through this first section, many of the details of his life after Nestor do not appear until later as he is waiting to die in the Hotel Splendour and dreaming about his earlier life—and when they do appear, they are introduced out of chronological order.

Clearly, Hijuelos is describing the relationship between an experience that produces a song, and the way that that song takes on a role in the lives of characters once it has been written and recorded. In his study of American audio recording in the twentieth century, Tim Anderson notes that recordings of musical performances originally "manifested an anxiety, an uneasiness that every musical recording must confront at the act or reproduction: that the lack of a live performer would constitute a substantial aesthetic gap" (119). Anderson notes that the rise of high-fidelity recording technology pushes the experience of music further and further away from the authenticity of the original performance, making the recording "a purer, ideal musical experience that strained undesirable elements out of the concert-going experience. Specifically these elements included noisy audience members and inconsistent acoustic spaces" (128). As a result, the record becomes a musical artifact independent of any prior experience that it records. *Mambo Kings* reflects this shift from original experience to recorded artifact. The translation of the experience of love into the hit record "Beautiful María of My Soul" is the central event of the brothers' lives. And yet, what drives the novel is not the love itself but rather the afterlife of that love in the form of a recording. The song gives Nestor and Cesar recognition for the rest of their lives; it is covered by a number of famous singers like Nat King Cole. "You can still hear it on the Muzak tapes, stuck between an unbearably cheerful pipe-organ version of 'Guantanamera' and '*Quizás, Quizás, Quizás!*' in supermarkets, shopping malls, airports, and bus-terminal lounges everywhere" (154). Cesar is able to scrape by economically because of the royalties that he continues to receive from the song for the rest of his life. Aside from the ghostly dissemination of the song in airports and supermarkets, the physical recording of the album also appears through Cesar's later life: "By the mid-seventies, most of these records had vanished from the face of the earth. Whenever Cesar would go by a secondhand store, or a 'classic' record rack, he would search carefully for new copies to replace the ones that had gotten smashed or lent out or given away or just worn out and scratchy from so much use. Sometimes he found them for 15 cents or 25 cents and he would walk happily home, his bundle under his arm" (15–16).

Part of the shift from focus on firsthand experience to the afterlife of the media object reflects Hijuelos's evident belief that any narrative is constructed retrospectively. When narrating a central event of the novel, a scene where Desi Arnaz is invited back to the Castillo house for a late-night dinner and invites the brothers to be on the show, the narrative is strangely uncertain:

Or perhaps they'd simply met Arnaz, who liked their music and, approaching them at the bar, said, "Would you fellows like to be on the show?" All business, with the fatigue of responsibility showing on his face. Or perhaps he had an air of weariness and exhaustion about him that reminded Cesar and Nestor of their father, Don Pedro, down in Cuba. Perhaps he had sadly yawned and said, "*Me siento cansado y tengo hambre*—I am tired and hungry." Whatever happened, he and his wife accompanied the brothers uptown to the house on La Salle Street. (130)

This gap in the narrative continues a theme introduced earlier in the scene, where the brothers discover that they share a mutual friend back in Cuba, leading them to imagine earlier meetings: "And then in the way that Cubans get really friendly, Arnaz and Cesar reinvented their pasts so that, in fact, they had probably been good friends" (127). This theme of reconstructing the past is reflected in the design of the novel. Past events and experiences remain relatively inaccessible in this novel, knowable only by the traces that they leave behind in concrete events: the visit to the apartment, the invitation to appear on the show. These traces have their clearest embodiment in the objects that circulate within the community: music records and television reruns.

Physical records and broadcast reruns, then, have a life of their own in this novel, and it seems clear that *Mambo Kings* is really a novel about their circulation rather than about the musical inspiration of these two men. According to Hijuelos's view of the medium, it would seem that music becomes the subject matter for a novel most powerfully when it gives rise to recordings that can circulate within the community and activate the social relations that are naturally the driving force of the novel. Focus on media circulation occurs over and over again in contemporary fiction and helps to explain why the media ecology is an important part of the plot and thematics of these novels, rather than merely a reflection of anxiety about the relevance of the novel. As this novel makes clear, the focus on circulation subtly transforms the way these novels give meaning to experience. This change is embodied in the television appearance of the two brothers that is such a central event in the novel; the appearance is not merely the mechanism of their fame but also a narrativizing of their music. On this show the brothers are cast as Alfonso and Manny Reyes, friends of Ricky Ricardo visiting from Cuba, and thus folded into the domestic narrative of *I Love Lucy*. Lucy greets the brothers and serves them cookies in their apartment while waiting for Ricky, who then prompts them to announce their song: "Did you fellows decide which song you're going to do on my show at the Tropicana?" (140). In many ways, this is what *Mambo Kings* does as a whole: it takes a song and gives it a narrative context. It does this not by telling the story of the inspiration for the song, but by examining the afterlife of the song as it circulates as a recording through a whole community. More than in Reed's novel, here we can see the narrative implications of emphasizing the circulation of a representation of experience. Those implications are inherently connected to the limits of the medium of music, which becomes an artifact whose history can be known only by attending to the stories (novels, televisions shows) into which it is inserted.

Mambo Kings brilliantly shows how attention to the life of a media object within a community is essential to understanding the nature of that medium. To understand the nature of music—especially recorded music—analyzing the medium in a vacuum is meaningless. Instead, we must think about the way that music moves through a community and through individual lives, from being rebroadcast on television to appearing in the discount bins in used record shops. Hijuelos affirms Ryan's insistence that a crucial component of any medium is the use that a culture makes of it. Perhaps the only limitation of *Mambo Kings* in comparison to the other media novels I discuss is that its central example is a medium so obviously different from writing. Although Hijuelos evokes the limitations of print narrative in the way that he has organized time in his novel, contrasts between writing and music are indirect and rather limited. To show the circulation of writing at work in a media novel, I turn to Tom Robbins's *Still Life with Woodpecker*, which shares with *Mambo Kings* an interest in the circulation of a medium among its users. Specifically, Robbins's novel offers a comic mediation on the book as an object, and does so by invoking other, visual media. Specifically, Robbins introduces into his story the central object of a pack of Camel cigarettes, the visual design of which prompts dreams in his heroine that link the plot of the story to the physical object of the book.

Still Life with Woodpecker tells the story of the twenty-year-old Princess Leigh-Cheri, the daughter of King Max and Queen Tilli Furstenberg-

Barcalonas, exiled from their unnamed nation and living with the support of the U.S. government in Seattle. The young Leigh-Cheri is an idealist who gradually falls in love with Bernard Mickey Wrangle, a redheaded outlaw who goes by the name "the Woodpecker." The novel uses this political framework largely as a backdrop for the romantic dynamics between the two main characters. The "general conflict between social idealism and romanticism" (150) gradually becomes a more specific inquiry into the nature of love in the "last quarter of the twentieth century [which] was a severe period for lovers" (3). As Robbins announces at the outset of the novel, "There is only one serious question. And that is: *Who knows how to make love stay?*" (4). This question is made dramatic when the Woodpecker is arrested for a bombing. A plea bargain gets Wrangle a ten-year sentence and makes him eligible for parole in twenty months. Leigh-Cheri decides to replicate the harsh conditions of Wrangle's cell in her parents' Seattle home, moving to an attic and removing all furniture except a cot, a forty-watt light bulb, a chamber pot, and a single package of Camel cigarettes. This time in the attic plays a crucial role within the novel, and it is the point at which the visual design of the package emerges as a major element of the story. The time that Leigh-Cheri spends in the attic is thematically significant because temporal rhythms are an important element of the story. This period represents a turn from the linear time (measured in solar terms), which we associate with traditional plot, toward a cyclical time, which the novel links with romance and the moon. Indeed, Robbins brings these together by observing about her single source of light in the attic, "Bernard had told her that the light of a full moon was equivalent to a forty-watt bulb at fifteen feet" (152).

Much like *Mambo Kings*, Robbins's novel connects this story and its relatively conventional narrative interest in love with the circulation of a media artifact. The primary media artifact that gives *Still Life with Woodpecker* its focus is the visual design of the Camel cigarette package. But this visual medium is introduced only after Robbins raises the issue of the production of the physical book. Robbins cites the imaginary complaints of "intelligent persons" who simply want a "good fast paced story" (167), and defines the linearly developing plot as a commodity that fulfills a narrow and immediate desire. Earlier in the novel, Robbins associates loveless sex with junk food: "There is lovemaking that is bad for a person, just as there is eating that is bad. That boysenberry cream pie from the Thrift-E

Mart may appear inviting, may, in fact, cause all nine hundred taste buds to carol from the tongue, but in the end, the sugars, the additives, the empty calories clog arteries, disrupt cells, generate fat, and rot teeth" (107). Robbins seems to have something similar in mind with the "fast paced story," which likewise promises to satisfy an immediate desire. It is in this context that Robbins's metafictional comments on the composition of his novel are best understood. Robbins frames his story by talking about the new Remington SL3 typewriter on which he will be composing *Still Life with Woodpecker*. At the beginning of the novel, it seems as if this new piece of technology will make writing the novel almost effortless: "This baby speaks electric Shakespeare at the slightest provocation and will rap out a page and a half if you just look at it hard" (ix). Not surprisingly, over the course of the novel, Robbins becomes disillusioned with the typewriter. He admits that "it's a superb tool—for the proper desk in the proper office" (34) and begins to imagine a device for writing that better matches the creative task that he is involved in:

> Perhaps what a novelist needs is a different sort of writing imple-
> ment. Say, a Remington built of balsa wood, its parts glued togeth-
> er like a boyhood model; delicate, graceful, submissive, as ready to
> soar as an ace.
>   Better, a carved typewriter, hewn from a single block of sacred
> cypress; decorated with mineral pigments, berry juice, and mud; its
> keys living mushrooms, its ribbon the long iridescent tongue of a liz-
> ard. An animal typewriter, silent until touched, then filling the page
> with growls and squeals and squawks, yowls and bleats and snorts,
> brayings and chatterings and dry rattlings from the underbrush; a
> typewriter that could type real kisses, ooze semen and sweat. (35)

Robbins's impossible, fanciful "writing implement" is quite the opposite of the practical and efficient electric typewriter that he is using for the novel. And, in fact, at the end of the novel, Robbins realizes that he has made a mistake in trying to compose on the typewriter when he begins summarizing the novel's themes: "But wait a minute. Hold on. I've been trapped. This is the very kind of analytical, after-the-fact goose gunk the Remington SL3 cut its teeth on" (271). Robbins concludes the novel by handwriting the last three pages, having realized that the efficient tool of the Remington pushes his book in directions that he does not want it to go. It seems as if the fast-paced plot that Robbins associates with Leigh-Cheri's practical but unimaginative audience is of a piece with the efficient, electric writing that the Remington seems so eager to turn out.

In both stories discussed in this section, the inadequacy of the conventional articulation of story into discourse is the primary issue around which the narrative is constructed. Robbins does much the same thing as the other two writers do: turn to the artifactuality of the representation, to the life of the story after it has been articulated. The central moment for this swerve is the time that Leigh-Cheri spends in her attic with the Camel package. The princess becomes fascinated with the package and eventually reads into its design secret messages about a conspiracy crossing the ages and suppressed by historians. Initially, her interest in the package arises from boredom. Having settled into her imitation cell, she "had to confess she could still feel on her neck the tepid breath of boredom. At that moment, something caught her eye" (160). Robbins's link between the package and boredom is significant, since Wrangle has associated dullness and totalitarianism (151); it seems as if both the anarchist and the dreamer are motivated by the desire to escape the dull, the efficient, and the practical. The Camel package becomes a place where Leigh-Cheri can dream: "Mostly, though, she just sat holding it, staring into its exotic vistas, populating its landscape, colonizing it, learning to survive there" (166). In fact, this passing mention of learning to survive in the imaginary desert of the Camel package turns out to be surprisingly literal. At the end of the novel, Leigh-Cheri and Wrangle are reunited after a misunderstanding keeps them apart. They are trapped, however, in a modern-day pyramid that Leigh-Cheri's fiancée has constructed for her as a wedding gift; the only way out is to dynamite the door, something that both are convinced will kill them. They desperately try the dynamite anyway and miraculously survive with only damage to their hearing, but while unconscious from the blast they have exactly the same dream of being at a desert oasis. It appears that "when he and Leigh-Cheri fell to the floor right before the blast, he experienced the sensation that they had fallen into the Camel pack" (266–67), and both wonder "whether at the instant of explosion it [the Camel pack] had sheltered them from death" (268). This whimsical conclusion to the novel not only confirms the power of dreams but also uses this dream space to turn back on the demands of the fast-paced plot. Here dreams provide a thoroughly illogical solution to the forward movement of the narrative.

In some ways, Robbins's interest in whimsical dream space within the visual design is of a piece with the other two novels that I have discussed. Both are interested in the life of the representation after the act of writing (or design) has ended. But Robbins's use of the Camel pack is also more complex than either of these cases, because this dream space raises some of the disruptive but fundamentally narrative concerns that were central to stories like "Duck Tape" and *Vineland*. Specifically, Robbins is interested in the spatial dimensions of the packaging. He spends most of the time describing the odd exoticism of the pyramid and camel scheme on the front of the package. Robbins describes the package as Leigh-Cheri begins to study it in her boredom:

> Having nothing else to read, Leigh-Cheri eventually reads the rest of the package: *Camel: Turkish & Domestic Blend Cigarettes: Choice: Quality: Manufactured by R.J. Reynolds Tobacco Co., Winston-Salem, N.C. 27102, U.S.A.; 20 Class A Cigarettes*; and the famous inscription that has graced the rear panel of the package since its creation in 1913 . . . ; *Don't look for premiums or coupons, as the cost of tobaccos blending in Camel Cigarettes prohibits the use of them.*
>
> She tried to count the *e*'s in that sentence, running into the same difficulty that has plagued many another package reader: almost nobody counts them accurately the first time. Staring at the camel, she detected a woman and a lion hidden in its body. On tiptoes, she held the pack before the one clear windowpane and saw in its reflection that the word CHOICE reads the same in its mirror image as it does on the pack, it is not turned around by the mirror. That might have tipped her off that the Camel package crosses dimensional boundaries, the line between matter and anti-matter, but she failed to grasp its significance right away. It was just another parlor game. As when she searched for additional camels on the package. (There are two behind the pyramid.) (162)

Leigh-Cheri's playful and obsessive concern with the details of what otherwise seems to be a simple commercial object is typical of the movement away from efficiency toward dream space. In fact, on the next page Robbins mocks the promises of a package of Cheerios: "If you are not satisfied with the quality and/or performance of the Cheerios in this box" (163), questioning "what might be meant by the 'performance' of the Cheerios" (163). The language of performance is clearly connected to efficiency and the use of tools, and thus precisely the opposite of what the Camel package offers to the princess. In particular, the package works by opening up a space for dreaming. This is evident in the playful suggestion that two additional camels hide behind the pyramid on the package. Such a suggestion makes a certain kind of sense within the three-dimensional space that is represented here, but it seems wildly illogical as a claim about the package itself. Like Leigh-Cheri, Robbins seems to be drawn into the space of the package and to entertain rules for that space that clearly violate the design logic of the package. After all, no designer would have put in camels that were invisible to viewers. Such a decision would be frivolous, unnecessary, and wildly inefficient.

Robbins pushes this use of the Camel package further, however, and describes it not merely as a space for dreaming but also as an object itself. It would seem like an interest in objects would be for Robbins just another example of an ethics of efficiency and the search for good tools. However, by the end of the novel Robbins is able to announce (at the prompting of his analytical Remington) that one of the themes of his novel is "a breakthrough in relations between animate and inanimate objects" (271). Robbins explains that our relation to objects is also complex and rich: "Caught in the earth's gravitational web, the moon moved around the earth and could never get away. Yet, as any half-awake materialist well knows, that which you hold holds you. Neither could the earth escape the moon. The moon conducts our orchestra of waters, it is keeper at the hive of blood. In a magnetic field, every object exerts force on every other object. The moon is an object, after all. Like a golden ball. Like a pack of cigarettes" (168–69). This passage ends by reminding us that the package of Camels is both a space for dreaming and an object that we hold in our hands. Normally, we ignore the objects that influence us. Robbins's reference in this passage to the golden ball harks back to a fairy tale recounted earlier in the novel about a girl who promises to take care of a toad if he will retrieve the golden ball that she dropped into a pond. Naturally, once the ball is retrieved the focus of the story shifts to the girl's unwillingness to follow through on the promise, and the ball never appears in the story again:

"The story initially made a big deal about the ball, only never to mention it again, but it was the characters who were important, the ball was just a prop, a toy, an *object*" (141). Fast-paced narratives use props all the time, treating objects as tools to move the story along. Elsewhere, after Leigh-Cheri becomes "sensitized to objecthood" (220), she can appreciate how an "absolutely unnecessary [object] becomes absolutely genuine" (228–29). We can see this thinking at work in Robbins's comments about the ideal writing instrument that I quoted earlier. Where the Remington strives to be a tool in the most efficient and blandest terms possible—Robbins complains, for example, that its black paint is boring, and eventually has it repainted red (123)—he wishes for a writing tool that is also an interesting object because it is hand-carved, made from an interesting material, or alive.

It is clear that the book itself is such an object for Robbins. Leigh-Cheri's dreaming about the Camel pack is obviously a model for our relationship to the novel, and moves the narrative from a concern with the difference between story and discourse to an interest in the way that discourse then circulates after the act of creation is completed. What *Still Life with Woodpecker* adds to our discussion of the circulation of media objects is an emphasis on the way that these objects then transform other narrative categories specifically associated with writing—in this case, the setting for the narrative, which becomes a kind of hybrid space between the actual world of the novel's action and the dream space of the Camel package. In this regard, Robbins's novel looks more like the challenging and frequently disruptive narratives that I discussed in the previous chapter, and anticipates the extensive use of other media to analyze the nature of written narrative that I will describe in the next chapter. Robbins makes clear that stories of circulation afford methods of investigating the basic components and categories of the novel.

Media Circulation and Theories of the Novel

Narratives focused on the circulation of media objects, then, work against the basic promise of the novel: to tell a story about something that already happened. In the introduction I suggested that media appear in contemporary fiction as a way to define the role of writing in today's media ecology and in the process to give the novel a vocation. Let us now turn to one last novel that engages with some of the most traditional definitions of the novel in order to explain how narratives of media circulation confront and transform these definitions. Toni Morrison's *Jazz* is more explicit than any of the novels that we have discussed in this chapter in contrasting the circulation of media objects to the traditional role of the narrator in giving shape to the "discourse" of the story.

Morrison organizes her novel around the relationship between private lives and public knowledge, in particular about rumor and the social games of secrecy and disclosure. In doing so, she invokes Mary McCarthy's observation in her essay "The Fact in Fiction," which I cited in the introduction, that "the novel's characteristic tone is one of gossip and tittletattle" (453). McCarthy goes on to explain that what she has in mind more than anything is the style of narration in classic, realist novels in the European tradition: "Most of these writers were people of high principle; their books, without exception, had a moral, ethical, or educational purpose. But the voice we overhear in their narratives, if we stop to listen for a minute, putting aside preconceptions, is the voice of a neighbor relating the latest gossip" (453). Morrison's novel likewise depends on a narrator who strives to understand the characters on which she spies. At the end of the novel, the narrator/author confesses: "I thought I'd hidden myself so well as I watched them through windows and doors, took every opportunity I had to follow them, to gossip about and fill in their lives, and all the while they were watching me" (220). Against this very traditional novelistic concern and the structure of discourse that it depends on, Morrison offers music.

Jazz tells the story of a love triangle between fifty-year-old Joe Trace, his wife, Violet, and an eighteen-year-old girl, Dorcas. Joe and Violet moved to "the City" (unnamed) as a young married couple, leaving behind friends and family in Virginia. Gradually loneliness and regret drive them apart, and Joe seeks comfort and, especially, companionship in the flirtatious but shallow Dorcas. The novel itself opens after this relationship has come to its climax. Joe shoots Dorcas, in part because she had left him but also because he is confused by his feelings; as the narrator puts it, "He fell for an eighteen-year-old girl with one of those deepdown, spooky loves that made him so sad and happy he shot her just to keep the feeling going" (3). Violet scandalizes the neighborhood even further by showing up at Dorcas's funeral and attacking the corpse's face with a knife. From this initial opening, the novel tunnels back into the past, exploring Joe's family and how he met Violet, and gradually unpacking the feelings and events that lead to Dorcas's death. In fact, the novel builds toward the direct narration of Dorcas's death (about which we know only indirectly) before returning to the novel's present to narrate how Joe and Violet overcome their grief and separation, and find some measure of peace and happiness. The final image of the couple is as an example of "public love"—affection clearly manifested for all to see, and thus an object of envy for the narrator: "I envy them their public love. I myself have only known it in secret, shared it in secret and longed, aw longed to show it—to be able to say out loud what they have no need to say at all" (229). As this passage makes clear, one of the central issues in the novel will be the degree to which we can know other people, and how we get insight into their lives.

This tension between the public and private runs through contemporary media novels; it has already been an explicit issue in stories by Sukenick and Robbins and will be an important element of the final chapter. Instead of setting up a strict distinction between public and private knowledge, Morrison suggests that they are pieces of a whole. Early in the novel one of Joe and Violet's neighbors, Malvonne, discovers that her son has robbed a mailbox. When she finds the bag of hastily opened letters behind his bed, she goes about trying to make amends by putting the letters back in the mail. However, "a few of them required action on Malvonne's part" (42). An application to law school has had the one-dollar application fee removed, "so she added a note in her own hand, saying, 'I do not have the one dollar right this minute, but as soon as I hear that you received this application and agreed that I should come, I will have it by then if you tell me you don't have it and really need it'" (42). To another letter she appends extra postage to hurry a late message along. In another case, she "decided to mail it [a love letter] with a note of her own attached—urging caution and directing daddy's attention to a clipping from Opportunity Magazine" (44). These postal messages straddle the line between public and private conversation. Indeed, the love letter is sent from one apartment in a building to another, making the physical travel irrelevant and implying that it is the semipublic nature of the communication that is important: "Malvonne did not know what made her waste a three-cent stamp other than the pleasure of knowing the government was delivering her heat" (44). Although there is clearly a difference between gossip and public accounts, between whispered and mailed romance, Jazz implies that they are ultimately parts of a whole continuum, different ways of finding out about the lives of others.

The line between the public and private is important for the characters mostly as part of a game of secrecy and disclosure in which they participate. Dorcas is especially direct in playing this game. Part of her reason for throwing over Joe and pursuing the younger and more popular Acton is because she is ashamed to talk about Joe to her friends: "What I wanted to let him [Joe] know was that I had this chance to have Acton and I wanted it and I wanted girlfriends to talk to about it. About where we went and what he did. About things. About stuff. What good are secrets if you can't talk to anybody about them? I sort of hinted about Joe and me to Felice and she laughed before she stared at me and then frowned" (189). Dorcas's seemingly contradictory rhetorical question, "What good are secrets if you can't talk to anybody about them?" captures the structure of gossip and knowledge in the novel. Most characters pursue knowledge of others, and allow others to know about their private lives, as part of a social game. Earlier in the novel Joe remarks, "I know most men can't wait to tell each other about what they got going on the side. Put all their business in the street" (121). In this regard, the narrator's opinion about the importance of gossip and the relative uselessness of newspapers mimics the common attitude of characters in the book, that secrets are a game and that private life is invigorated by being made public.

It is in the context of this dynamic between public and private knowledge that music in *Jazz* must be understood. Our best descriptions of music in the novel come through the judgmental voice of Alice Manfred. When she thinks about racial violence in the city, she blames music: "Alice thought, No. It wasn't the War and the disgruntled veterans; it wasn't the droves and droves of colored people flocking to paychecks and streets full of themselves. It was the music. The dirty, get-on-down music the women sang and the men played and both danced to, close and shameless or apart and wild. Alice was convinced and so were the Miller sisters as they blew into cups of Postum in the kitchen. It made you do unwise disorderly things. Just hearing it was like violating the law" (58). Although Morrison is far from suggesting that music causes civil disorder, it does seem that "dirty, get-on-down music" pushes people in directions that are not entirely of their own planning or control. Late in the novel, as Dorcas is dancing at the party where Joe will shoot her, Morrison notes, "They agree on everything above the waist and below: muscle, tendon, bone joint and marrow cooperate. And if the dancers hesitate, have a moment of doubt, the music will solve and dissolve any question" (188). Music represents a kind of activity that is not under complete control but which connects individuals. When Joe and Violet get to the City, they are struck by this shared rhythm to life: "Even if the room they rented was smaller than the heifer's stall and darker than a morning privy, they stayed to look at their number, hear themselves in an audience, feel themselves moving down the street among hundreds of others who moved the way they did, and who, when they spoke, regardless of the accent, treated language like the same intricate, malleable toy designed for their play" (32–33).

Music, then, embodies this process of losing yourself in a larger social whole. This whole is not, however, necessarily a good thing nor supportive of community in our traditional ways of thinking about it. Again, the City seems to capture the ambiguous value of these connections. Joe and Violet are struck by "the amazement of throwing open the window and being hypnotized for hours by people on the street below":

> Little of that makes for love, but it does pump desire. The woman who churned a man's blood as she leaned all alone on a fence by a country road might not expect even to catch his eye in the City. But if she is clipping quickly down the big-city street in heels, swinging her purse, or sitting on a stoop with a cool beer in her hand, dangling her shoe from the toes of her foot, the man, reacting to her posture, to soft skin on stone, the weight of the building stressing the delicate, dangling shoe, is captured. And he'd think it was the woman he wanted, and not some combination of curved stone, and a swinging, high-heeled shoe moving in and out of sunlight. (34)

This passage describing a holistic desire that builds through the environment rather than simply being the result of attraction to an individual is echoed continuously in Morrison's descriptions of music. The rhythm of the City is musical, and pulls people out of neat, "private" selves into actions they might not want to do. Morrison's description of spring in the City makes this point most clearly: "It's the time of the year when the City urges contradiction most, encouraging you to buy street food when you have no appetite at all; giving you a taste for a single room occupied by you alone as well as a craving to share it with someone you passed on the street. Really there is no contradiction—rather it's a condition: the range of what an artful City can do" (117–18). Like music, the City pulls individuals into larger patterns, even though at the same time it inspires very individual desires and attractions.

Even in this very general form, music causes problems for traditional novelistic descriptions of individual lives, since these lives are not quite the individual stories that we normally expect. The narrator initially uses music as a way to describe the lack of control that the characters have in the City: "Take my word for it, he [Joe] is bound to the track. It pulls him like a needle through the groove of a Bluebird record. Round and round about the town. That's the way the City spins you. Makes you do what it wants, go where the laid-out roads say to. All the while letting you think you're free; that you can jump into thickets because you feel like it" (120). By the end of the novel, however, the narrator recants this metaphor and admits her mistake: "So I missed it altogether. I was sure one would kill the other. I waited for it so I could describe it. I was so sure it would happen. That the past was an abused record with no choice but to repeat itself at the crack and no power on earth could lift the arm that held the needle. I was so sure, and they danced and walked all over me. Busy, they were, busy being original, complicated, changeable—human, I guess you'd say, while I was the predictable one" (220). What is remarkable about this passage is that the same musical language that is used to characterize the determinism of Joe's life is used in the end to describe how he and Violet are "changeable"—they "danced and walked all over me." This passage makes clear, then, that music is more than just a metaphor for amoral social rhythms.

What, then, is it about music that pulls Joe and Violet back together, and that makes it a force for rejuvenation rather than ultimately destructive desire? To answer this, we have to move away from general musical language toward the concrete artifacts of the medium that circulate in the community. The crucial change in the novel occurs when Felice begins to visit the still estranged and mourning Joe and Violet. She provides some information about Dorcas that is comforting to Joe in particular—that Dorcas allowed herself to die rather than seeking medical treatment, and that her final thoughts were of him—but more than this she seems to shake the couple out of a stasis into which they had fallen. At the beginning of the novel, the couple is haunted by the girl whose picture they keep on the mantle: "They each take turns to throw off the bedcovers, rise up from the sagging mattress and tiptoe over cold linoleum into the parlor to gaze at what seems like the only living presence in the house: the photograph of a bold, unsmiling girl staring from the mantelpiece" (11–12). Felice's visits seem to allow Joe to separate Dorcas from other young women (Joe stirs for the first time when Felice says, "I'm not like her!" [209]) and to begin to talk about the guilt he feels. This healing reaches its climax when "somebody in the house across the alley put a record on and the music floated in to us through the open window" (214). Joe and Felice dance, and this prompts a series of promises that reconnect Joe and Violet to the outside world: Joe will go back to work to buy a Victrola, and Felice will return to visit and bring records.

This scene is clearly central to the novel's representation of healing, and yet the reason why music is a force for healing here is not obvious without the context provided by the other narratives of media circulation that I have been discussing. Clearly music functions in this scene, as it does throughout the novel, as a way to connect people, to move them out of their private grief and isolation. At the same time, however, connection is dangerous in other places, since it fosters a desire disconnected from love. What is different about music in this scene? The dynamic here is first and foremost a triangle, with Felice, Joe, and Violet all involved. This three-part relationship seems different and more powerful than the isolated rhythms that Dorcas pursues in her secret romances, first with Joe and then with Acton. In this way, music at the end of the novel functions not as a rhythm that goes on without the characters' control, but as an object that is *used* by the characters in the story, that helps to set up a scene or provide an occasion for social interaction. This is why music in the novel is almost always recorded music—music embodied in physical objects to be circulated and used by characters—and ultimately located within a very domestic space. After all, the music in this crucial scene filters from the outside, but it becomes an occasion for healing as part of the domestic space of the parlor. Indeed, we could say that the very limits of this particular form of music—its embodiment in a particular object, its availability to those few characters who can hear it through the walls of the apartment—give it such a powerful place within the novel and allow the characters to connect to the social world beyond themselves.

Morrison's narrator, then, seems to be struggling to strike a balance between the spaces of the City and the home, and is able to do that because of the way that *recorded* music is able to transform this space. The novel traditionally depends on the very private space of the home, in which broader social issues are sharpened and examined. Morrison's narrator reflects this very traditional definition of the novel as organized around gossip. Her failure in the end to understand her own characters points to the limits of this way of thinking about the novel. Specifically, Morrison implies that gossip is organized around a narrative trajectory that moves from private motivation to public confrontation. That trajectory, in turn, depends on the belief in a prior, personal story that is articulated into discourse by the more public figure of the narrator. Morrison, however, shows that the line between story and discourse, between life and representation, is much more fluid. Music intervenes into these private spaces, pulling individuals out of their lives and into patterns that extend beyond them. Those patterns are not, however, set in stone—not "tracks" that individuals must follow. Instead, those individuals participate in the experience and circulation of these recordings. That circulation, then, becomes a part of the story.

Elsewhere in the novel, Morrison makes clear that the traditional novelistic search for sources, a past "story" that stands behind the discourse of the narrative, is an expectation shared by characters and narrator alike. The novel moves from the present of Joe and Violet's stasis over Dorcas's death into their family background, their decision to travel to the City, and eventually back into the story of Joe's mother. Early in the novel Joe's name is associated with his mysterious family origins; he gives himself the last name Trace because he has been told that his parents "disappeared without a trace" (124). Joe is connected to his own family origins, and yet at the same time as defined negatively: he is what is left behind, what they went off without. The strange aporia that is at the heart of his story is gradually unpacked as we learn that Joe is the child of a "wild woman" who lives in the brush near the Virginia farm where he meets Violet. Joe's wild mother is a particularly appropriate origin for the story, since she is unnamed (less than a Trace) and rejects the domestic space exemplified by Joe and Violet's apartment; she "live[s] outside like that all year round" (179). In fact, the nearest we come to a meeting between Joe and his mother is a scene in which Joe finds the warren in which his mother has been living, and discovers a small trove of distinctly domestic objects: "A green dress. A rocking chair without an arm. A circle of stones for cooking. Jars, baskets, pots; a doll, a spindle, earrings, a photograph, a stack of sticks, a set of silver brushes and a silver cigar case" (184). Joe's own origins turn on this search for a mother and a domestic space. Appropriately, he finds one but not the other; his mother has literally displaced herself from this fundamentally novelistic location and left him with nothing but a few artifacts in place of the story of origins that he came looking for. The story of Joe's mother is framed as part of an account of another man's search for his origins. Golden Gray, a half-white man linked to Violet's family, travels in search of his father, Henry LesTroy, and accidentally finds Joe's wild, pregnant mother in the brush and grudgingly cares for her. This search for origins itself is significant, since Henry's name quite literally associates this background with the construction of a narrative, a *story*: "Henry Lestory or LesTroy or something like that" (148). This trip into Joe's family background is the heart of his traditional "story," where we assume that hidden secrets about his past will explain his present and even define his future. And yet, Joe's story is not explained by Henry Lestory; ultimately the quest for Henry is someone else's, and the "traces" of Joe's origins are left undefined and ambiguous.

Jazz shows, then, how radically attention to the circulation of media objects can transform our understanding of the nature and purpose of the novel, and how exploration of the issues raised by media can push the novel beyond the search for origins and inquiry into private life that have been the novel's most conventional goals. It makes clear that any inquiry into the nature of a medium and its potential for storytelling must emphasize the role of that medium within a cultural context—how the society of the time imagines the medium, and how the basic artifacts of that medium take on a role within the lives of individuals. Again and again we will see that an understanding of the nature and limits of writing refers us out to the larger cultural spaces in which the novel operates.

Contemporary Experience and Participatory Culture

The theme of circulating media objects can be characterized as an innovation in the narrative structure of contemporary fiction. However, it should be clear that this issue of circulation is not in and of itself a layer of textuality—as, for example, the addition of a dramatized narrator seems to be a distinct element of the text—but instead a component of plot that is linked to narrative concerns. In other words, for all that circulation raises issues about how we tell stories, it is still ultimately the *subject* of the story rather than some new textual feature. However, as I have noted before, the novel has a long tradition of representing media objects like found manuscripts and letters. In emphasizing the circulation of media, the contemporary novel is exploiting and extending a feature that has been part of novelistic discourse from its beginning.

However, as we move beyond the boundaries of the contemporary novel, the circulation of media objects can indeed produce much more dramatic changes to our interaction with narratives. Craig Saper has suggested that the circulation of art and writing has evolved into its own aesthetic principle. Saper notes that some contemporary practitioners of "mail art" have established peer-to-peer systems for exchanging art and writing. Saper unpacks the implications of this move and offers the suggestive notion of "intimate bureaucracies" to describe these networks: "The participatory decentralization becomes a mantra of mail-art networks, and the collective endeavors of assemblings become the vehicle to express this decentralized bureaucratic form. These forms of organization as well as aesthetic achievement represent a paradoxical mix of artisanal production, mass-distribution techniques, and a belief in the democratizing potential of electronic and mechanical reproduction techniques" (22). Here is a form of art that takes the circulation of visual and written texts as the very basis for its "aesthetic achievement." If the novels we have discussed in this chapter thematize this circulation, turning it into an element of the plot, the writers and artists described by Saper enact this circulation more literally in the kinds of artistic communities that they create.

We need not look only to high art to see how important the circulation of texts is in contemporary culture. In particular, I have in mind Henry Jenkins's characterization of fan fiction as a "participatory culture." In *Textual Poachers*, Jenkins examines the way that fans of television programs have built up a culture around particular shows—some current and some long-since canceled—frequently engaging in elaborate analysis of the story and furthering the plot and characterization by writing their own narratives set in the story world. Jenkins explains that he conceives of fans as "readers who appropriate popular texts and reread them in a fashion that serves different interests, as spectators who transform the experience of watching television into a rich and complex participatory culture" (23). Jenkins notes that this use of popular culture in such a serious way cuts against the distinctions we take to be the basis of taste: "Fan culture muddies those boundaries, treating popular texts as if they merited the same degree of attention and appreciation as canonical texts" (17). Such fan practices draw into question not only the difference between "serious" and "trivial" artistic products but also the distinction between fandom and academically validated forms of criticism and study.

What is especially important about Jenkins's study of fan culture is the emphasis that it places on the circulation of texts within these subcultures. Jenkins notes that fans exchange their own writings and their commentary on the series as part of a larger social experience. Particularly significant is Jenkins's suggestion that this exchange can be seen as a form of gossip: various forms of gossip are "exchanged because of their practical value in perpetuating fan culture and because they offer new ways of thinking about the programs. They also provide an outlet through which fans can voice their frustrations or laugh over their embarrassments" (81). For Jenkins, the content of these comments is less important than the social experience that they create: "The manifest content of gossip is often less important than the social ties the exchange of secrets creates" (81). It is probably not a stretch to suggest that the kind of participatory culture that Jenkins describes is similar to the circulation of narrative objects that I have been describing: both mark a shift away from the stories themselves to what is done with them, to the life that those stories take on after they have been written. In his more recent work, Jenkins has argued that this shift toward the circulation of stories through communities is part of a more general embrace of digital technology and networking; this "*collective intelligence*" is a "*dress rehearsal for the way culture might operate in the future*" (*Fans, Bloggers, and Gamers*, 134). Many critics have seen networks of production and circulation to imply a fundamentally different way of thinking about creativity and thought. In describing "The Literary Assemblage," John Johnson describes a networked vision of writing: "If Deleuze says that writing is only 'one flow among others,' it is precisely to stress that it occurs in a necessary relation with something exterior to it. In other words, writing is always a writing with: it happens as part of a conjunction and circulation of effects, specifically in relation to a machinic assemblage or particular configuration of bodies making or enabling desire to flow" (15). Matthew Fuller describes this trend within literary criticism this way: "literature becomes a part of a subset of media, and thus of discursive storage, calculation, and transmission systems" (4).

It is not hard to see this interest in the circulation of media objects as a response to the problems of experience that I raised at the beginning of this chapter. If we seem to live today in a world in which immediate, personal experience is a problematic concept, then the stories we tell will be less a matter of getting back to an original moment and more a matter of the way that we use stories. The fan cultures that Jenkins describes seem to be a particularly extreme but powerful articulation of this shift, since the original texts are valued mostly for their ability to prompt exchanges within the community. More importantly, Jenkins's theory shows us that the cultural *use* is an essential component of contemporary thinking about media. From fan use of popular culture texts to the emphasis on circulation within the media novel, we have come to recognize that the limits and potentials of a medium depend first and foremost on the role that those media take on within a culture.

3   Defining the Vocation of the Novel through Narrative Elements

The general outline of how the contemporary U.S. novel uses media other than writing should now be clear. Once the novel had lost its traditional vocation, any choice by a writer must be evaluated against its rhetorical effectiveness. Novels can use media for a variety of storytelling purposes, and contemporary writers can appeal to other media to reveal the potential and limits of writing. We have seen how many of these novels thematize the circulation of the media object within the story world to explain the cultural meaning of the medium of writing. In the remainder of this book, I will explain how the limits of the written medium of the novel give it a place within the media ecology: what particular qualities of writing the novel emphasizes (this chapter), how the focus on limits differs from the promises of electronic textuality (chapter 4), and what this all means for our understanding of reading today (chapter 5).

When contemporary novels describe the circulation of media objects, they are frequently challenging some basic qualities of written narrative. *Still Life with Woodpecker* and *Jazz* both provided examples of these challenges. Robbins's novel draws our attention to the space of written narrative to get us to think differently about the experience of reading; Morrison's novel critiques the traditional image of the controlling narrator who exposes characters to public knowledge. A key link was revealed that I now want to focus on: the connection between the narrative *use* of media objects and the exploration of the limits of traditional narrative categories. I have argued that the rhetorical and universal definitions of narrative that emerged after 1960 are not, in fact, so different. We can see some confirmation of this, since the rhetorical use of the Camel package or the jazz record in these two novels has nonetheless raised theoretical concerns about plot and narration in general. By reflecting on such theoretical definitions of the basic building blocks of written narrative, contemporary writers are able to redefine the vocation of the novel.

In a recent article on "exporting" narrative concepts from one medium to another, Werner Wolf provides a model for these media novels. Wolf notes that narratology frequently applies narrative concepts developed for one medium to another. A classic example is the attempt to export the concept of the "narrator," which seems natural and even inevitable in the novel, to film, where it is much more problematic. Wolf asks which narrative concepts seem to have the greatest potential for fruitful and meaningful application "beyond verbal storytelling" ("Metalepsis," 84) and suggests that such narrative concepts will form a continuum: "On the one hand there are phenomena that are more genre- or mediaspecific, such as the narrator who tells a story, phenomena that are intrinsically related to the defining core of verbal storytelling. . . . On the other hand there are phenomena that are rather more transgeneric and 'transmedial.' Their conceptualization may have originated in narratology, too, but it is characteristic of them to have only a loose or accidental connection with verbal narratives" (86). Wolf describes the issue that concerns media novels: the relationship between core narrative concepts and specific media. Indeed, this essay suggests that narratologists and novelists today are frequently struggling with the same questions about the role of media in our storytelling. The novels that we discuss throughout this book but especially in this chapter narrow Wolf's question. They describe the qualities that these core narrative concepts take on when presented through writing as part of a novel. They do this in order to investigate the nature and limits of the novel, and in the process define its place within the contemporary media ecology. I will show contemporary novelists at work exploring the nature of written narrative through an inquiry into these core narrative concepts. I will follow the model provided by Morrison's novel, which invoked and discarded a conventional explanation of the vocation of the novel (gossip) before going on to offer a meditation on the nature of written narrative. Each of the stories that I analyze in this chapter rejects some conventional justification of the novel, and instead turns to an inquiry into the nature of writing in order to redefine the potential and limits of the novel. Because the novels treated in this chapter work by investigating the basic elements of written narrative, I have organized the discussion around the terms interrogated. Specifically, I have chosen five traditional terms—description, setting, world, character, and plot—and five stories that investigate their role in the novel.

Contemporary media novels do indeed coalesce around a quality of writing they find to be centrally important to the novel's vocation today: the ability to represent the absent, potential or unrealized. Other media like music, painting, or photography have considerably more difficulty in showing what is absent, and contemporary media novels gravitate toward this element as they explore the vocation of fiction. This quality of writing has a twofold significance. Not only does it define a central strength of the novel that will help to give it a role in the contemporary media ecology, but it also explains why the novel is especially able to embrace its own limits. The novel is good at pointing to what is missing, to what is beyond its own means of representation. Coupled with its focus on circulation and social use, this makes the novel particularly able to describe the way that its stories can take on a role within a context larger than itself. Ultimately, this provides a compelling description of the vocation of the novel today, the misguided elegies for which I will try to answer in the final chapter.

Description

One way to justify the value of fiction is by emphasizing its ability to prompt reader judgment and evaluation. In the introduction I cited Wayne Booth's *The Rhetoric of Fiction* as part of the post-1960 narrative landscape. Booth took it upon himself to defend novels against an overly strict emphasis on reader judgment. Citing Henry James, Booth summarizes this attitude: "What he requires is intelligence, discrimination, and analytical interest, and although . . . he is willing to accept responsibility in raising the reader to his level, he still presupposes a reader ready for the proper analytical response" (121). Subsequent narratologists have followed Booth in respecting the many different ways that reader judgments can be activated. But it is a nearly universal assumption that the ability to prompt critical thinking and evaluation is essential to the intellectual and ethical value of the novel. James Phelan speaks for many of us when he describes our response to even a simple story like Cinderella as guided by the judgments we make about characters: "We become engaged on Cinderella's side because . . . we judge Cinderella positively and her stepmother negatively—we value her traits of character and do not value those of her stepmother. As 'Cinderella' proceeds beyond its first paragraph, the narrative not only reinforces these initial judgments but also relies on them to influence significantly our hopes and desires for

Cinderella to escape the tyranny of her stepmother" (*Experiencing*, 1–2). Phelan concludes this opening example by suggesting a general thesis: "The judgments readers of narrative make about characters and tellers (both narrators and authors) are crucial to our experience—and understanding—of narrative form" (3).

What would it mean to write a *novel* that did not depend on this central role of reader judgment? A fascinating if little known inquiry into this possibility is Kenneth Gangemi's *The Interceptor Pilot*. Gangemi's novel is striking because it is essentially the description of a film. Here, for example, is the novel's opening: "The beginning of the film is set at a Naval Air Station somewhere in the western United States. It could be any one of the southwestern or Rocky Mountain states: Arizona, New Mexico, Utah, Nevada, Colorado, Idaho, Wyoming, or Montana. The reason is mainly cinematic. The film will be in color, and the setting might as well be one of great natural beauty. It will be a western landscape of sagebrush and semi-desert plains and striking mountains" (7). This passage is typical of the novel as a whole. Gangemi describes a film without actually providing a traditional script. In fact, he seems to go out of his way to avoid presenting the kind of line-by-line dialogue that would make up the bulk of a traditional film script. Gangemi also departs from the minor subgenre of the *ciné-roman*, the predominantly French novels based on already existing films.[1] Here is another passage from later in the novel that gives a better feel for how Gangemi handles dialogue and character interaction:

We will see that Wilson and the other professor, whose name is Miller, are good friends who often have lunch together. Professor Miller is one of the minor characters in the film. He will be seen as a leftist, but one who is more genial than militant. He will be portrayed quite favorably.

The camera moves in towards the two men and their conversation begins to be heard. They are talking politics, as they often do, and have resumed an old debate. We will see that Professor Miller is further to the left than Wilson.

Cut to a shot of Miller as he looks at Wilson and says, "What have you decided about Korea?" Cut to Wilson. He tells Miller that he hasn't decided anything. Cut back to Miller as he smiles and says, "Well, it's perfectly clear to *me*." (16–17)

Gangemi's novel is actually less like a script than the description of a film that might then be inserted into a larger novel—something we see in Vladimir Nabokov's *Laughter in the Dark* and Mark Danielewski's *House of Leaves*. At the same time, the description is not framed by the actions of characters viewing the film but is instead directly addressed to the reader. The approach is very unusual.[2]

In the novel James Wilson is a navy pilot who served with distinction in Korea, but he is haunted by the civilian deaths he caused and is so disturbed by the escalation of the Vietnam War that he joins the North Vietnamese military and flies combat missions against his own country. We understand Wilson's seriousness when a friend is shown Wilson's collection of materials on Korea: "He is obviously impressed by the quantity of material. Besides the many books on Korea, there are stacks of files and clippings. It is all evidence of years of study" (20). One of the effects of embedding the film within written narrative is that we are very aware of what information we have and, in particular, how we are supposed to respond. Indeed, Gangemi describes not objects or characters so much as our reactions to them. Instead of letting us come to our own evaluation about them, Gangemi tells us exactly why an element is in the film and what we will think about it. The first passage from the novel does this in a relatively mild way; we are told why the film is set in the Rocky Mountain states. Gangemi does not ask us to imagine the scene and then, perhaps, we will realize it is visually striking. Instead, he simply tells us that it will be striking. Likewise he tells us that Miller is a minor character and that we will view him favorably.

Even this brief summary of the novel reveals that Gangemi challenges our ability as readers to come to our own decisions about characters. This assault on our expectations about the importance of reader judgment becomes part of a broad inquiry into the nature of *description* as a component of writing. In fact, of all the narrative terms that I discuss in this chapter, description is the most important because it is the element of narrative most deeply entwined with writing—it falls most clearly on the "mediaspecific" end of Wolf's continuum of narrative concepts with export potential. Some critics have argued that description itself is unique to writing; after all, the word refers to writing (from the Latin *scrībere*, to write) and not to representation in general. In his defense of the idea that films describe, Seymour Chatman summarizes the objection: "Because narrative film keeps characters and props persistently before our eyes and ears with virtually limitless sensory particularity, there seems no *need* for films to describe; it is their nature to show—and to show continuously—a cornucopia of visual details" (*Coming to Terms*, 39). Chatman goes on to argue that films can achieve some of the same effects, but the key feature of description in writing is clear despite Chatman's protest: in writing, populating the background world through description takes time at the discourse level, and simply fills up page space. Description is an activity, in other words, and cannot happen in the background.[3] Michel Beaujour emphasizes this particularly well when he notes "description's seemingly uncheckable tendency to turn into micro-narratives" (33). Philippe Hamon concurs, and notes that the agency most at work within a description is that of the narrator: "To describe, then, is a 'to describe for'; it is a textual praxis, both coded and aimed, opening onto concrete, practical activities" (6). Hamon and Beaujour both emphasize the way that description can become an activity within the text that runs parallel to, and can even rival, the main narrative.

Gangemi's unusual novel suppresses the traditional gap between description and narrative, with profound implications for reader agency. *The Interceptor Pilot* is essentially *all* description. Tamar Yacobi notes that description "is normally theorized as subordinate to the forward-moving action" (619), and it is in observing these forward-moving actions that readers feel most active in exercising their judgments—what Phelan called "our hopes and desires for Cinderella to escape the tyranny of her stepmother." Beaujour notes that, in contrast, description is an activity in which we most see the *writer's* agency. This is the point at which the novel seems so different from film, where the settings, objects, and even characters appear on screen independent of the director's direct effort. After all, as any one with a home movie camera knows, it's easy to film a scene accidentally; we are much less likely to write a description accidentally. Usually we are able to move back and forth between these two forms of information in the text, appreciating and using the description provided by the narrator to understand the narrative world while at the same time forming judgments that we hope to see borne out over the course of the story. In fact, we could say that written narrative depends on keeping the writer's descriptive agency in check so that readers have the freedom to form their own judgments. It is just this gap that is missing in *The Interceptor*

Pilot. It is impossible, for example, not to see Miller positively. At one point we are told about a budding romance between Wilson and a woman he meets in Hanoi: "They are looking at each other, they are both smiling. All the signs are there, and we can see that a love affair is in progress" (85). Gangemi's novel as a whole routinely deploys events where "all the signs are there." In collapsing narration into description, Gangemi suppresses the reader's ability to come to independent decisions about characters and events.

It is virtually impossible for readers to distance themselves from these judgments. In part, this is because we have no other source of information to use to reject these judgments. Even more important, we cannot get distance from these assertions because Gangemi is describing our reactions to the story. Phelan notes that in second-person narratives addressed to "you," readers are likely to distance themselves from the *you* being described when reactions become more specific: "The fuller the characterization of the you, the more aware actual readers will be of their differences from that you, and thus the more fully they will move into the observer role" (*Narrative as Rhetoric*, 137). The design of Gangemi's novel works against this distance, since he is describing a *potential* film, explaining where it will be set, how the characters will be portrayed, how we will respond. Everything about the film is potential, and as a result it is harder for us to see the description of audience reactions as referring to some character that we are merely observing. Gangemi seems essentially to be promising that if the film is produced correctly, we *will* have these responses. The only way we might not see Miller positively, or not recognize the signs of Wilson's romance, would be because of some incident in the production of the film (such as a poor performance by one of the actors), which is beyond the scope of Gangemi's book. This description of future reactions is quite unusual, and makes it considerably more difficult for the reader to hold these responses at arm's length and merely observe them.

Reducing reader agency reflects the novel's themes of control, skill, and bureaucracy. Wilson's impressive collection of books and clippings on the subject of Korea suggests that he has thought through the subject and come to a difficult decision. Later in the story, for example, we see an interview with the American commander Richards after Wilson has begun flying for North Vietnam. The reporter is currently handling public relations for the navy. In the interview Richards is serious and methodical, and demonstrates a sophisticated understanding of the strategic problems raised by Wilson, all the while giving him credit for his training and skill. In contrast, the reporter tries to take the interview in a different direction:

> Cut back to the journalist as he rapidly writes in his notebook. He finishes writing, looks up at the Commander, and then abruptly changes the subject. He begins to inquire about Wilson's personal life when he was in Korea. The journalist asks a number of questions, and Commander Richards is surprised at a few of them: whether Wilson drank very much, what he did when on leave in Japan, and so on. We can see that the Commander is annoyed by the way the journalist rephrases some of his answers. Nothing derogatory is revealed, however, and the journalist seems to be vaguely disappointed. (74–75)

Like Wilson, Richards goes about doing what he takes to be his duty with seriousness and technical skill, while the reporter clearly hopes to manipulate information for some predetermined end. In this regard, Wilson's carefully organized set of clippings reflects the care with which information reported in a newspaper or press announcement needs to be handled. Handling these is a technical matter like flying an aircraft. Like Richards but unlike the reporter, Wilson is able to look at his subject methodically and dispassionately. Indeed, the novel consistently contrasts subjective agency to an impersonal and technical skill that eventually becomes indistinguishable from bureaucracy. We are told of debates about how to respond to Wilson:

> Various courses of action have been discussed, numerous plans have been proposed.
> At last one plan has been agreed upon. It has its risks and its disadvantages, but it is the one favored by the most influential advisors. It is also the course of action that the fewest people oppose. The decision has been made, and the machinery of the government has been set in motion. (106)

This very indirect and corporate agency seems to be embodied in Gangemi's novel as well, since nowhere do we see room for readers to respond individually. Instead, the structure of the film-within-a-novel and the reactions attributed to the reader feel like "machinery" that has been "set in motion."

Restricting audience response and attenuating reader and writer agency, then, has thematic significance to *The Interceptor Pilot*, since Gangemi evidently wants to describe a world in which ethical response to a situation follows almost mechanically from knowledge of its circumstances. But in rejecting the reader's role in forming judgments, this novel violates one of our most basic assumptions about the vocation and value of the novel. Rejecting this common vocation for the novel allows Gangemi to explore the nature of written language—especially the way that writers subordinate their own activity to the judgment of the reader. By keeping description in check or by attributing it to a potentially unreliable narrator, the conventional novel makes possible the reader's evaluation of the story. The need to exert this restraint is particularly important to written narrative because, unlike film or photography, nothing appears within the frame of the novel without the action of the writer's description.[4] Without exercising restraint on description, reader agency vanishes. The resulting loss of agency puts the reader of *The Interceptor Pilot* in a very strange position indeed. It is difficult to read this novel without feeling the irritation of our limited information and constrained responses. Gangemi puts the reader in such an unusual position in part because this suppressed agency has thematic relevance to his story, and in part because he is interested in the unique powers and limitations of writing. But in the process, we should notice an aspect of this novel that reoccurs throughout this discussion: an interest in writing's ability to represent the absent, the possible, or the unrealized. Describing *potential* reactions is essential to the unusual position the reader occupies in this narrative, and we will see such absent elements of the story used in many different ways in the stories discussed in this chapter. This facility at representing the absent is the central quality of writing that allows the novel to dramatize its own limits and connections to other media within the contemporary ecology.

Setting

When we think of American fiction that makes use of other media for innovative narrative effect, Robert Coover's short story "The Babysitter" is likely to be among the first that comes to mind. In it, an unnamed girl arrives to watch the three young children of a couple who are going to a nearby friend's house for a party. The girl's young body is the fetishized object of male lust and is pursued by the girl's boyfriend (Jack), his friend (Mark), the husband (Mr. Tucker), and even the young boy (Jimmy) who is among those that she is watching. Each weaves around the babysitter sexual fantasies and fears. Jack imagines seducing and at the same time rescuing and protecting her, sometimes from Mark (216) and sometimes from Mr. Tucker (230); Mark imagines an orgy (222) and at the same time a rape (225); Mr. Tucker imagines the girl attracted to his sexual experience (215) or at least subject to his manipulation (225–26). The story is told in a series of short, one-paragraph sections that coalesce into several mutually exclusive possibilities: the boys arrive and are greeted by a receptive babysitter; the babysitter is frightened by the boys and fights them off; Mr. Tucker arrives to save the babysitter, to seduce her, or to be exposed for trying to seduce her; and the babysitter manages the evening beautifully, allows it to become sexual, or loses control of the children and kills the youngest (either by suffocating it with her hand [235] or allowing it to drown [237]). While the evening begins with each character locked in his or her own fantasy of how the night will develop, during the story more of these fantasies and fears merge. In the end the host of the party blithely announces to Mrs. Tucker, "What can I say, Dolly? . . . Your children are murdered, your husband gone, a corpse in your bathtub, and your house is wrecked. I'm sorry. But what can I say?" (239)

Coover's story is a postmodernist classic, a particularly clear and famous example of the way that innovative contemporary writing can frustrate our expectations about fiction. Our frustration with this story arises not primarily from confusion, since the language and structure of the narrative are actually quite straightforward once we recognize that the various story lines will not be resolved into a single arc. Some of our irritation with this story is no doubt the result of plot uncertainty: we want to know *what happens*, but Coover refuses to give us a simple answer. But this story's appeal to the reader is not primarily epistemological but rather affective—we are offered a story of sexual desire, frustration, and fear, but none of these strong emotional investments are resolved in the end. Indeed, Coover invokes the most cliché elements of potboiler romances and erotica, promising us a lurid story that will satisfy our most common but disreputable reasons for reading. Robyn Warhol has noted that, while such emotional responses are central to the appeal of much of our reading, literary critics have largely ignored them and the issues they raise: "If popular narratives deploy formulas to invoke predictable patterns of feeling in their devotees, what shapes do those patterns take? If audiences of thrillers and action-adventures experience again and again the pounding heart and pallor of the fight-or-flight reaction; if readers of long-running serial novels and viewers of soap opera continually oscillate between hope and curiosity on the one hand, boredom and annoyance on the other; if fans of marriage-plot films and novels and other forms of sentimental fictions repeatedly indulge in having a good cry, what traces of those affects will their bodies carry over the long term?" (xvii–xviii). Coover evokes these common (if critically disregarded) reasons for reading fiction in "The Babysitter" but frustrates our reading by refusing to provide the affective resolution that we have come to expect.

The key to Coover's challenge to the conventional link between the pleasure of reading and the forward motion of the plot is a rethinking of the nature of setting in the narrative. This story is fundamentally defined by its domestic setting, which prompts and organizes the male desires that circulate through the story: the construction of private and public places (Jack and Mark watch the babysitter from outside the house voyeuristically), the organization of several different domestic spaces (especially the couch as a site of seduction and sexual opportunity), and the way that the same object (the bathtub) can be both an object of duty (getting the children ready for bed) and a source of pleasure and indulgence. The central element of the setting that organizes and describes these desires is the Tuckers' television set. The television mostly shows one of three very conventional plots: a Western about a "lean-jawed sheriff" (214), a spy mystery about masked assailants "down forbidden alleys. Into secret passageways" (224), and a romantic drama about "a man married to an aging invalid wife, but in love with a younger girl" (227). Obviously, these conventional plots of romance, danger, and social expectation parallel the very conventional sexual plots that each of the males develops about the babysitter. The babysitter is an object of lust, aggression, and wistfulness in these overlapping and contradictory plots because American culture thinks about young female sexuality in all these ways. The television embodies these various plots and gives them a place within the domestic space of the house. With its stories that run on and on, even though no one is paying attention to them, the television embodies a world whose plots are external to the characters. Indeed, the second sentence of the story describes the television as a mystery: "From other rooms come the sounds of a baby screaming, water running, a television musical (no words: probably a dance number—patterns of gliding figures come to mind)" (206).

Coover is interested, then, in how desire is built into the spaces of the home. The television amplifies the desires by connecting them to conventional plots, but it complicates this space constantly by introducing other plots and drawing characters away to other spaces. The domestic space is overlaid with "forbidden alleys," the dance floor where "a man in a tuxedo and a little girl in a flouncy white dress are doing a tapdance together" (209), and the brawl between the sheriff and a "dark beardy one" (214). Part of the dizzying quality of the story results from the characters' split attention to their current situation and the spaces implied by these television stories. In essence, there is no simple place where the events of the story take place, because the television is constantly beckoning the characters "from other rooms" into other plots. In using such a dispersed notion of setting, Coover is actually exploiting tensions that are already implicit in the nature of literary setting. In other words, like Gangemi, Coover's challenge to a traditional vocation for fiction (involving the reader emotionally in the pleasure of the text) leads him into an inquiry into a fundamental element of narrative in writing—in this case, setting.

The multiplicity of spaces in setting is especially powerful in the novel. When Ruth Ronen tackles the issue of literary setting, she begins with the principle that writing creates many different layers of space: "Fictional constructs of space are the products of the integration of dynamic bodies of spatial information" ("Space," 421). Ronen distinguishes between the frame and the setting. The frame "is a fictional place, the actual or potential surrounding of fictional characters, objects and places" (421); a setting, conversely, "is the zero point where the *actual* story-events and story-states are localized" (423). Ronen recognizes that many different kinds of frames surround the setting and distinguishes between secondary frames, inaccessible frames, distant frames, and generalized spaces. In the case of a theatrical stage set, setting can be defined fairly easily by reference to the space that the stage is taken to represent: a living room, a train station, a battlefield. Although other spaces may be suggested by the theatrical set—a doorway may suggest a next room, a painted backdrop may represent a far-off forest—the line between the immediate setting of the play and these distant spaces is quite clear.

In the novel, however, setting is defined entirely through language, and consequently the line between the near and the distant is more porous. Language can leave a setting initially vague, and only gradually can it fill in details that allow the reader to visualize the space more specifically.[5] In contrast, Jason Mittell notes that film cannot generally leave the details of its setting undefined: "A film's visual and auditory representation of a storyworld generally contains all of the elements that comprise that setting, while a novel will selectively present details that convey necessary narrative information and set an effective tone" (161). Even more powerful and remarkable is writing's ability to introduce negatively defined spaces. Paul Werth cites a Hemingway story in which the absence of gunbearers is mentioned: "If Hemingway had not mentioned them, then obviously they would have played no part whatsoever in our mental picture. . . . This is now a fact for which we expect an explanation: the gunbearers have been pointed out, and we will want to know why" (10–11). It is certainly possible for theater or film to introduce spaces that are undefined, negated, or not part of the immediate setting of the story, but these spaces will be introduced through character dialogue rather than through theatrical set design or the filmic shot—like Hamlet's university life at Wittenberg, which is mentioned but never seen in the play.

Setting in the novel, then, is more complex than in other media like film and theater because our sense of both setting and frame—both concrete location and other spaces invoked—is constructed through language. At the same time, setting and frame serve to anchor our understanding of the story. We have no physical boundaries and props that define the concrete setting of the written story. The result is a dynamic process of separating figure and ground; as David Herman observes, "changing judgments about what is important can lead to inversions of what counts as figure and what counts as ground in both the perceptual field and the realm of emotional response" (*Story Logic*, 277). Frame and setting are *others* to each other, and consequently involved in a dynamic interaction. This will especially be the case in written narrative, because the spaces that we construct as we read are so tenuous and susceptible to revision. Given that this complexity is both a quality of writing and, at the same time, inherently connected to narrative itself, it should be no surprise that contemporary novels concerned with media frequently focus on setting as a structurally complex element of the narrative.

The complex, layered space that writing is especially good at describing is necessary to the television's particular role in the domestic space of the story, since it constantly beckons characters into other spaces and other plots. This is why television is also the device by which Coover is able to signal the gradual loss of control over narrative. At the beginning of the story, each character is captured by his or her unrealistic imagination of how the evening will develop; as the evening progresses, the fears that come with these desires take on more and more importance to the story. Initially, the characters exercise control over the television—the babysitter uses the Western to pacify Jimmy (211) and later chooses casually between a ballgame, murder mystery, and the romantic drama. As the story goes on, however, characters (especially the babysitter) begin to feel more and more alienated from the plots that are developing on television: "By the time she's chased Jack and Mark out of there, she's lost track of the program she's been watching on television. There's another woman in the story now for some reason. That guy lives a very complicated life. Impatiently, she switches channels" (230). Snippets of action on the television suggest links and motivations that the babysitter does not grasp, and instead of being involved in the plot, more and more the babysitter simply uses the television to drown out the children that she is supposed to be tending: "People are shooting at each other in the murder mystery, but she's so mixed up, she doesn't know which ones are the good guys. She switches back to the love story. Something seems to have happened, because now the man is kissing his invalid wife tenderly. Maybe she's finally dying. The baby wakes, begins to scream. Let it. She turns up the volume on the TV" (231). The babysitter's desire for "something" to happen "finally" reflects her growing alienation from the plots in which she is involved.

The spaces evoked by television in Coover's story, then, are always elsewhere. In chapter 2 we noted Brian McHale's similar observation that the television is an "ontological pluralizer." This *elsewhere* can be another room or another story entirely. In this regard, Coover's use of television is exactly the opposite of what we see in other stories of characters getting caught up in fantasy worlds, like Walter Mitty, who loses track of the everyday world for the sake of the imagination. In "The Babysitter," conversely, these plots are always incompletely understood and someplace else—part of some world that the characters feel they belong to but are not sure that they quite understand or know how to find.[6] The spaces of Coover's story organize characters' desires and courses of action. This link is essential to the story's use of setting, since we have seen that it is the nature of written narrative to construct not just a simple location as the setting of the story but also the surrounding, often more general, spaces. These spaces are not the concrete locations of the theater set but instead are those implied by the plots that encircle, unrealized, the main action of the story.

Just as we saw with Gangemi's novel, Coover rejects a conventional and compelling definition of the novel, that of sweeping us up into the "pleasure of the text." After rejecting this vocation for fiction, Coover turns to a theoretical exploration of problems in our understanding of setting as it appears in writing. In the process, he discovers that writing is especially good at representing the way that our lives are woven out of desires and the other spaces they imply. Coover's story also shares with Gangemi's novel an interest in what is *not there* in the story: the other spaces that call to characters while they are caught up in the activity of child care or routine socializing. In *The Interceptor Pilot* we noted that Gangemi reaches beyond the traditional boundary of the text and describes not merely characters and events but responses that the reader is expected to have. Just as Gangemi describes an experience that we have not had, Coover is able to describe spaces that are not part of the story but which haunt the narrative anyway. For both writers, this ability to represent the absent appears to be central to writing. Coover's story demonstrates that the ability to represent what is missing is a way of describing a larger network of relations. The setting of Coover's story gestures toward spaces that are beyond the scope of the story itself to describe; the living room, in this sense, is a kind of node in a system of locations far exceeding anything that appears in the story itself. Likewise, this focus on the absent allows the novel to use its limits to show how it connects to systems of media relations larger than itself.

World

Susan Daitch's *The Colorist* is an exemplary media novel, since it is a compendium of contemporary media forms. The novel is told in the first person by Julie Greene, whose job it is to color a comic about a superhero called Electra. The comic is on shaky economic footing, and shortly after the novel begins it is canceled and Julie and her friend Laurel Quan Liu, the inker, are fired. The search for employment carries Julie and Laurel into a variety of artistic odd jobs, and they eventually end up working for a shady company that makes reproductions of artworks and archeological artifacts for sale in museum gift shops. This overall plot design allows Daitch to explore the nature of cartooning as an art form, especially in its relationship to mundane economic concerns like audience and distribution—what I described in chapter 2 as the circulation of a narrative. Julie notes, for example, "Electra hadn't changed much since the beginning of the series, on the premise that one audience grew up and was replaced by another" (15). After the comic is canceled, Julie and Laurel continue the story privately between themselves, and it is here that Daitch explores the medium as a way to tell stories.

To this interest in comics, art, and writing is added another key medium: photography. Julie's roommate is Eamonn Archer, a photographer who becomes interested in gun smuggling and piracy, and who consequently tries to use his photography as a form of investigation. Eamonn's opinions about photography provide the perspective of another medium against which cartooning and writing can be evaluated. In fact, his own desire to remove photography from a concern for its audience and even subjects provides a remarkable contrast to Julie's struggle to make a living as a colorist. Eamonn "only partly believed in the audience's right-to-know anyway" (35). For Eamonn, the photograph has a kind of absolute quality that makes no reference to the context in which the photograph is taken or received. He explains further: "*The camera never lies, you know,* Eamonn had said when he first showed me his pictures. . . . *They also tidy up, make accessible, and establish distance because they remove the firebombed pub from its context,* he admitted" (70). Julie goes on to note that "negatives, prints just back from the lab" had "no captions, no titles on the margins or on the back. These were disassociated from printed language. The power of specific site and circumstance was lost" (70–71).[7]

In this regard, photography is the opposite of writing, which is directly engaged with the contemporary world. Eamonn associates writing with context, the "specific site and circumstance" that a caption would bring. The only example that Daitch gives of writing in the novel, in fact, is oblique. When Laurel and Julie are particularly hard up and have been out of work for a long time, Laurel considers prostitution. She approaches a woman (who works under the name Janet Ling) who offers to sell Laurel her black book describing her customers: "Opposite each name in the book was a description of what she should expect to do and how much each usually paid" (124). Julie becomes interested in these descriptions: "I tried to look at the black book as if it were a notebook for a writer. The names were fictional, made-up characters for a novella. That characters were traded like baseball cards between different 'writers' was a demonstration of inventiveness" (130). The "notebook" of this prostitute embraces all those aspects of recording that Eamonn denies in his photographs; it is an economic document that connects the "artist" with a network of clients. In fact, the descriptions that Janet Ling offers are ultimately nothing but the "site and circumstance" that she must adopt in order to complete the job. And, unlike Eamonn's photographs, these descriptions are hypothetical and dangerously contingent. Ling warns against meeting some of the men too many times: "He starts off undemanding, but when he gets short-tempered and offers more money, it's time to cut out, unless you're really desperate" (127). This notebook, then, connects Ling (as well as Julie and Laurel) to an economic network and to a dangerous and contingent work that is quite different from the pure artifact that Eamonn strives toward with his photographs.

Like the other novels we have discussed in this chapter, *The Colorist* appeals to but also challenges a common and familiar vocation for the novel—in this case, that of unifying a variety of characters who represent different elements of contemporary life into a single fictional world. The claim that the novel can embrace a wide range of social life and bring together figures from different classes, races, and nations is a familiar and conventional justification for the novel's place within liberal culture. As Georg Lukács remarks, "The novel is the epic of an age in which the extensive totality of life is no longer directly given, in which the extensive totality of life has become a problem, yet which still thinks in terms of totality" (56). The novel's ability to link together disparate elements of contemporary life is implicit in M. M. Bakhtin's influential definition of the novel as concerned with heteroglossia: "*It is precisely the diversity of speech, and not the unity of a normative shared language, that is the ground of style*" in the English novel (308). Bakhtin's theory is a more sophisticated articulation of what has been a longstanding and conventional justification for the novel. W. J. Harvey summarizes this view of the novel in *Character and the Novel* (1965): "We may fairly say that the novel is the distinct art form of liberalism, by which I mean not a political view or even a mode of social and economic organization but rather a state of mind. This state of mind has as its controlling centre an acknowledgement of the plentitude, diversity and individuality of human beings in society, together with the belief that such characteristics are good as ends in themselves" (24). One traditional definition of the work of the novel is to find connections between these heterogeneous elements of conventional life.

What is jarring about Daitch's novel is that the different characters brought together are not part of some coherent fictional world, but are instead elements of many different worlds. The most obvious example of this is, of course, the narrative about Electra—which initially reflects the rules of a comic-book world. We might also include Eamonn's investigative photography about gun smuggling, which likewise seems to reflect a different world with its own shadowy and mysterious rules that he never quite grasps. In fact, as part of his investigation Eamonn travels to Dublin and then to Belfast on the thinnest of instructions: "Eamonn wasn't sure what he expected to find in the North. He and [smuggler] Freddy Driscoll hadn't much use for each other, really. Driscoll's plans were too deliberately vague. *A photographer could be useful.* Driscoll had given him a number to call in Dublin, but though he dialed it many times over several days, no one ever picked up" (106). Eventually Eamonn is given the task of photographing individuals at a particular intersection in Belfast, but the reason for doing so and what will become of his photographs are never explained, and he abandons the task without ever discovering the plot in which he is participating. In *The Colorist*, in other words, the characters seem to inhabit different worlds with their own rules. In fact, Daitch describes Eamonn and Electra in the same terms: "A sense of powerlessness put him on the train traveling north and this was new. He hadn't ever felt like Electra, sent successfully all over someone's idea of space and finally assigned by the colorist to failure on earth. Now, on the train, he did" (106–7). The reason why those worlds are so different is evident in this mention of "someone's idea of space": each character is associated with a different medium (writing, comics, and photography), which seems to obey completely different (and often mysterious) rules.

Daitch's use of these three media focuses on the connection between a story and its larger world. Writing and photography define two poles that delineate the nature of representation in *The Colorist* and, in particular, the relationship between a medium and its circulation in a larger economic world. The distinction that Julie notes between the photograph and the caption, between pure abstract image and specific written context, between artifact and economics, is one that cartooning seems to bridge. Discussing a scene involving Electra that "was done in red," Julie summarizes the exchange: "Eamonn would say Electra's redness when she fought was the mock red of a bloodless revolution. In the comics, I would say, color is never an entity by itself, color is never a message without a sign. . . . There was no conflict between word and image in Electra's bit of space. Artificial and highly stylized, there were no contradictions between what was said and what was seen" (50). The conflict between word and image is precisely what Eamonn has dwelt on, and his (sarcastic) attempt to assign reference to the color red in the comic is typical of his aesthetics, which sees any reference as reductive. Julie, however, describes a medium in which representation is not at odds with the scene described—precisely because the medium has the power to stylize the world. The comic seems to strike a middle ground between specific historical reference and pure ahistorical aesthetics, to maintain the idea of reference to a system while at the same time making that system more general and stylized.

When describing the worlds created by these different media, Daitch focuses particularly on implied situations and plots, and especially on the logic behind them. The importance of such logic is noted in passing by Laurel when she and Julie are working on their private Electra. Discussing the possible directions for their story, Julie proposes that some of the characters must have credit cards: "Laurel asked if I had ever seen a credit card in a comic like *Electra*. Money didn't exist in a graphic way, but it was very important as a concept" (154). This exchange nicely encapsulates the kind of logical constraints that the two women work under as they construct their narrative. Money may not appear in the story, but it defines a condition of the world that is represented, and thus it exerts a logical pressure on the way the narrative can develop. The example of credit cards in particular is especially effective, since credit itself is the *idea* of currency even in the absence of physical money or assets.

It is this implied logic of the fictional world that Electra inhabits where

Daitch most clearly speculates on what makes writing unique among the other media she invokes in her novel. To understand why this implied logic is so important to writing, we should consider the nature of fictional worlds as a narrative concept. In chapter 1 we touched on the issue of fictional worlds in the discussion of Sukenick's short story "Duck Tape." That story interrogated what it means for something to be "in" the story: is merely a mention of a lawyer enough to make him part of the story world? This interest in fictional worlds is especially powerful because the concept is overwhelmingly based on language rather than other representational media. How, philosophers have asked, is it possible to refer to a thing that does not exist? Thomas Pavel notes that Bertrand Russell simply concluded that it is impossible for statements about fictional entities to have any truth value at all (13–14), but most philosophers since have been at some pains to reclaim validity for such statements. This ranges from speech-act theorists who conclude that references to fictional entities are simply *pretended* or represented speech acts (Walton, 81), to other philosophers like Alexius Meinong who has claimed that our definition of objects of reference needs to be extended and that existence should be understood as merely one of many possible qualities that an object can have (Crittenden, 4). Into this very abstract debate, the concept of fictional worlds arises as a way to describe the conditions that allow such references to work. As Marie-Laure Ryan explains, "We know that the textual universe, as a whole, is an imaginary alternative to our system of reality; but for the duration of the game, as we step into it, we behave as if the actual world of the textual universe were *the* actual world" (*Possible Worlds*, 23).

Because the field emerged from questions about reference to nonexistent objects, theories of fictional worlds tend to describe the nature of such worlds in terms of the entities they contain. To take a common example, we may ask whether it is possible for a fictional world to contain an impossible object, such as a square circle, which "effectively prevents us from considering fictional worlds as genuine possible worlds" (Pavel, 49). Clearly, such worlds must imply principles of logic that make some objects possible and others impossible. Such logic has received limited attention. Pavel's sophisticated theory of fictional worlds stands out in this regard for recognizing that different worlds imply different types of logic. He notes, for example, "In the ontology of the sacred, the plenary reality of the sacred domain is crucially opposed to the precarious existence of the profane. Sacred beings not only obey different laws than do sublunar creatures, but their way of being is fundamentally different" (60). This passage makes clear that implied laws are a fundamental but frequently invisible element of fictional worlds. The example that Daitch raises about the nature of money implicit but unstated in Electra's fictional world is, in fact, a particularly complex and interesting case of an implied logic at work within a fictional world. Ryan specifically addresses the role of money in her treatment of the implicit logic of the chivalric romance. If fictional worlds obey the principle of minimal departure—we assume that they are the same as our world except when we are explicitly told that they are not—then "knights errant need to sleep and eat and pay for services unless otherwise specified" (*Possible Worlds*, 53). Ryan goes on to argue that this case represents an overly strict application of the principle of minimal departure, and amends this principle "to prevent the invasion of textual universes by unwanted species and individuals." Such a species will only be transferable from the actual to the fictional world if "the appropriate environment for [it] is set up in the" textual world (53). Ryan's invocation of the "appropriate environment" resonates with Pavel's idea of sacred beings obeying their own implied physical laws: both describe the rules that organize the fictional world. Such rules exist in the fictional world but may never manifest themselves in the actual objects of the world: a fictional world organized by the principles of capitalism will have a different logic than a fictional world organized feudally, even if the inventory of objects in that world is exactly the same.

The best way to think about the logic that organizes fictional worlds is provided by Lubomír Doležel's appeal to action theory in *Heterocosmica*. Actions are organized around intentions and goals: "Intention in and for acting orients the agent toward the future, directs him or her to proceed from a given initial state to an anticipated end state" (58). These goals and intentions in turn are structured by the social circumstances in which they are placed, and they depend on the rules implied by those circumstances. Doležel gives an example from Dickens: "In the novel *Little Dorrit*, Charles Dickens constructed a fictional world where the persons' capacity for intentional and purposeful acting is severely impaired. Two global conditions are responsible: rigid social organization and a propensity for accidents. Dickens' narrative is propelled by the agents striving to cope with the oppressive conditions reigning in the world into which they have been thrown" (81). In particular, Doležel's account helps to explain how cultural rules may limit actions and shape the nature of the fictional world. When Doležel refers to an "action-system polarity" at work within such worlds (112), he identifies in the system the crucial component that organizes the logic of fictional worlds. This system of constraints manifests itself particularly clearly in the modal structures that I mentioned briefly in chapter 1. What we think of as *a* fictional world is in fact a tissue of many worlds. Ryan explains this by placing the "textual actual world" as the basis of this fictional world and then describing the various potential worlds that can surround that world and reflect a series of constraints. Deontic systems determine what is allowed, axiological systems determine what is good, epistemic systems define what can be known, and so on. Each of these systems produces modal worlds: our systems of knowledge structure what can be known (the K-world), our axiological systems determine our wish world (W-world), and the deontic system determines our obligation world (O-world) (*Possible Worlds*, 111). These various nonactual worlds surround the textual actual world, and structure the actions of the characters. When Doležel refers to a system that makes action possible, he is clearly describing the logical constraints upon such modal worlds: "Agents of the actual world have to deal with a tangled bundle of modal restrictions" (114), whose structure reflects the cultural system in which they operate.

Daitch's primary insight in *The Colorist* is that, while any narrative can imply such modal worlds—virtually every narrative will involve characters considering possible actions, reflecting on social expectations, and so on—writing is particularly capable of analyzing those modal structures. Ryan has suggested that the ability to project such modal worlds is fundamental to our sense of the value and "tellability" of a story in any medium: "The appeal of the trip [metaphorically through a novel] depends not so much on the immediate surroundings of the road actually followed as on the glimpses it permits of the back country, and of the alternative roads it invites the reader to travel in imagination" (*Possible Worlds*, 174). Most narrative forms can project nonactual states of affairs; we might think of the ubiquitous thought bubble in the comic book or the dream sequence in film.[8] Although such visual narratives refer to hypothetical or imagined events, making those references is usually easier and more natural in language. Ryan explains: "Pictures may admittedly find ways around their lack of propositional ability to suggest specific properties (for instance, through caricature), but there are certain types of statements that seem totally beyond their reach. As Sol Worth argues, pictures cannot say 'ain't'" ("Introduction," 10–11). Even though other media can project various modal worlds that surround the present (textual actual world), writing gives us more tools for analyzing their relationships. Consider, for example, the convoluted opening sentence of Henry James's "The Beast in the Jungle": "What determined the speech that startled him in the course of their encounter scarcely matters, being probably but some words spoken by himself quite without intention—spoken as they lingered and slowly moved together after their renewal of acquaintance" (277). A statement is described and then withdrawn (it "scarcely matters") and further modalized in terms of mere possibility ("being probably but some words") and subordinated to their intention ("quite without intention"). Writing can create complexly nested worlds much more easily, and especially can analyze their relationships.[9]

Daitch puts this power to work in her novel, allowing Julie and Eamonn to analyze in dialogue and their written Electra narrative what could not be discussed in the original comic book. This analysis is especially focused on money, which is not merely one of the logical constraints that shape the Electra story but *the* central issue in the private Electra story that Julie and Laurel create, and the element of narrative that Daitch's *written* story about this comic book is especially good at revealing. In fact, when Julie tells Eamonn about writing the private Electra story and, in particular, on bringing the character to Earth, his first response focuses on the concept of money: "Before he left, as I was idly drawing, not even aware of his imminent departure, Eamonn had said that if I insisted drawing her on earth, I should at least have Electra learn the value of currency immediately. He advised that she should try to blend in as much as possible. To have her wandering around Manhattan would only cause trouble" (75). In Julie and Laurel's story, Electra gets into just this sort of trouble because, as she travels back to Earth, she loses some of her memory: "*In his* [the villain Orion's] *frustration he pounded the controls of his spaceship, and a fragment of an amnesia-inducing ray pierced Electra's thermaglass window. It was only a small bit of a ray, but it erased the part of her brain that stored the memory of Dr. Atlas"* (67). Once on Earth, her ship having *"disintegrated as it fell through the Earth's atmosphere"* (67), Electra is lost and directionless. Zippered into her suit is a package of thousands of dollars, labeled "Useful on Earth," but Electra abandons them in Central Park because she does not know what to do with them. She wanders around New York, living on the street and *"constructing her possessions from what other people threw away"* (91).

Electra emerges as a figure blind to the economic context because of her originally stylized medium, and it is essential to Daitch's use of that medium that it is only when it is inserted into writing that this context emerges and can be analyzed. Late in the novel Electra makes her temporary home in a movie theater where she has some shelter and the chance to scrounge enough food to eat. Earlier I noted that money was relevant to the comic "as a concept," and this part of her narrative seems concerned with trying to take greater account of the "concepts" that define the world of her story and the possible actions that she can take there: "If any of them [their characters] ventured out of the movie theatre to beg or look for food, he or she would risk not being able to get back inside. In the cold, it was a difficult decision to have to consider: sacrificing food for shelter or relinquishing shelter for food. These were circumstances her original publisher had ignored. There had always been money and food in space. At Fantômes, Laurel had never drawn so much as a sandwich or a dime, but it was understood the characters had access to whatever ensured basic survival under ordinary circumstances" (154). Julie and Laurel return to their Electra story with a greater interest in the rules of "ordinary circumstances" and particularly in the logic within these circumstances that functions invisibly, implicit but never described on the page. In writing *about* the comic, however, Julie and Laurel are able to articulate the abstract economic context of this stylized world. Exploring this context provides the impetus for their writing, which becomes a way of solving the sort of storytelling problems that we have seen authors encounter again and again: "Even now, she had free license to draw all of them as millionaires but couldn't logically get them out of the movie theatre" (154). Because written narrative describes possible choices and hypothetical worlds, it is particularly drawn to these kinds of economic forces, to all those rules that impose themselves on the events of the story.

Once again, we see in *The Colorist* a story that is fascinated by something that is not simply "in" the story. Gangemi described audience reactions that may not have occurred; Coover describes plots that haunt the narrative without ever quite becoming the story; and Daitch describes rules according to which her world works but which remain abstract and shadowy presences. In all three stories, an inquiry into the strength and limitations of writing leads to an interest in what is absent, potential, or unrealized in the text. Even more importantly, the novel emerges as the medium most capable of describing the relations between media (comics, photography, and the novel) precisely because it is able to articulate these absent, abstract systems at work between and beyond any one form of representation.

Character

Like many contemporary novelists, Kurt Vonnegut's career cycles through other media—from music in a minor way in *Player Piano* to painting more centrally in *Bluebeard*. *Breakfast of Champions* is typical but also more extreme, since in this story Vonnegut intersperses his own hand-drawn images. He admits in his introduction that these images, drawn with a felt-tipped pen, are crude and immature (5), and it is clear that they do not simply serve as traditional illustrations for his novel. Vonnegut interrupts his narrative to introduce them, pointing indexically to their place on the page rather than allowing them to exist independently and outside narrative time, as is traditional in illustrations. I have avoided discussing novels with other media elements inserted into them—contemporary novels like Carole Maso's *The Art Lover* or Jonathan Safran Foer's *Extremely Loud and Incredibly Close*, both of which include images—because I am more interested in the *idea* of media as it is described by these writers. Vonnegut's image-strewn book initially seems like an exception to this principle, but it quickly becomes apparent that he is not interested in the drawings themselves, which he admits are poorly executed. Instead, Vonnegut focuses on the decision to create and include these drawings. Vonnegut explains that "scrawl[ing] pictures" (4) in this book is a way to get the past out of his mind: "I think I am trying to clear my head of all the junk in there—the assholes, the flags, the underpants. Yes—there is a picture in this book of underpants. I'm throwing out characters from my other books, too. I'm not going to put on any more puppet shows. I think I am trying to make my head as empty as it was when I was born onto this damaged planet fifty years ago" (5). *Breakfast of Champions* is, then, about the decision to put these images down on paper and include them amid Vonnegut's story. The images that Vonnegut includes in this book represent the collective American past, as well as those parts of Vonnegut's own past that were shared by others of his generation. Thus, many of the images in the book are national symbols like the American flag or the torch of liberty. Even Vonnegut's crude drawing of the pornographic come-on about photographs of "wide-open beavers" is offered as part of a cultural history: "When Dwayne was a boy, when Kilgore Trout was a boy, when I was a boy, and even when we became middle-aged men and older, it was the duty of the police and the courts to keep representations of such ordinary apertures from being examined and discussed by persons not engaged in the practice of medicine. It was somehow decided that wide-open beavers, which were ten thousand times as common as real beavers, should be the most massively defended secret under law" (23–24). Images like these—both highly visible public symbols such as the flag and fetishized and banned images of female genitalia—are part of a collective past that Vonnegut is describing. Vonnegut focuses on how we know the world through collective images.

By using these images as building blocks for his novel, Vonnegut has created a narrative that rejects one common purpose of the novel: to describe "possible worlds" that illuminate our actual world. Vonnegut actually invokes this common way of thinking about the novel in the science fiction written by his main character, Kilgore Trout. Typical is the plot of Trout's most popular book, *Plague on Wheels*, which describes a planet inhabited by creatures that look like automobiles and are powered by internal combustion engines. After the planet exhausts all its resources, the creatures try to get visitors from the planet Zeltoldimar to carry one of their eggs to another planet, but the "smallest egg they had was a forty-eight pounder, and the space travelers themselves were only an inch high, and their space ship wasn't even as big as an Earthling shoebox" (26–27). The Zeltoldimarians do, however, promise to keep alive the memories of these automobile creatures, and eventually they carry a description to Earth, not realizing that "human beings could be as easily felled by a single idea as by cholera or the bubonic plague" (27). Although hardly an instance of the sort of realistic possible futures that we associate with science fiction, nonetheless Trout's hypothetical narratives work by creating a story and situation, developing the logical actions of characters who function as "possible people" in that world, and even offering a moral lesson that follows from the events.

It is clear that Vonnegut is unable to follow this vocation for the novel because he feels overwhelmed by the detritus of culture. As a result, the illusion of a meaningful plot falls away and we are left with characters who are artifacts from Vonnegut's own childhood imported into the story. Unable to allow his characters to function in the roles that they were given, Vonnegut intervenes constantly and thus exposes the origins of his characters, not in a realistic possible world but in the very personal obsessions and purposes of the author. Vonnegut himself appears as a character late in the novel when he buys a drink and watches the confrontation between two major characters, and is possibly recognized as the author by one of them (247). The novel ends by Vonnegut magnanimously freeing his characters. As he explains, "'I am approaching my fiftieth birthday, Mr. Trout,' I said. 'I am cleansing and renewing myself for the very different sorts of years to come. Under similar spiritual conditions, Count Tolstoi freed his serfs. Thomas Jefferson freed his slaves. I am going to set at liberty all the literary characters who have served me so loyally during my writing career'" (301). If Vonnegut has been shaped by the building-block images that he has received from culture, in turn his story is a product of the elements he has created and manipulated. Vonnegut's reference to slavery picks up on a running concern with race and the exploitation of others by government and business interests. Here is Vonnegut's summary of the founding of the U.S. government: "The sea pirates [European colonists] who had the most to do with the creation of the new government owned human slaves. They used human beings for machinery, and, even after slavery was eliminated, because it was so embarrassing, they and their descendants continued to think of ordinary human beings as machines" (11). Vonnegut links conventional methods of narrative construction to the exploitation of human beings. In fact, as the novel moves toward its conclusion, Vonnegut is more and more explicit about how he has orchestrated the events of the novel for his own purposes. He foreshadows the end of the novel in this way: "Here was what was going to happen to Wayne in about four days—because I wanted it to happen to him" (210).

It seems clear, then, that like the other writers discussed in this chapter,

Vonnegut is rejecting a traditional vocation for the novel and is instead turning to a common narrative element—in this case, character—whose link to writing he interrogates. Initially, the link between character and writing may seem tenuous. Films, radio dramas, graphic novels, stage plays, video games, and even paintings can all have characters in much the same way that a traditional print novel can. There are, however, a number of ways that character becomes complicated when presented through writing. Part of our experience of characters in written narrative involves the dual awareness that they are both like people and not really people. Mieke Bal explains:

> Characters resemble people. Literature is written by, for, and about people. That remains a truism, so banal that we often tend to forget it, and so problematic that we as often repress it with the same ease. On the other hand, the people with whom literature is concerned are not real people. They are fabricated creatures made up from fantasy, imitation, memory: paper people, without flesh and blood. That no satisfying, coherent theory of character is available is probably precisely because of this human aspect. The character is not a human being, but it resembles one. (115)

Phelan formalizes this duality when he distinguishes between the *synthetic* and the *mimetic* qualities of fictional characters. Opening *Reading People, Reading Plots* by citing David Lodge's example of a slippery character named Brown or Green or Grey, Phelan observes that

> Brown-Green-Grey is neither real nor the image of a real person but rather is a construct, designed as an amusing display of authorial ingenuity which will also make Lodge's argumentative point about the importance of language in fiction. Although our awareness of, say, Hamlet, or Huck Finn, or Clarissa Dalloway, as made-up is not foregrounded to the degree it is with Brown-Green-Grey, we can recognize that such an awareness is part of our apprehension of them as characters. Part of being a fictional character, in other words, is being artificial in this sense, and part of knowing a character is knowing that he/she/(it?) is a construct. I will hereafter call the "artificial" component of character the synthetic. (2)

Phelan goes on to note that our awareness of the synthetic function of the character—the fact that the character is created by the author in a skillful or unskillful way, for specific narrative or poetic purposes—is balanced against the understanding of the character as a possible person, what Phelan refers to as the mimetic component of the character.

In the novel, then, there is a tension between characters as objects of representation and characters as tools for telling a story. This tension is implicit in any form of narrative, of course, but it is especially powerful in written narrative because sorting out the various voices telling the story is such a central element of reading. Patrick O'Neill captures this complexity particularly well in his cross-media analogy of the author as director: "Even in the case of the most obviously objective external narrator, that is to say, what we normally think of as an entirely univocal narrator is thus always more accurately thought of as being a *compound* narrative instance, composed of the implied author as the 'director' behind the narrative and the narrator as its 'performer'" (68). The tension between author and narrator is less central to other narrative forms because in most we are not usually encouraged to treat the vision of the narrator as an artifact in (potential) conflict with the implied author. David Bordwell has argued particularly forcefully against importing linguistic models of narrator and implied author into discussions of film. He criticizes the use in film theory of Émile Benveniste's analysis of ways that language can signal its circumstances of enunciation, including the situation of the speaker and listener. Applying such linguistic categories rests on an unjustified analogy; why, he asks, "is the employment of linguistic concepts a necessary condition of analyzing filmic narration?" (23). More broadly, he concludes that "since any utterance can be construed with respect to a putative source, literary theory may be justified in looking for a speaking voice or narrator. But in watching films, we are seldom aware of being told something by an entity resembling a human being" (62). Other critics have responded to this claim and have demonstrated the value of the concept of a narrator in film, especially when dealing with varieties of unreliable narration. Seymour Chatman makes a strong case that film can have the same elements as written narrative: "In short, for films as for novels, we would do well to distinguish between a *presenter* of the story, the narrator (who is a component of the discourse), and the *inventor* of both the story and the discourse (including the narrator): that is, the implied author" (*Coming to*

Terms, 133). But Chatman's examples make clear that the ironic distance between implied author and narrator is considerably less common in film than in written narrative; in written narrative we almost always entertain the suspicion that the narrator is an imperfect agent of storytelling, but creating doubts about what we are being shown on the screen is used less frequently and is usually more disruptive. More importantly, Bordwell is correct in suggesting that such distinctions seem to import categories that are more natural to writing. Donald Larsson has noted, for example, that among the cinema's "unique properties" is the fact that it is a *"collaborative medium"*: "Film undermines literary notions of the solitary author. As a *multi-track* medium, [it] relays information (that is, *narrates*) through all the technical means available to the medium, thus undermining literary notions of a single narrator of an entire text" (n.p.). Given the collaborative origin of film, it is harder to identify a single "implied author" as a component of the story. We can say that suspicion about reliability is not one of the "affordances" of film, even though film audiences can be made suspicious through special techniques.

Written narrative, then, is especially good at drawing our attention to how a story is being told, and thus of making us aware of the *use* being made of core narrative concepts—chief among them, characters. Vonnegut seems to have had exactly this tension between the realistic and the tool-like qualities of characters in mind when he wrote *Breakfast of Champions*. The characters in this novel clearly depend on the speaking voice implicit in the act of enunciation. Indeed, Vonnegut shows us that writing is especially likely to use characters as tools precisely because writing is the medium that we think of as fundamentally personal and intimate. O'Neill's description of the implied author as a "director" responsible for the design of the whole novel reminds us that we always imagine such a designing intellect behind every story, but Vonnegut shows us that the stronger our sense of the author's personal investment in the story, the more mechanical that story's characters will be. Vonnegut insists on this investment at every turn, from his very personal concern for his fiftieth birthday and his adolescent fascination with sexual images, to the way that he has hand-drawn the images that appear in the book. Instead of accepting the traditional idea that the novel is a possible future of realistic people, Vonnegut describes the novel as a way of making the private public. In doing so, the novel's characters come to be mere storytelling tools.

I take it as an important detail that Dwayne Hoover owes his origins to typesetting:

> [Hoover] himself had been adopted—by a couple who had moved to Midland City from West Virginia in order to make big money as factory workers in the First World War. Dwayne's real mother was a spinster school teacher who wrote sentimental poetry and claimed to be descended from Richard the Lion-Hearted, who was a king. His real father was an itinerant typesetter, who seduced his mother by setting her poems in type. He didn't sneak them into a newspaper or anything. It was enough for her that they were set in type. (45)

The promise of print is to move the private act of seduction (and sentimental self-expression) to the larger world. For Hoover's mother, this idea—merely the idea—that her poems might be printed and read by others is very powerful. Vonnegut's character Hoover is an embodiment of the movement from private to public, since he is both an invention of print (that is, a fictional character) and figuratively born from type. This seems to be Vonnegut's general understanding of print, which for him is what allows thoughts to move from private obsession to public display. In fact, even when he is referring to his own drawings, Vonnegut emphasizes his own personal reasons: "I am programmed at fifty to perform childishly—to insult 'The Star-Spangled Banner,' to scrawl pictures of a Nazi flag and an asshole and a lot of other things with a felt-tipped pen" (4–5). The pictures themselves are less important than the decision to draw them, to put them onto the page; this is the real story that Vonnegut is telling, and by implication the story at the heart of every piece of writing.

Vonnegut's use of drawing, then, shifts the vocation of the novel from the description of a possible set of events to a public articulation of the private thoughts and experiences of the author. As we have seen in all the other examples from this chapter, this shift is made possible by an inquiry into one basic narrative element (character) and how it appears within the medium of writing specifically. Thus, like all the stories discussed in this chapter, Vonnegut's use of another medium ultimately becomes a way to talk about what makes the novel unique. His effort to position writing within a whole media ecology by looking at how characters make the private public is perhaps most concisely captured in a scene early in the novel. Over the course of the novel, as Vonnegut has Trout travel toward his meeting with Hoover, the literal justification for his meeting is so that Trout can participate in a symposium entitled "The Future of the American Novel in the Age of McLuhan" (55). Trout dismisses the topic without knowing who McLuhan is and reframes the discussion in practical economic terms: "Does this McLuhan, whoever he is, have anything to say about the relationship between wide-open beavers and the sales of books?" (55). Vonnegut takes what seems to be a fundamental theoretical question about the novel today—the place of the written word in the larger media ecology that includes the visual—and instead turns it into a question of the relationship between private fantasy (wide-open beavers) and the public marketplace.

Vonnegut's emphasis on writing's ability to stage the transition from the private to the public also helps to complicate and deepen the link between writing and the articulation of the absent, possible, or unrealized. The focus on the manipulation of characters by an author who normally resides offstage in most novels has much in common with Coover's interest in the spaces and desires that surround his story's immediate setting; both writers describe a force that is absent but deeply influential on the concrete objects that make up the story. But Vonnegut also reminds us that an interest in these absences takes us outside the story itself to the culture in which the story circulates. In each of the four stories discussed thus far, what is absent in the story—that which writing is so good at describing—is also the point at which the book enters into a circulation within contemporary society. In Daitch, this world is represented by the cultural logic of money; in Coover, it is the conventional plots through which characters live, in Gangemi, it is the film's ability to impose on the reader an experience he or she may not feel; and in Vonnegut, it is the personal origins of the artifact that readers hold in their hands. In each case, an interest in the limits and potentials of the medium of writing takes us outside the story to its place within a larger world.

Plot

Don DeLillo's *White Noise* is one of the best-known media novels and is frequently taken to be a classic statement about the role of television in contemporary culture. As one character in the novel remarks, echoing Coover's story and McHale's claim that television is an ontological pluralizer, "For most people there are only two places in the world. Where they live and their TV set" (66). The particular way that DeLillo uses television as a device to deflect the inevitability of plot provides a capstone example of the pattern that we have seen throughout this chapter: a media novel challenges a conventional definition of the novel by investigating a general narrative concept, in this case, plot.

DeLillo's novel tells the story of Jack Gladney, who teaches Hitler Studies at a small college, as he negotiates the place of death and dread in contemporary life. Early in the novel a toxic spill near his house forces an evacuation during which Gladney is apparently exposed to a chemical called Nyodene Derivative or Nyodene D, which might eventually cause his death. The nature of Nyodene D is kept vague and shrouded in medical doublespeak:

"We'll know more in fifteen years. In the meantime we definitely have a situation."

"What will we know in fifteen years?"

"If you're still alive at the time, we'll know that much more than we do now. Nyodene D. has a life span of thirty years. You'll have made it halfway through." . . .

"So, to outlive this substance, I will have to make it into my eighties. Then I can begin to relax."

"Knowing what we know at this time."

"But general consensus seems to be that we don't know enough at this time to be sure of anything." (140–41)

Gladney is oppressed by dread of his own mortality, a fear which both industrial capitalism and the medical bureaucracy only heightens by wrapping any information in this layer of uncertainty. Although initially this sort of noninformation seems to be a form of legal self-protection, over the course of the novel it becomes clear that the American marketplace profits from fostering a sense of fear—even if that fear concerns the products of the marketplace itself. As Gladney notes, "Terrifying data is now an industry in itself. Different firms compete to see how badly they can scare us" (175). Medical tests, industrial products, and disaster preparation drills become part of a whole economy. As Gladney's wife, Babette, remarks, "It is all a corporate tie-in. . . . The sunscreen, the marketing, the fear, the disease. You can't have one without the other" (264).

DeLillo evokes a classic definition of the novel as negotiating our sense of inevitability. Indeed, this is so conventional a justification for storytelling in general that it seems to be built into the very nature of plot itself. More than any of the other terms discussed in this chapter, plot seems to transcend writing to provide a general principle not just for storytelling, but for our experience of our lives. As the phenomenologists claim, our experience of the world is a matter of organizing time around a "temporal horizon."[10] DeLillo's concern with inevitability, regardless of the medium in which it is studied, is a common element of theories of plot. In *Time and Narrative* Paul Ricoeur has argued that we can turn time into plot only because our prenarrative experience of time already has been structured; as Ricoeur writes, "*We are following therefore the destiny of a prefigured time that becomes a refigured time through the mediation of a configured time*" (54). Probably the best-known articulation of the contradictions of inevitability in plot is Peter Brooks's psychoanalytic theory. According to Brooks, plot is fundamentally about ending: "The sense of a beginning, then, must in some important way be determined by the sense of an ending. We might say that we are able to read present moments—in literature and, by extension, in life—as endowed with narrative meaning only because we read them in anticipation of the structuring power of those endings that will retrospectively give them the order and significance of plot" (94). Although narrative looks ahead to the ending to make sense of plot, plots in turn depend on delay and repetition to "suspend temporal process" (100). Brooks sees this irony as a reflection on our attitudes toward death: "We emerge from reading *Beyond the Pleasure Principle* with a dynamic model that structures ends (death, quiescence, nonnarratability) against beginnings (Eros, stimulation into tension, the desire of narrative) in a manner that necessitates the middle as detour, as struggle toward the end under the compulsion of imposed delay, as arabesque in the dilatory space of the text. The model proposes that we live in order to die, hence that the intentionality of plot lies in its orientation toward the end even while the end must be achieved only through detour" (107–8). This paradoxical response to the passage of time, in which we rush to the end for closure and meaning while dreading and delaying that movement at the same time, clearly applies to all forms of narrative—whether it is the eight-hundred-page Victorian novel or the ninety-minute summer blockbuster movie.

DeLillo certainly seems to agree with Brooks's understanding of plot as inevitably moving toward but fearing its end. Early in the novel, Gladney shows a collection of film material as background for his course, Advanced Hitler. At the end of the showing, he offers the following generalization: "All plots tend to move deathward. This is the nature of plots. Political plots, terrorist plots, lovers' plots, narrative plots, plots that are part of children's games. We edge nearer death every time we plot. It is like a contract that all must sign, the plotters as well as those who are the targets of the plot" (26). The association of plotting and death is naturally important, given the fundamental theme of the dread of death. In fact, as the novel progresses Gladney's colleague Murray suggests that plotting is part of the human drive to control (and thus deny) nature: "To plot, to take aim at something, to shape time and space. This is how we advance the art of human consciousness" (292). Although plots move deathward, the desire to create plots reflects the nature of human consciousness, the ability to be aware of the world and to challenge rather than merely to accept nature. Murray frames this as a fundamental conflict between people, each of whom strives to plot the death of another in order to protect themselves from death. To the suggestion that "there are two kinds of people in the world. Killers and diers" (290), Gladney responds: "Are you saying that men have tried throughout history to cure themselves of death by killing others?" (290). Murray concludes that "To plot is to live" (291), even though that means bringing the death of another.

Television will provide DeLillo with an unlikely way to challenge inevitability through the particular features of writing. As we saw with Pynchon and Coover, television is first and foremost an element of domestic space, and in *White Noise* it especially provides comfort in changing times through verbal descriptions.[11] At one point after a shopping trip Jack sees his daughter, Steffie, "in front of the TV set. She moved her lips, attempting to match the words as they were spoken" (84). Likewise, as the family listens intently to the radio during announcements about the toxic spill, they carefully parse every word and change in terminology, as the toxic cloud goes from being called a "feathery plume" to a "black billowing cloud" to an "airborne toxic event" (111–17). As the family evacuates their house, reports about the medical effects of Nyodene D on the radio have the power to induce the symptoms in the listeners: the daughters "only get them [the symptoms] when they're broadcast" (133). Like radio, television is not a visual medium, or even primarily technological; it is, rather, a speaking voice and thus fundamentally verbal. The most common narrative use that DeLillo makes of the television is when he has the television intrude, characterlike, into dialogue going on at the same time. In the middle of a discussion between Jack and Babette about which erotic story one would read to the other, "Someone turned on the TV set at the end of the hall, and a woman's voice said: 'If it breaks easily into pieces, it's called shale. When wet, it smells like clay'" (28). DeLillo goes even further in using television as a kind of character that interjects the irrelevant into dialogue a page later: "I began to feel an erection stirring. How stupid and out of context. Babette laughed at her own lines. The TV said: 'Until Florida surgeons attached an artificial flipper'" (29). This passage may at first seem to be simply an example of Barthelme-like postmodern absurdity, but I think that the role of television in this scene is very important for the way that the novel handles the task of storytelling. For DeLillo, the television isn't an alternative medium for telling stories but rather an object in the lives of the characters that complicates, deflects, and renders absurd their concerns and plans.

Televisions in *White Noise* never tell stories but rather intrude into the lives of the characters as a reminder of things they may have forgotten, denied, or wished for. In turning television into a voice that interrupts the story, DeLillo makes it into a distinctly *novelistic* element very much a part of the long tradition emphasizing character voices in written narrative. He does this, I think, because he recognizes that the tools for resisting a sense of inevitability in plot are provided particularly well by the medium of writing. Indeed, the notion that writing might be particularly able to resist inevitability should not be a surprising one, given my earlier discussion of fictional world theory. Writing seems to be especially good at suggesting and organizing modalities of the world. Extended to the topic of plot, we could say that the novel can more easily suggest alternative and nonactual plots than other media can. Gary Saul Morson has offered up this quality of language as a fundamental challenge to traditional understandings of plot, and as an ethical response to the sense of inevitability.[12] The term he offers for this is *side shadowing*: "In sideshadowing, two or more alternative presents, the actual and the possible, are made simultaneously visible. This is a simultaneity not *in* time but *of* times: we do not see contradictory actualities, but one possibility that was actualized and, at the same moment, another that could have been but was not. In this way, time itself acquires a double and often many doubles. A haze of possibilities surrounds each actuality" (118). Morson sees this ability to create side-shadowed possibilities in a narrative as particular to language: "In its inclusion of contrary-to-fact expressions and tenses, our language displays an appreciation of potentialities in excess of actualities—of the *surplus of temporalities*. In this sense, we may speak of the wisdom of tenses. Time ramifies, and the present we know is one of many possible presents" (119). I have suggested that, while other media can certainly project possible outcomes and alternative possibilities, writing provides the novel with especially powerful tools for representing and discussing those possibilities. We might say that plot becomes most fundamentally connected to the nature of writing when it most thoroughly exploits the possibilities of side shadowing.

In *White Noise*, then, television is antinarrative—something that stands outside the seemingly inevitable trajectory toward death that defines plot. We can see this especially clearly at the end of the novel, where DeLillo uses television to sidestep a seemingly inevitable revenge. Gladney discovers that after human trials were canceled, Babette received from the project manager a supply of an experimental drug (Dylar) that eases the fear of death. Babette met the manager (Willie Mink) in a cheap motel where she trades anonymous sex for her supply of the drug. When Jack discovers this (and especially when he discovers the name of the man and the motel where they met), he is driven by two contradictory urges—to petition Mink for a supply of Dylar to suppress his own fear of dying, and to take revenge on Mink for having sex with his wife. Babette, in fact, refuses to give Gladney Mink's name because she believes that he will simply want revenge for this infidelity: "We all know about men and their insane rage. This is something men are very good at. Insane and violent jealousy" (225). And, in fact, Jack gradually develops a plan to confront and kill Mink in the motel room where he continues to stay after having been fired from the Dylar project. As Jack plans for revenge on Mink, he finds that planning itself raises his spirits: the plan was "elegant. My airy mood returned" (304). The decision to shoot Mink seems to confirm Jack's discussion with Murray earlier in the novel about how plots move deathward. It seems that Jack has fallen into the most predictable plot imaginable, to take the life of someone else to stave off death. And yet, at the motel, Jack's plan doesn't work out the way that he imagines. Mink is eating Dylar by the handful while watching television. Side effects of the medication include memory loss and the inability to distinguish between words and their referents. Mink is, therefore, at Jack's mercy; when he calls out "Falling plane," Mink "looked at [him], gripping the arms of the chair, the first signs of panic building in his eyes" (309). In his increasingly deranged state of mind, Mink becomes televisionlike, tossing out non sequitur lines that mimic the random dialogue that pops up throughout the novel:"'And this could represent the leading edge of some warmer air,' Mink said" (313).

The stage is set, in this climactic scene, for a confrontation between the grand narrative plot of death, about which Jack and Murray seem so confident, and the antinarrative or side-shadowing nature of (novelized) television. Jack's plan goes awry because once he has shot Mink and placed the gun in his hand to make it look like an accident, Mink simply shoots Jack. Pulled out of his plotting by the vivid pain of the gunshot wound, Jack seems to return to reality: "I looked at him. Alive. His lap a puddle of blood. With the restoration of the normal order of matter and sensation, I felt I was seeing him for the first time as a person" (313). We could see this shift as simply a matter of doing away with narrative and its obsession with death. But as the scene progresses, Gladney continues to manipulate the events. He drags Mink to the hospital, where he announces the shooting in very different terms: "We're shot" (315). The plot that he has been constructing has shifted radically by this point, changing from a confrontation between two men to a shared event. Likewise, Jack is able to manipulate the scene—and thus to erase his own guilt from the botched revenge that he has planned—because of Mink's Dylar-induced suggestibility:

"Who shot me?" he said.
"You did."
"Who shot you?"
"You did. The gun is in your hand."
"What was the point I was trying to make?"
"You were out of control. You weren't responsible. I forgive you."
(314–15)

In contrast to the mess that he makes in pursuing his revenge, Jack is able to manipulate the scene much more effectively after he has joined Mink as a victim. This seems to mark a shift in the nature of plotting, a step outside the kill-or-be-killed mentality that Jack and Murray seem to agree on for much of the novel. He is able to do this precisely because the reality of the scene is so malleable, and so subject to the narration that Jack is able to exploit.

In this regard, DeLillo's novel is like all the others discussed in this chapter. *White Noise* takes a narrative concept—in this case, plot—and uses another medium to reflect on the strengths and limitations, paradoxes and contradictions, implicit in that concept as it applies to the novel. DeLillo does this, like the other authors do, because he resists one traditional understanding of the novel—in this case, as a means of creating a sense of inevitability. As he looks to escape this inevitability, DeLillo discovers that writing is particularly good at embodying the side shadows that surround the main plot. It is for this reason that television appears in the novel, not as some radically "other" element of the story, but as the most novelistic thing possible—a speaker that intervenes into dialogue. The seeds of this freedom are always implicit in writing, DeLillo suggests, but it takes their embodiment in the unlikely object of the television to make us recognize it.

Novelists as Media Theorists

Much of this chapter has depended on comparing the potentials and limitations of different media. I have attributed to writers like Daitch, DeLillo, and Gangemi insight into the nature of writing, comics, film, and television. As I explained in the introduction, those differences are affordances rather than absolute qualities. There are many ways that comics can suggest modalities, film can project side-shadowed narratives, and so on. Nonetheless, the broad conclusion that these writers have come to seems to be generally fair: writing is especially good at representing the absent, the potential, or the unrealized. Perhaps the best, most concise example of this is provided by the novel *The Book of Illusions*, where Paul Auster's main character works as a translator for a Chateaubriand book whose title he wants to translate as *Memoirs of a Dead Man*. Chateaubriand hopes to find a publisher willing to get him an advance on a book that will not be published until after his death: "The plan failed, but response to the book was extraordinarily good. The *Memoirs* became the most celebrated unfinished, unpublished, unread book in history" (63). All writing, Auster implies, has this ghostly quality precisely because it is so good at representing what is missing, possible, or unrealized. In turn, it is precisely writing's facility at representing what is absent that allows it to address its points of interface with other media. As we saw especially clearly in Daitch and Gangemi, the description of these absent forces points to the larger social world in which it participates. The novel's facility at describing what is absent makes it particularly good at recognizing other media and thus at describing media limits. Later, in chapter 5, I will focus on the way that the novel's limits connect it to media and social circulation outside itself to redefine what it mean to read today.

Finally, we need to recognize the limitations of the conclusions about media that I have developed in this chapter—especially those about media other than writing. The texts discussed here are first and foremost novels. The writers who produced these novels have generally worked in the medium of written, fictional narrative, and most have only limited direct experience with producing work in other media. This means that they have a great deal more to say, and they say it with a great deal more power and authority, when speaking about writing and the novel than about other media. It also means that there is considerably less agreement among contemporary novelists about the nature of these other media independent of writing. In other words, we can see a general pattern emerge among many writers about the role of the novel today, but we would be hard pressed to find agreement among these same novelists about the nature of film, television, or the comic book.

Consider the case of photography. We saw that in *The Colorist* the photograph was the very opposite of writing—divorced from context and narrative. But when Richard Powers builds his novel *Three Farmers on Their Way to a Dance* around an eponymous photograph, it is to reveal the way that this photograph contains and also becomes part of the story of the three farmers and their descendants. Likewise, Daitch's understanding of the iconic simplicity of the comic book is echoed but also complicated by other media novelists. In *Krazy Kat*, for example, Jay Cantor sees the innocent simplicity of this 1930s comic strip in roughly similar terms to those assigned to the colors of the Electra comic book. But Cantor also suggests a psychoanalytic depth hidden beneath the romantic pursuit of Ignatz Mouse by Krazy Kat: "She had known it immediately, with the force of sight. *There were more sides to them, sides that were hidden by the sides she saw.* They had *backs,* and not just in a way, like her and Ignatz" (20). Conversely, when Frederic Tuten writes *Tintin in the New World,* his interest in the comic strip medium is primarily in the ageless youth of his borrowed protagonist rather than in the simplicity of the medium. The same qualifications apply to media novels about film. While for Gangemi, film seems to be largely a matter of controlling audience reaction, for Ronald Sukenick in *Blown Away,* films are a reflection of the studios that produce them. For Mark Danielewski in *House of Leaves,* film is private and above all documentary; the fictional film in that novel is titled *The Navidson Record.* And we have already seen that Pynchon in *Vineland* treats television as similar to film, while DeLillo and Coover use television located in the home, which differentiates it from film.

Thus, media novels are ultimately *novels* and are therefore concerned fundamentally with the nature of writing. Although many of the novels discussed in this and other chapters make valid observations about other media, those observations are almost always partial and a product of the idiosyncratic needs of the author and of the particular novel in which they appear.

4 Writing Beyond the Media Limit?

The contemporary novelists whose works we examined in the previous chapter have approached the limit of what the novel can do. Gangemi's use of film, Coover's use of television, or Daitch's use of comics each contemplated another medium and then turned back to the novel the wiser. It should go without saying that another way to respond to these limits is to leave writing and move on to another medium. Some have done so for purely financial reasons, like William Faulkner's writing for Hollywood in the 1930s and '40s, while others have seen in another medium aesthetic possibilities, like William Burroughs's use of tape recording as a tool for randomizing language. But few of the writers discussed in this book have done this, in large part because, as we have seen, their interest in other media is ultimately a search for the vocation of the novel in the contemporary media ecology.

A more complex and pervasive response to the limits of writing is to see recent technology as transcending the differences between media. The idea that the transition from page to screen might fundamentally alter the boundaries and nature of writing is implicit in the debate that has emerged around what is commonly referred to as "new media": the mixture of writing, image, audio, and video that is made possible by the computer screen.[1] In 1992 Robert Coover famously associated hypertext with "The End of Books": "The novel . . . as we know it, has come to its end. Not that those announcing its demise are grieving. For all its passing charm, the traditional novel, which took center stage at the same time that industrial mercantile democracies arose . . . is perceived by its would-be executioners as the virulent carrier of the patriarchal, colonial, canonical, proprietary, hierarchical and authoritarian values of a past that is no longer with us" (706). Coover's summary is, of course, somewhat tongue-in-cheek, but this passage does capture the sense felt by many that new media do not constitute just *a* new medium, but instead a fundamental commentary on the limits of writing. Since the description in 1977 of the hypothetical Dynabook (a proto-notebook computer) as "a metamedium, whose content would be a wide range of already-existing and not-yet-invented media" (Kay and Goldberg, 403), writing about new media has been more a matter of exploring possibilities—often utopian—than analysis of actual texts. As Mark Amerika remarks, "The artificial intelligentsia that has evolved around new media practice is all about reconfiguring the way we think about art and, in this way, closely resembles the Conceptual Art movements of the 1960s and 1970s" (23).

Throughout this book I have embraced the somewhat dated term *multimedia* for this new form of electronic communication. In fact, some have argued that we would be better served by moving away from reference to the media that make up this electronic communication and instead should emphasize the senses to which each medium attends. In her analysis of "multiple sensory modalities" in digital texts, Maribeth Back calls for just this shift: "In this argument, use of the term 'multisensory' rather than 'multimodal' or 'multimedia' is deliberate: an attempt to pull critical analysis in new media toward consideration of the human body's interface systems as well as cultural systems" (161). I argued in the introduction, however, that the terms *multimedia* and, to a lesser extent, *new media* represent an attempt to articulate the media ecology rhetorically, and thus that we should not dismiss imprecise terms like these without recognizing their historical value. Because I am interested in the attempt to use this cluster of new communicational technologies to comment on the limits of writing, the imprecise and even contradictory qualities of these terms are especially important, since they help to reveal the rhetorical work being done with them.

The question of what sort of unique features will emerge out of these new technologies is, of course, an unsettled debate. There has been an especially vigorous argument within narrative studies in particular about whether video games should be seen as part of an established storytelling tradition, or whether we should put aside the expectations and terms developed from prior media and instead look for the qualities unique to these new media. It may well be that ten or twenty years from now, claims that video games are variations on the novel or that online video is a variation on film will seem as quaint and dated as the use of theatrical staging in early films. Here I will steer clear of this debate and instead focus on a much narrower feature of new media evident in Coover's essay: the tendency to see these new technologies as moving us beyond the limits of any one medium. We might recall from the introduction Friedrich Kittler's vision of a postmedium future: "*Optical fiber networks.* People will be hooked to an information channel that can be used for any medium—for the first time in history, or for its end. Once movies and music, phone calls and texts reach households via optical fiber cables, the formerly distinct media of television, radio, telephone, and mail converge, standardized by transmission frequencies and bit format" (*Gramophone* 1). One promise of new media is that writing will become simply one part of an undifferentiated mixture of media made possible by the computer interface and networked transmission. In many ways, much of the commentary on new media is as much about the limits of writing that we are trying to leave behind as it is about the shape of a new medium. This is why, except in the case of video games, new media have produced more theory than practice—more interesting discussions of the possibilities of the medium than beloved works that demonstrate those possibilities.

This vision of writing as integrated into some larger medium, where the boundaries between text, audio, and video fade, represents a competing understanding of writing's place within the contemporary media ecology. In this chapter we will look at the difference between these two visions of writing today. There are three ways that new media appear to supplement writing and to transcend the limits of print: to store and retrieve information as part of a complete *encyclopedia*, to connect texts and readers together in a *network*, and to allow users to experience another body through a virtual *transparency*. This vision of writing transformed by new media is in fact problematic. We have seen that a focus on media limits allows the novel to articulate how it is *used* and takes a place within the community through which it circulates. Precisely this issue of the use of media returns again and again to haunt the idealized vision of a medialess electronic future. In each of the three promises of new media, the dynamics of the use of media are articulated better by a contemporary media novel, and the debates about writing in a new media context remain bound to the limits of writing and the novels I have been describing.

Encyclopedism

The first potential of new media is what we might call *encyclopedism*, the idea that electronic media will provide not only a more efficient way to archive information but also fundamentally different ways to access it.

From its beginnings, the encyclopedia has been an object that expresses the possibilities and limitations of the print medium. For example, Catherine Rubincam observes that the Graeco-Roman genre of encyclopedic world histories confronted the problem of searching through papyrus rolls. The Greek historian Ephorus partially solved this problem in the fourth century BC by becoming "the first prose writer to choose the number of rolls among which he wished to apportion his text, and write those divisions into the text by insertion of a preface to each bookroll" (129). For a long time, the encyclopedia embodied the abstract and idealized goal of organizing knowledge into a whole. This striving was easier to recognize before the advent of the alphabetical principle of the modern encyclopedia, when medieval encyclopedists depended on general systems like the division into traditional disciplines (cosmology, geography, zoology, and so on) or more whimsical principles like Empedocles's four basic elements (earth, air, water, and fire) or even the six days of creation (104–8). But even in Diderot's alphabetically organized *Encyclopédie* the goal of providing a vision of human knowledge as a whole is evident in its "système figuré" engraving (fig. 1).

In many ways, the history of the encyclopedia over the last two hundred years has been a gradual acceptance of the limits of our ability to organize knowledge in this idealistic way. Except in a few rare instances, like *Encyclopedia Britannica*'s propaedia, modern print encyclopedias have discarded the hope of a single principle or table that organizes all knowledge. In the twentieth century the encyclopedia became the very embodiment of what Joan Shelley Rubin refers to as "middlebrow" cultural striving, like any other self-improvement scheme: the Book-of-the-Month Club, the Harvard Classics, the Little Leather Library of the "Thirty World's Greatest Masterpieces." Today the *Encyclopedia Britannica* advertises itself as a way to complete mundane tasks: "For school homework, research projects, home study and more," promises its Web site. We could say that, in a small way, these encyclopedias have accepted the limits of their print medium and their rather reduced place within the contemporary media ecology.

New media have intervened into this trajectory in a surprising way. The advent of the electronic encyclopedia on CD-ROM in the 1990s briefly rejuvenated dreams of totalizing knowledge. When the 1992 *New Grolier Multimedia Encyclopedia* launches, we are presented with our main menu

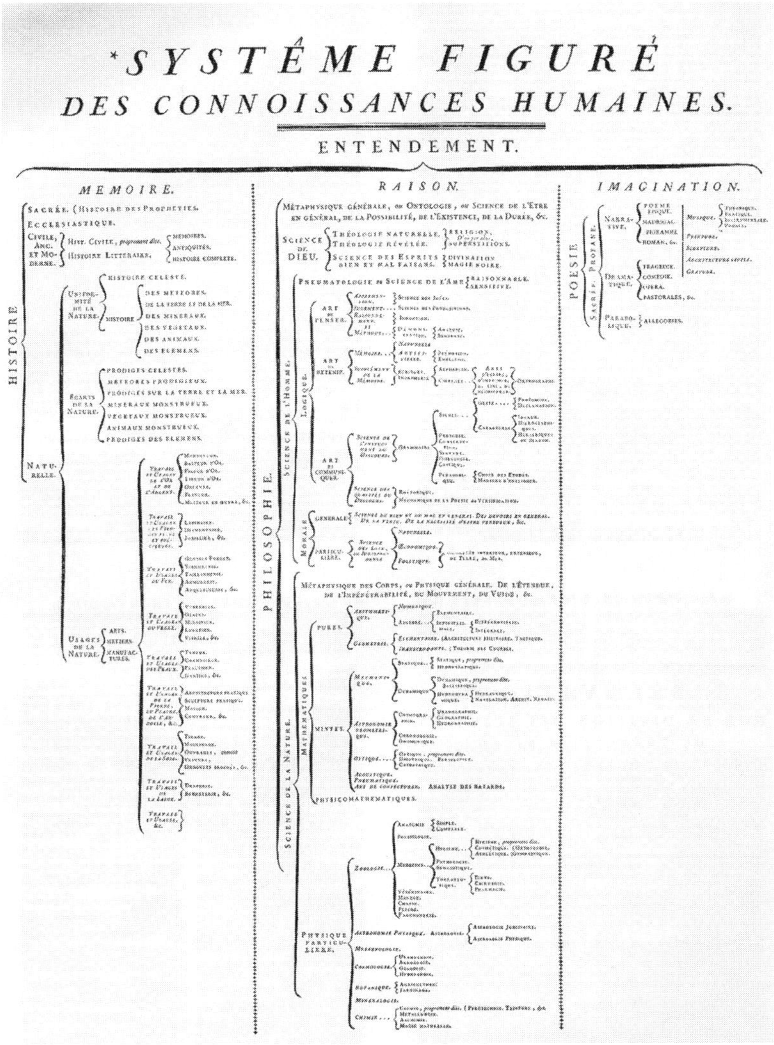
*SYSTÊME FIGURÉ
DES CONNOISSANCES HUMAINES.
ENTENDEMENT.
MEMOIRE.
RAISON.
IMAGINATION.
HISTOIRE
PHILOSOPHIE.
POESIE

1. Diderot's "Systême Figuré."

and discover that the hope of organizing knowledge into a single table or image has returned. Although the *Word Search* option is front and center in this menu and functions much like it would later in *Wikipedia* or Google, other options in this menu such as *Browse Article Titles* and *Knowledge Tree* suggest that the encyclopedia designers are searching for different ways that users might interact with the information on the disk.

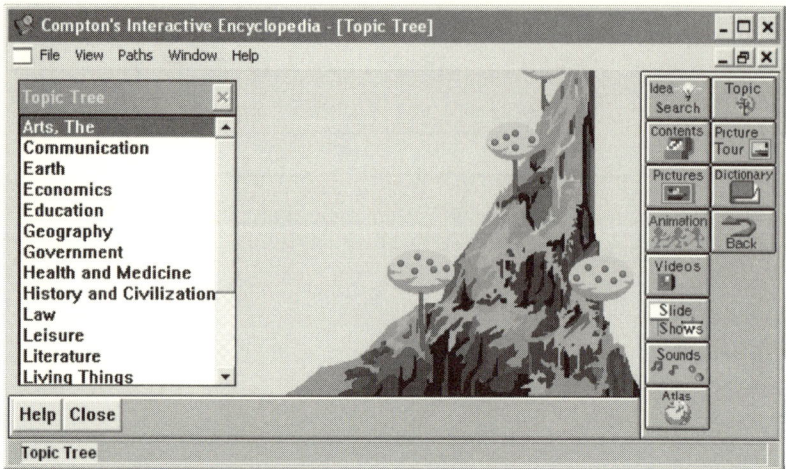

2. *Compton's* "Topic Tree." Used with permission of Encyclopedia Britannica.

The same knowledge tree is a prominent part of the 1992 *Compton's Interactive Encyclopedia* (fig. 2). In 1996 *Encarta's* interface looks more sophisticated, but its structure is essentially the same, retaining the dual *Word Search* and *Category* options (fig. 3). In fact, the issue of how users will interact with this information is even more obvious in *Encarta*, since the program itself launches with an introductory screen before we encounter the main *Find* options. This opening screen foregrounds the issue of what users will *do* with the encyclopedia, allowing them to *Experiment, Explore History,* and *Play a Game* (fig. 4).

Robert Fowler speaks for many when he describes the way that electronic encyclopedias bring with them a fundamental change of metaphors for how we imagine knowledge: "Though they preserve the traditional arrangement of lemmata, it hardly matters; associated tools allow you to whiz around the disc and instantly connect anything with anything. You can reorganize the encyclopaedia according to your personal whim. Untrammeled free association is the preferred method of learning" (25). What also strikes me as especially important about Fowler's description of the changing metaphors for the encyclopedia is that this shift resurrects the possibility of envisioning knowledge as a whole. If the encyclopedia gradually became a reference work useful mostly for doing book reports for school, the advent of the CD-ROM version suddenly suggests that the encyclopedia can be something more. Although Fowler's description of

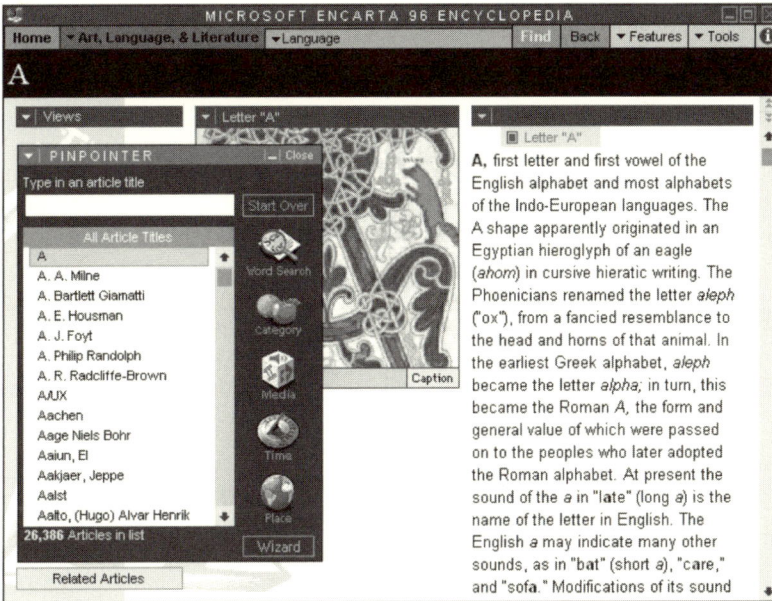

A

▼ | Views   ▼ | Letter "A"

▼ | PINPOINTER |_| Close

Type in an article title

[Start Over]

All Article Titles

A
A. A. Milne
A. Bartlett Giamatti
A. E. Housman
A. J. Foyt
A. Philip Randolph
A. R. Radcliffe-Brown
AJUX
Aachen
Aage Niels Bohr
Aaiun, El
Aakjaer, Jeppe
Aalst
Aalto, (Hugo) Alvar Henrik
26,386 Articles in list

Related Articles

Word Search

Category

Caption

Media

Time

Place

Wizard

▼ |

▣ Letter "A"

A, first letter and first vowel of the English alphabet and most alphabets of the Indo-European languages. The A shape apparently originated in an Egyptian hieroglyph of an eagle (*ahom*) in cursive hieratic writing. The Phoenicians renamed the letter *aleph* ("ox"), from a fancied resemblance to the head and horns of that animal. In the earliest Greek alphabet, *aleph* became the letter *alpha;* in turn, this became the Roman *A,* the form and general value of which were passed on to the peoples who later adopted the Roman alphabet. At present the sound of the *a* in "late" (long *a*) is the name of the letter in English. The English *a* may indicate many other sounds, as in "bat" (short *a*), "care," and "sofa." Modifications of its sound

3. *Encarta* main search screen. Used with permission from Microsoft.

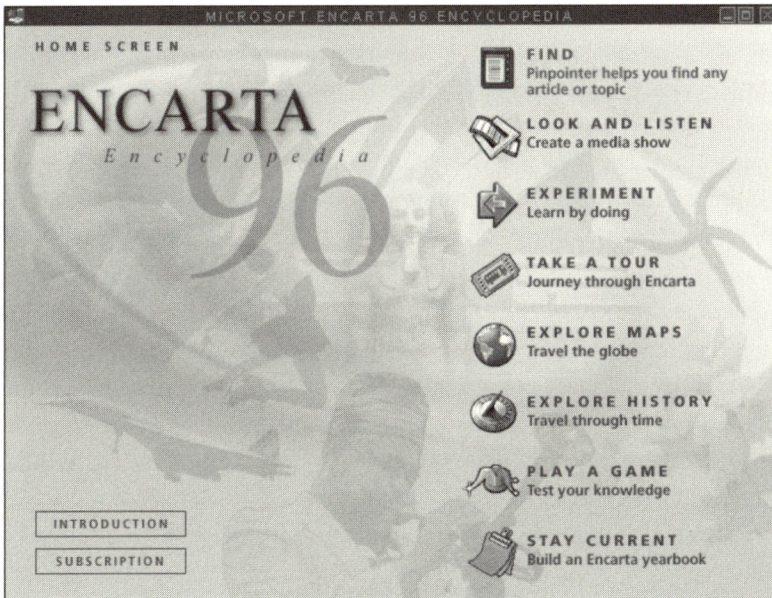

HOME SCREEN

ENCARTA
Encyclopedia
96

FIND
Pinpointer helps you find any article or topic

LOOK AND LISTEN
Create a media show

EXPERIMENT
Learn by doing

TAKE A TOUR
Journey through Encarta

EXPLORE MAPS
Travel the globe

EXPLORE HISTORY
Travel through time

PLAY A GAME
Test your knowledge

STAY CURRENT
Build an Encarta yearbook

INTRODUCTION

SUBSCRIPTION

4. *Encarta* opening screen. Used with permission from Microsoft.

reading the encyclopedia and connecting ideas "according to your personal whim" may seem dismissive, implicit here is a positive description of *reading* the encyclopedia as a personal experience with continuity over time—something that seems to have escaped the encyclopedia since the advent of the alphabetical system of organization. *Encarta's* list of activities that users can do with the encyclopedia seems to capture this idea perfectly.

What, ultimately, is different about the CD-ROM encyclopedia that inspires these old dreams of a total vision of knowledge and a consequent escape from the limits of the print medium? Today we are likely to say that the key element is the ability to search the database in a powerful and sophisticated way; this is what makes Google or *Wikipedia* different from the library card catalog or encyclopedia, both of which were limited to predefined subject headings. This is why *Wikipedia* is so beloved by students: searching is easy, fast, and takes no specialized knowledge about the organization of categories or keywords. But from the perspective of two decades ago when the CD-ROM encyclopedia was first emerging, the unique quality of the electronic medium was not the issue of search, but instead the *multimedia* nature of the text. Again and again these early electronic encyclopedias were marketed according to their ability to integrate video, maps, sound, and games in a way that was unthinkable in earlier texts. It is a striking shift simply to consider the title of the early and recent electronic encyclopedias. From *The Grolier Multimedia Encyclopedia, Encarta: The World Standard in a Multimedia Encyclopedia*, and *Compton's Interactive Encyclopedia* we have moved to *Wikipedia*, which describes itself simply as "The Free Encyclopedia." At the very beginning of the CD-ROM encyclopedia, then, the presence of several media within the text was linked to the possibility of creating a total vision of knowledge. Encapsulated here is the promise of new media to escape the limits of individual media. I argue that the evolution of the electronic encyclopedia away from other media and toward the centrality of the function of the text search is a reembracing of the textual, written nature of these electronic documents.

The link between multiple media and the reorganization of information into a new way of reading is evident in all of these early electronic encyclopedias. *Encarta's* main search dialogue allows users to browse or search by media type (fig. 5). This is also an option available earlier in *Grolier* and

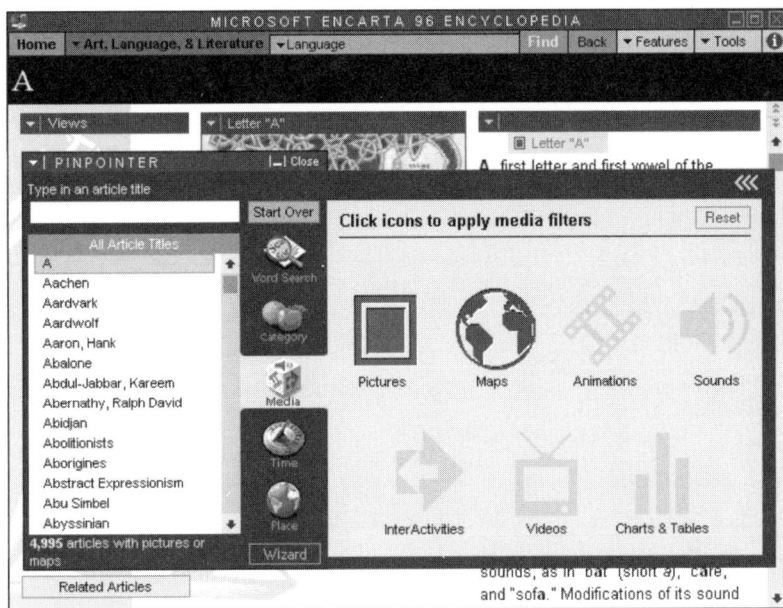

5. *Encarta* media filter. Used with permission from Microsoft.

Compton's. In this regard—and upon reflection, in a very strange way—media are treated like general knowledge categories. One of the central ideas of the pre-alphabetical encyclopedia is that gaining a whole vision of human knowledge means organizing that information into subjects and then grasping the relation between those subjects. The organization of *Encarta* implies that exactly the same thing is true of media: if we can group our knowledge into different forms of media and then understand their relation to each other, we can grasp human knowledge as a whole. This is a dream built into the very idea of multimedia: that by collecting enough different media we can create a fullness without the kinds of media limits that have marked the novels discussed in this book.

An even better example of the link between the totality of information and the merger of media is the redesign of the *Compton's Interactive Encyclopedia* in the later 1990s. What is initially striking about the 1997 *Compton's* is its multipane organization. Many of its organizational elements reflect what we have already seen in *Encarta* and *Grolier*: we have access to a *Timeline*, *Atlas*, and *Topic Tree* that offers to organize the knowledge we encounter in different ways. And, like those other

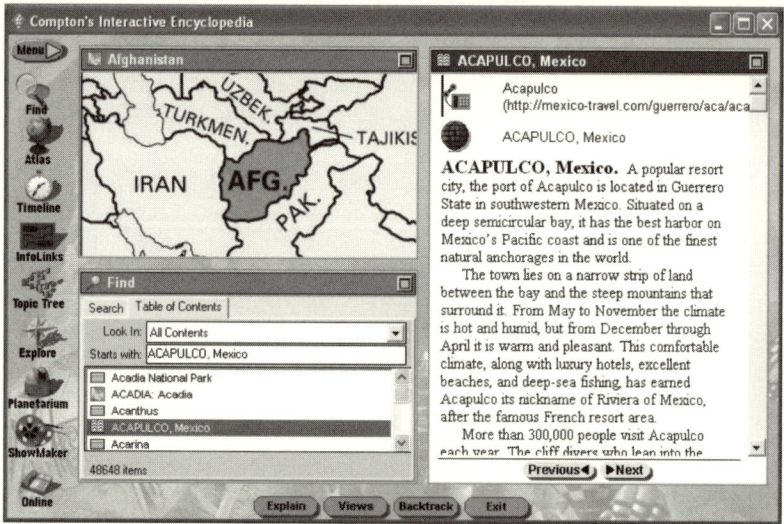

6. *Compton's* multipanel design. Used with permission of Encyclopedia Britannica.

encyclopedias, *Compton's* uses these organizational options essentially as a way to filter the articles to which users have access. However, what makes *Compton's* different is that the three panes that make up the primary user interface remain visible at all times. When users select an entry, it opens in the appropriate pane depending on its media type: the top pane for images, the right pane for text. The result can be disconcerting, since the user will frequently have incompatible forms of information on the screen at one time (fig. 6). What seems to me especially important here is that this design creates the illusion of informational fullness. The user's screen is literally only filled when accessing media of several types. Although most entries do not have items from each media type, this interface design suggests that such completeness is the ideal toward which the encyclopedia strives. The perfect multimedia encyclopedia, in other words, would have text, image, audio, and video available for every topic. Then the coverage of this topic would appear complete, and the user's screen would coincide with the outside world that is being described.

With the rise of new media, the multiplicity of media forms have come to embody our idea of the totality of human knowledge precisely because they promised to transcend the limits of any one form of representation.

That the mixture of media might be thought of in this way comes as no surprise given the rhetorical construction of media ecologies we have discussed throughout this book. This new and positive way of thinking about the media ecology is one reason why the electronic encyclopedia briefly sparked a renewed interest in creating different ways to access information, and promised to move the encyclopedia away from the dull reference work that is best used to help schoolchildren write reports. Once we begin to imagine a different way to use the encyclopedia, we also begin to think about uniting our disparate information into a single vision of the world. In many ways, we seem to be back in the world of synesthesia and the unity of media that Wagner and Kandinsky have noted (see chapter 1). What seems especially important about this competing articulation of the media ecology is that it sees new media as the location where these idealistic possibilities are articulated. In bringing together multiple media, the CD-ROM encyclopedia promised to go beyond the limits of writing. In contrast to the my emphasis on media limits at the center of writing's place in the media ecology, new media promise a completely different understanding of writing today based on escaping those limits as part of a multimedia work.

It should be clear, however, that much of this potential is a matter of rhetorical framing rather than qualities inherent to the medium itself. In fact, when we look more closely at the direction that the electronic encyclopedia has gone over the last decade, we see that designers of these documents in many ways are discovering the problems in this promise of media without limits, and that these problems are to a large extent entwined with denying the specific contours and limits of writing. After all, *Wikipedia* defines itself not as a multimedia encyclopedia but merely as a free encyclopedia. What happened to the utopian claims of the multimedia encyclopedia? To answer this question, let us turn back to contemporary fiction—specifically to Pynchon's *Gravity's Rainbow*—which explores the same possibility of a multimedia encyclopedic aesthetic and similarly comes to recognize the problems of mixing media to achieve a total vision of knowledge. Specifically, Pynchon's novel embraces just what these new media theories want to ignore: our encounter with the specific qualities of writing itself and the ways they are embodied in the particular media object of the novel with which we interact. In turning to Pynchon's novel, we follow Edward Mendelson's 1976 article "Encyclopedic Narrative: From Dante to Pynchon," wherein Mendelson describes a genre that includes works like Dante's Comedy, Cervantes's *Don Quixote*, and Herman Melville's *Moby-Dick* and suggests that each national literature develops a single literary work that is encyclopedic. Such works "attempt to render the full range of knowledge and beliefs of a national culture, while identifying the ideological perspectives from which that culture shapes and interprets its knowledge" (1269). Although Mendelson assigns this genre a long historical sweep, he seems particularly interested in Pynchon's novel. Indeed, his title emphasizes Pynchon, as does the way that Mendelson is willing to bend the rules of the genre—Pynchon is, for example, a *second* American encyclopedist (after Melville) and thus should be unnecessary in his scheme. He clearly sees Pynchon's novel as the first that self-consciously deploys the encyclopedic style: "Pynchon has now written, for the first time, an encyclopedic narrative that emphatically calls attention not only to its own structure but also to the social and psychological processes that give books like his their cultural position" (1275). What seems to be especially important about Pynchon's novel, and what makes the novel especially relevant in discussing the electronic encyclopedia, is something Mendelson fails to emphasize: that *Gravity's Rainbow* connects its encyclopedism to media. Pynchon contemplates using other media as a way to organize our knowledge, but as we will see, ultimately returns to the limitations and dynamics inherent to writing.

Among the many structuring oppositions in the novel, *Gravity's Rainbow* contrasts two different kinds of order embodied, respectively, in the whole motion of film and the combinational principle of chemistry and language. The more obvious of the two is the overarching order implied in Pynchon's title: the "rainbow" of *Gravity's Rainbow* describes a single arc whose whole motion is determined beforehand. Pynchon in fact refers repeatedly to the way that the total flight path of the v-2 rocket is determined at the moment the engines shut off (*Brennschluss*); the rest of the flight is determined by inertia and gravity: "Ascending, programmed in a ritual of love . . . at Brennschluss it is done—the Rocket's purely feminine counterpart, the zero point at the center of its target, has submitted. All the rest will happen according to laws of ballistics. The Rocket is helpless in it. Something else has taken over. Something beyond what was designed in" (223). Within the novel's imagery, the arc of gravity's rainbow can be broken into particular moments only by the work of calculus, which is described as a "method of finding hidden centers, inertias unknown" (302). Pynchon associates wholes based on such a seamless arc with film. Throughout the novel film shares with the flight of the rocket both the appearance of total movement and the ability to be broken down into particular still moments. As Hanjo Berressem notes, "A film sweeps the subject from image to image, shrouding over the invisible bars between frames and evoking the illusion of continuity" (157). Pynchon describes films used to analyze the rocket's flight: "In the daily rushes you would watch the frames at around 3000 feet, where the model broke through the speed of sound. There has been this strange connection between the German mind and the rapid flashing of successive stills to counterfeit movement, for at least two centuries—since Leibniz, in the process of inventing calculus, used the same approach to break up the trajectories of cannonballs through the air" (407).

In contrast to film's whole arc, which is only broken down arbitrarily in the still image, Pynchon describes those forms of organization that depend on elements that can be linked together to form larger complexes. The most obvious of these is chemistry, which provides the narrative framework for Pynchon's central story of Tyrone Slothrop. As an infant Slothrop is conditioned to get an erection when exposed to a particular kind of plastic, Imipolex G, and this conditioned response ends up implausibly allowing him to predict when the V-2 rockets will strike in London on the basis of his own sexual encounters. Throughout *Gravity's Rainbow* Pynchon treats chemistry as a way of creating new molecules from the recombination of existing parts.[2] In turn, this combinational model of chemistry is associated with language:

How alphabetic is the nature of molecules. One grows aware of it down here: one finds Committees on molecular structure which are very similar to those back at the NTA plenary session. "See: how they are taken out from the coarse flow—shaped, cleaned, rectified, just as you once redeemed your letters from the lawless, the mortal streaming of human speech. . . . These are our letters, our words: they too can be modulated, broken, recoupled, redefined, co-polymerized one to the other in worldwide chains that will surface now and then over long molecular silences, like the seen parts of a tapestry." (355)

Elsewhere, Pynchon remarks about the "German mania for name-giving, dividing the Creation finer and finer, analyzing, setting namer more hopelessly apart from named, even to bringing in the mathematics of combination, tacking together established nouns to get new ones, the insanely, endlessly diddling play of a chemist whose molecules are words" (391). Although Pynchon emphasizes the German origin of both calculus (which pauses the arc of flight) and the combinational structure of language, these two kinds of totality seem to be natural opposites, and to be naturally embodied by film and language, respectively.

Of course, this simple binary of film and language is a radical simplification of Pynchon's novel, and it ignores other media like the comic book (in particular, the Plasticman and Floundering Four sections of the novel) and music (especially evident in later sections of the novel when Slothrop takes up the harmonica and "is closer to being a spiritual medium than he's been yet" [622]).[3] But what interests me more than an inventory of media in *Gravity's Rainbow* is the way that these competing totalities are framed by the novel as a whole. Like the CD-ROM encyclopedia, *Gravity's Rainbow* defines totality by the integration of competing organizing schemes. Both juxtapose different media with their own claims to totality—the timelines or maps in the encyclopedia, the total arc of "gravity's rainbow" in the novel—in order to create a broader model of knowledge that no one medium can provide. Equally striking is the fact that neither work ultimately provides an explanation about the relationship between these media. It is easy to see this in the electronic encyclopedia, where the various types of media in *Encarta*'s "media filter" obey no principle of completeness. After all, *Pictures*, *Maps*, and *Charts & Tables* are all visual representations of information and seem less distinct than *Videos and Sounds*. These media are organized not according to the senses addressed (visual or aural), the source (historical artifacts versus the produced information of the chart or graph), nor their modes of use (the passive consumption of the video and sound or the activity of the *Interactions*). Likewise, critics have noted that Pynchon ultimately does not unify the different media models that circulate through the novel. Joseph Tabbi explains that Pynchon refuses to integrate his metaphors into one system while at the same time "locat[ing] each trajectory in its particular historical circumstance": "It is true that each trajectory is defined not in itself but in relation to any and all of the other trajectories in the novel. Yet the entire constellation, which is imaginary but congruent with flight paths that were actually taken by v-2 rockets, suggests that multiple readings and interpretations can in fact converge on a vanished historical reality" (93).

But Pynchon does not simply introduce these two media as alternatives that must be chosen, or as ways of organizing information that are supplementary and add up to some transmedia fullness. Instead, as the novel develops, writing reasserts itself as the media framework in which the story must be imagined. Doing so is linked, in turn, to the agency of the characters: the ability to *act* in this media environment. One of the best examples of this occurs late in the novel, when Slothrop begins to discover graffiti scattered throughout Europe in the immediate wake of the war:

> He felt brave and in control. But then another message caught his eye:
> ROCKETMAN WAS HERE
> His first thought was that he'd written it himself and forgot. Odd that that should've been his first thought, but it was. Might be he was starting to implicate himself, some yesterday version of himself, in the Combination against who he was right then. (624)

Slothrop goes on to discover various forms of graffiti, including drawings that seem to be "*the A4 rocket*, seen from below" (624): "Crosses, swastikas, Zone-mandalas, how can they not speak to Slothrop?" (625). This graffiti appears to be an example of neither of the forms of organization that figure so prominently in the novel (language and film). While this graffiti does seem to be combinational in some sense, it obviously obeys no particular formal constraints; neither does it reflect some overarching narrative that gives it meaning. What seems most important, instead, is that it reflects a certain agency in the novel. After all, Slothrop's first response to the Rocketman graffiti is to assume that he had done it himself. There are a number of other, somewhat more whimsical examples of this kind of agency. Earlier in the novel, as Slothrop becomes more and more paranoid in the Casino Hermann Goering, he responds to the powers directed at him with graffiti fantasies: "'Fuck you,' whispers Slothrop. It's the only spell he knows, and a pretty good all-purpose one at that. His whisper is baffled by the thousands of tiny rococo surfaces. Maybe he'll sneak in tonight—no not at night—but sometime, with a bucket and brush, paint 'FUCK YOU' in a balloon coming out of the mouth of one of those little pink shepherdesses there" (203). Such vandalism reflects the particular use that characters make of media toward the end of the novel. A particularly well-known example is the way that Pirate Prentice and Roger Mexico misuse the combinational principle of language in their subversive disruption of Jeremy Swanlake's party, playing an alliterative game of asking for disgusting food: pus pudding, vomit vichyssoise, dandruff dressing (715).

That Pynchon offers such local and subversive uses of power as an alternative to totalizing systems is well established in the criticism on *Gravity's Rainbow,* and none of my observations here are particularly novel.[4] What is noteworthy about Pynchon's turn to the *use* of media and away from the large systems that organize our knowledge of the world is that it correlates with a similar evolution in the electronic encyclopedia over the last fifteen years. We have seen that the transition into the electronic format resurrected dreams of providing an overarching structure to what had become a rather mundane tool for book reports. The possibility that a mixture of media might create new totalities appears to have been short-lived, however. Or, to be more precise, we could say that the definition of total knowledge has changed as we move from *Encarta* to *Wikipedia.* We might at first think that *Wikipedia* has jettisoned the idealism of early electronic encyclopedias and embraced the mundane purposes of the traditional print encyclopedia; after all, students use *Wikipedia* as a resource for writing their papers—much to the dismay of many teachers. With its simple, text-based search query box and refusal to provide a knowledge tree, *Wikipedia* seems to be an attenuation of the hopes for a cohesive vision of human knowledge. Indeed, *Wikipedia*'s offer of a "featured article" on its front page seems to embody these lowered expectations.[5] Recent CD-ROM encyclopedias have largely followed *Wikipedia*'s example, moving media to the margins of the interface design and foregrounding a simple text box (fig. 7).

And yet, beneath the surface, *Wikipedia*'s community-based writing and editing of entries is a far more radical reconceptualization of the nature of the encyclopedia than the relatively superficial mixture of media

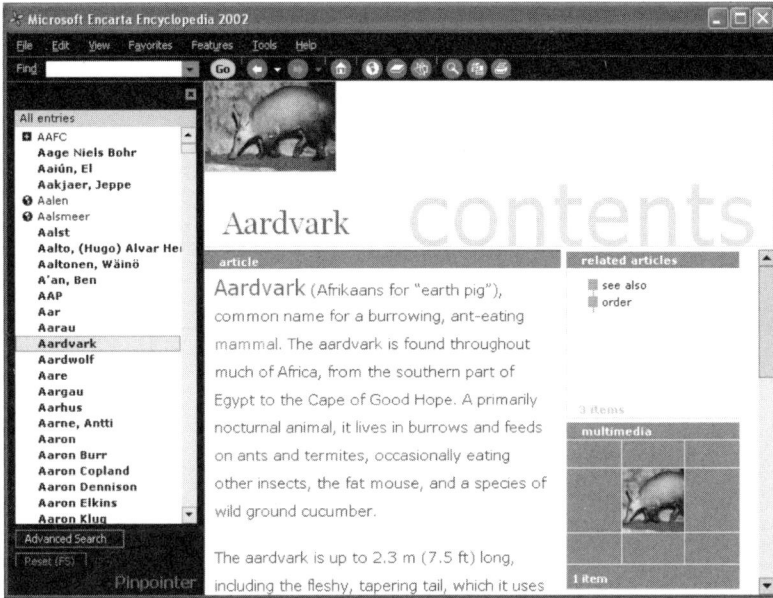

7. 2002 *Encarta* layout using a simple text box for searching. Used with permission from Microsoft.

in *Encarta* or *Grolier*. In particular, community editing transforms the encyclopedia from a work that tries to provide a whole image of human knowledge to one that is, by its nature, constantly in flux. Indeed, it is precisely this flux that is, paradoxically, the basis for *Wikipedia*'s claim to reliability, which is described in the site's *About* page:

> Visitors do not need specialized qualifications to contribute, since their primary role is to write articles that cover existing knowledge; this means that people of all ages and cultural and social backgrounds can write Wikipedia articles. Most of the articles can be edited by anyone with access to the Internet, simply by clicking the *Edit this page* link. Anyone is welcome to add information, cross-references or citations, as long as they do so within Wikipedia's editing policies and to an appropriate standard. Substandard or disputed information is subject to removal. Users need not worry about accidentally damaging Wikipedia when adding or improving information, as other editors are always around to advise or correct obvious

errors, and Wikipedia's software is carefully designed to allow easy reversal of editorial mistakes.

No edit to the encyclopedia here is damaging precisely because others are also constantly editing further—a remarkable way to frame the authority of the text. The totality of the knowledge represented in *Wikipedia*, then, is based precisely in the diversity of its contributors: "Wikipedia is written by open and transparent consensus—an approach that has its pros and cons. Censorship or imposing 'official' points of view is extremely difficult to achieve and almost always fails after a time. Eventually for most articles, all notable views become fairly described and a neutral point of view reached. In reality, the process of reaching consensus may be long and drawn-out, with articles fluid or changeable for a long time while they find their 'neutral approach' that all sides can agree on." This seems to me to be a quite different model for totality than is provided either by the knowledge tree or by the multimedia aesthetic of the early CD-ROM encyclopedia, and is in fact a totality that is remarkable for being independent of the ability of readers actually to grasp this knowledge. Instead, it is based entirely on the *activity* of its participants. Where the knowledge tree synthesizes the material in the traditional encyclopedia so that the reader can understand it, *Wikipedia* offers a totality that exists in the site but cannot be visualized directly. Like *Gravity's Rainbow*, the encyclopedia moves away from an idealized model of knowledge based on transcending the limits of specific media, and toward an emphasis on agency and use. Surprisingly, agency in the *Wikipedia* community depends not on the multiplication of the media used but instead on the exploitation of the nature and limits of text itself.

We can understand the meaning of the shift that we see in *Wikipedia* by again following the lead of *Gravity's Rainbow*. For a novel that makes use of so many other media, *Gravity's Rainbow* is a document that emphasizes its print nature to a surprising degree. Although the novel includes images, their diagramlike quality emphasizes their continuity with print and traditional typography.[6] A particularly good example of this is the very first image that appears in the novel, the "insignia the German troopers wore in South-West Africa when they came in 1904 to crush the Herero Rebellion. . . . For the Zone-Hereros it has become something deep . . . maybe a little mystical" (361) (fig. 8). As Pynchon explains, this image is

ıl device in red, white and blue

⬭ (V H E K Z)

ıia the German troopers wore ıı

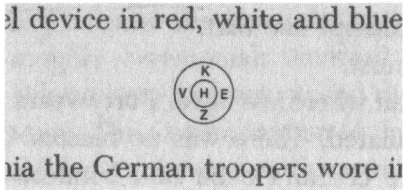

8. Textualized image in *Gravity's Rainbow*.

9. Filmlike section divider in *Gravity's Rainbow*.

;creen wipers brush the rain in a rhythmic b
nd time for home.

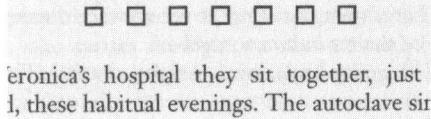

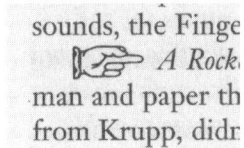

◻ ◻ ◻ ◻ ◻ ◻ ◻

eronica's hospital they sit together, just
1, these habitual evenings. The autoclave sir

sounds, the Finge
☞ *A Rock*
man and paper th
from Krupp, didn

10. Dingbat as graffiti in *Gravity's Rainbow*. All
three images from *Gravity's Rainbow* by Thomas
Pynchon. Copyright © 1973 by Thomas Pynchon.
Used by permission of Viking Penguin, a division
of Penguin Group (USA) Inc.

based on the five positions of the launching switch for the rocket. What
seems to be especially significant about this image is that it is nearly textual itself—primarily a matter of letters oriented within a diagrammatic
circle. Rather than representing an alternative to print, images here are
ultimately subordinated to print.

An even better example of the way that Pynchon subordinates the visual to print is his use of dingbats. Critics noted that the section dividers
in the novel resemble the sprocket holes on the edge of film (fig. 9).[7]
Important here, however, is the fact that these separators are also very
conventional typographical elements. Like the representation of graffiti
in the novel, these seemingly nontextual elements are transformed into a
conventional textual form. A more sophisticated example of this is Pynchon's subversive insertion of the index-finger dingbat bullet point, which
has been modified to use the middle finger (fig. 10). Like the reference to
film in the section-separating blocks, this finger dingbat inserts another
medium into print. And yet, in both cases that other medium appears via

a very conventional typographical element. From the beginning Slothrop has been associated with language and, in particular, print through his family, who are described as "word-smitten Puritans" (207) and involved with a paper company (285).

Ultimately, the competing media that appear within *Gravity's Rainbow* and that promise to provide alternative ways to organize human knowledge give way to the pragmatic principles of use, and in doing so come to reveal the way that writing itself is Pynchon's medium. In other words, the more the novel tries to take account of other media, the more we become aware that these other media are themselves being shaped by the form of the book: graffiti is turned into diagram, film into dingbat. Agency in this regard reflects the uses made possible by embracing the nature and limits of the medium of writing. Thus, I believe Pynchon is engaged in the same struggle with the limitations of his medium that we can see in the electronic encyclopedia. *Gravity's Rainbow* appears initially to offer us a multimedia aesthetic in which film, music, and language are all orchestrated to provide different forms of organization. Over time, however, those media are subordinated to the printed, textual nature of Pynchon's work. We are reminded that first and foremost we hold a book in our hands, and that any reference to the visual or to music is mediated by the potential of print on the page. The same has occurred over the last fifteen years as the promise of the multimedia encyclopedia has been worked through. Initially, designers of these documents treated different media as providing multiple organizational possibilities, and they saw the CD-ROM as a vehicle for uniting those media. Over time, however, the organizational possibilities of these other media have fallen away, and the document has coalesced around what we could take to be the central element of the electronic database medium: the search query.[8]

In striving to encapsulate human knowledge, the encyclopedia has chronically sought to incorporate other media—never more so than with the birth of the electronic encyclopedia. It has done so because it implicitly recognizes that human knowledge is more than just what is recorded in print. But in reaching out to these other media, encyclopedias are implicitly textualizing it, subordinating these other media to writing—most obviously, perhaps, in the subordination of image to its alphabetical entry in the traditional print encyclopedia. This schizophrenia reaches its zenith in the CD-ROM encyclopedia, where the hope of gathering competing media produces an interface that is fractured into many different panels and portals on the same information. In this regard, the electronic encyclopedia exemplifies the new media, since here is encapsulated the promise to transcend the limits of individual media. *Wikipedia*, conversely, seems to have gone quite the opposite direction in recognizing the key components of the online, primarily textual medium of the Web-based encyclopedia: the ease of typed search queries and the importance of constant editing. The unity of knowledge produced there is built not out of gathering together competing media, but out of how we *use* this writing—its constant revision by users—and organized around purposes directly linked to the way that users encounter it. In this sense, both instances of contemporary encyclopedism initially consider the possibility of transcending their "home" medium but ultimately embrace the strength and limitations of the written medium. *Wikipedia* is not, of course, precisely a print document, since it is networked and subject to continuous editing in a way that is impossible for a printed encyclopedia. But the recent history of the encyclopedia has been a gradual discovery of the value that arises from its easy and ongoing written editing. As we will see, new media frequently begin with the promise of transcending the limits of media but end with those limits reasserting themselves.

Networking

A second vision of media fullness promised by new media in contrast to traditional print is networking. We will recall that Kittler's definition of a media ecology in which the differences between individual media vanish starts from a vision of fiber optic networks, in which all forms of information travel in the same way. Likewise, we have already seen that *Wikipedia* improves on *Encarta* not only by accepting that it is ultimately a written document but also by embracing the way that it is different from print in linking users together, allowing for continuous revision of entries. Obviously, computer networks have emerged as a major element of contemporary culture, and like the CD-ROM encyclopedia, these networks promise to transform writing through different technologies of storage and transmission. But what it means to live in a networked age is harder to define than it seems at first. For most, claiming that contemporary society is networked means simply that we are connected to a degree that we have not been previously. In *Connected: Or What It Means to Live in the Network Society*, Steven Shaviro understands the network to translate to a state of constant connection: "It means that I haven't really withdrawn from the world after all. It means that I am nothing special. It means that I'm just the same as everybody else. The network has colonized my unconscious. It has made me into a tiny version of itself" (25). This idea that the nature of individual identity has been changed by media networks has been a part of new media theory since the beginning. In *Remediation*, Bolter and Grusin note, "A sense of presence of oneself to others and of the self to itself comes not through immediate visual perception, as it does in virtual reality, but through the feeling of being connected to others through the Internet" (258). Networked identity seems to carry us beyond the individual book into a series of exchanges and flows that will reconfigure the relationship between an individual audience and the circulation in which writing participates. Of course, many of these exchanges are implicit within writing, which likewise is meant to be exchanged, and likewise is subject to systems of dissemination and communication. After all, this is the complaint about publishing that Julie's boss at Fantômes makes about print in *The Colorist*. Like the fullness of the multimedia encyclopedia, the networked text seems to promise an escape from the limits of the circulation of individual media objects, which proved to be so central to the media novel (see chapter 2). Here instead are texts to be distributed instantly and everywhere, and thus unmarked by the details of circulation that we have seen time and again in the media novels we have discussed. What seems to be especially important about the networked text is an issue that usually remains in the background of most of this criticism: the way that networking changes how we map space. This issue is especially important, however, because it reflects the ways we imagine one work in relation to a larger society; ultimately, being able to visualize this depends on the media ecology. Mapping of the networked narrative reflects tensions implicit within print narrative as well. Just as the electronic encyclopedia ultimately came to reflect the potential of textual editing, so too do appeals to networked narratives ultimately depend on limits and potentials already implicit in print.

The previous section delayed introducing *Gravity's Rainbow* until the problems of the electronic encyclopedia were clear, but in this section I want to begin with a story that explores the topic of the network, because it will allow us to unpack the problems in the promises of the networked text more directly. Initially, what is most striking about Walter Abish's innovative short story "Ardor/Awe/Atrocity" is its organization. The story is broken into brief sections, each headed by three words beginning with a letter of the alphabet, moving from A to Z: "Ardor/Awe/Atrocity," "Buoyant/Bob/Body," and so on. Unlike the alphabetical organization of his novel *Alphabetical Africa*, this scheme appears to exercise no restraint over the story segments that appear under each heading. Each of these words (in their alphabetical order) is assigned a superscript number that looks like a footnote reference, and any time that the word appears within the story text it is marked by this reference number. Because of this numbering system, the story seems to have a cross-reference system that connects the different parts of the story to each other. The result is a tension between the static, encyclopedialike cross-referencing system and the narrative that takes place throughout these twenty-six sections. The story itself focuses initially on Jane, a young woman who has left her family behind in New York and moved to Southern California. The first half of the story narrates Jane's mundane emotional and sexual encounters in California before it shifts to follow Bob Down, a past friend of Jane who runs into her accidentally in the airport. The remainder of the story follows Bob and his acquaintances, especially focusing on his attempts to keep track of Jane. The story ends with one last shift, this time from Bob to the narrator, who explains "Bob[9] sent me a telegram inviting me to his wedding and then called me in New York to urge me to come" (57). Like the shift to Bob in the middle of the story, this change is striking because we had not previously been introduced to the character. Nonetheless, it is the narrator who wraps up the story, telling a surprised Bob that he read in the newspaper that Jane had died in a shooting. The narrator notes, "When he hung up, I realized that he hadn't mentioned my latest book. The novel is set in South California[10], a place I've never visited" (57). As a whole, then, the story moves away from its initial interest in Jane, toward more mediated knowledge about her, to end, finally, with newspaper reports and a novel written from secondhand knowledge.

Already it is clear that the media through which we encounter Jane's life will be a fundamental element of the story itself. Abish makes this theme quite explicit by describing characters obsessed with the television show *Mannix*, through which they view the whole of Southern California life: "People watch Mannix carefully, in order better to emulate the wealthy people he frequently visits in the graceful-looking haciendas of San Diego. Without Mannix, Southern California[7] would have no entrée to the wealth and power in L.A. and San Diego. Without Mannix Southern California[7] would be bereft of the distinction between ardor,[1] awe,[2] and atrocity[3]" (45). References to *Mannix* run throughout this story and clearly function as a metonymy for the way that media structure our experience of the real world. The reference to the sorting function of the words of the story's title also links the arbitrary arrangement of the story to media. Abish's story is not simply a critique of television. In fact the story opens by emphasizing the role of signs both in media and in everyday life. Jane drives through the Mojave Desert, worrying about the "persistent knocking sound" in her car's engine and what it might mean. She passes a hitchhiker holding a sign: "GOING MY WAY? EL LAY" (42). She notices a billboard with "a freshly cut[9] half of an orange, displayed in the center" (42), accidentally strikes a "large-sized gray furry animal" that runs across the road, and sees "a thin trail of blood on the highway" (43). Each of these signs points to some cause or possible future event, and Abish does not distinguish between the artificial sign of the billboard and the natural sign of the bloody highway. Abish's story, thus, is about meaning and how it is inserted into the landscape.

It is easy and perhaps natural to read Abish's story as reflecting Jean Baudrillard's description of the hyperreal postmodern landscape in which reality disappears under an "empire of signs": "Abstraction today is no longer that of the map, the double, the mirror or the concept. Simulation is no longer that of a territory, a referential being or a substance. It is the generation by models of a real without origin or reality: a hyperreal. The territory no longer precedes the map, nor survives it. Henceforth, it is the map that precedes the territory" (166). *Mannix* seems to function for Abish's characters as just this sort of "map that precedes the territory": "At what stage does the Southern Californian[7] convert the world around him into the flatness that resembles a movie screen. Everything the mind focuses on may be something it might have, on prior occasion, spotted on a screen. In time, the Southern Californian[7] will no longer ask, can I also do it? Instead he or she will want to know where, at what movie house, can it be seen?" (50). Television and film are therefore part of a whole system by which Southern Californians have their perception of possible actions and futures shaped for them: "With each new shopping center, with each new airport, with each new office building complex, Southern California[7] is expanding the range of the plausible. The immediate future,[16] the immediate immaculate[25] future[16] lies mapped[37] out in the brain cells as the suntanned people on the Coast carefully observe Mannix's arrival at an airport" (49).

We make a mistake, however, if we see Abish as simply identifying the hyperreal postmodern landscape; instead he emphasizes the material conditions of life in Southern California: "The question bears repeating. How[22] is it all done? How[22] is this miraculous way of life accomplished? The highway system is just one of the answers. The vast intricate[26] network[42] of roads in Southern California[7] facilitate the filming or, as it is sometimes called, the shooting[56] of a 'Mannix' sequel of sixty minutes minus time for commercials" (46). Abish's question of how the filming of *Mannix* is accomplished draws us back to exactly the sorts of issues that Baudrillard seems to ignore, back to the economic and cultural conditions out of which this hyperreal entertainment arises—a context that is figured directly in Abish's offhand remark that *Mannix* is filmed in a way that allows time for commercials. However, we should not go to the other extreme and simplify Abish's move to the material in his description of the highway as an unproblematic economic origin of characters' behavior. Although this turn allows him to draw our attention to the economic forces at work in the lives of the characters, it is also described in very abstract terms as a "network." Indeed, the similarity between this network and the map that Mannix provides for the characters is not accidental; in both cases, a system of organization is being imposed on the landscape. It is for this reason that the highway network and shopping center—both very physical and economically material entities—ultimately do the same thing as *Mannix*: ensure "the smoothly functioning process of a culture prepared for any eventuality, any disaster" (49). In this case, there seems to be little difference between the material "networks" that allow the movement of people and goods throughout Southern California, and the mental "map" that allows Southern Californians to anticipate and organize actions.

Abish's story reveals, then, one of the fundamental ambiguities of the network itself—the degree to which it is a material condition for contemporary life or merely a map of those conditions. In some ways, a network is simply a system of senders and receivers, and thus a vehicle for the circulation of media objects that I have described in previous chapters.

The current fascination with networking, described by Jenkins and Saper, is fundamentally connected to the issue of circulation (see chapter 2). The concept of the electronic network is an especially powerful formulation of this broader issue of circulation, however, because of its ambiguous materiality. In their recent book on networks and power, Alexander Galloway and Eugene Thacker see the network as an entirely material force beyond the human: "*Perhaps there is no greater lesson about networks than the lesson about control: networks, by their mere existence, are not liberating; they exercise novel forms of control that operate at a level that is anonymous and non-human, which is to say material*" (5). Abish also seems to embrace this understanding of the network as material, since it is precisely the fact that the network functions in the background, before any human actions, that distinguishes it from the particular narrative (*Mannix* episodes) that it makes possible. Indeed, the comparison between the anthropomorphic narrative of *Mannix* (can it be an accident that the television series invokes "man" by its title?) and the inhuman nature of the highway system that makes it all possible seems to be at the heart of Abish's question of "how" the show is filmed. Galloway and Thacker emphasize this quality of the network:

> The nonhuman quality of networks is precisely what makes them so difficult to grasp. They are, we suggest, a medium of contemporary power, and yet no single subject or group absolutely controls a network. Human subjects constitute and construct networks, but always in a highly distributed and unequal fashion. Human subjects thrive on network interaction (kin groups, clans, the social), yet the moments when the network logic takes over—in the mob or the swarm, in contagion or infection—are the moments that are the most disorienting, the most threatening to the human ego. (5)

The highway in this regard is quite the opposite of the humanity of Mannix.

And yet we know that this highway network is the product of human action; Abish is far from describing some natural force outside human control. Indeed, both Mannix and the highway system are products of human imagination and work. In this regard, we might compare this network to Bruno Latour's description of the "quasi-object" that is ambiguously material. Looking at "hybrid" natural phenomena like "the ozone hole story, or global warming, or deforestation" (50), Latour finds objects poised between nature and social formation: "Quasi-objects are much more social, much more fabricated, much more collective than the 'hard' parts of nature, but they are in no way the arbitrary receptacles of a full-fledged society. On the other hand they are more real, nonhuman and objective than those shapeless screens on which society—for unknown reasons—needed to be 'projected'" (55). These quasi-objects are not just abstract conditions but are structures that only come to life when they guide human action. The material ambiguity of the highway network is fundamentally connected to the nature of the actions that it makes possible. In the passage cited above regarding the highway system, notice Abish's focus on the word how: "How[22] is it all done? How[22] is this miraculous way of life accomplished?" (46). The highway exists to make action possible. This is something that Galloway and Thacker emphasize in their definition of the network. The network is described not by some conceptual model, but by the protocols that allow movement between its nodes: "*In the broadest sense, protocol is a technology that regulates flow, directs netspace, codes relationships, and connects life-forms*" (30). Characters understand the network—both the highway and the models provided by *Mannix*—because they can observe the actions that they make possible. This is a powerful if somewhat unlikely definition of the network that I want to emphasize: networks are organizations at the level of action, rather than traditional maps. It is for this reason that Galloway and Thacker say that "*protocol is twofold; it is both an apparatus that facilitates networks and a logic that governs how things are done within that apparatus*" (29).

It is easy to miss how radically the network changes our understanding of mapping. Normally the map is not the space itself but instead merely an attempt to conceptualize that space; as Alfred Korzybski remarked, "the map is not the territory."[9] Michel de Certeau depends on this distinction when he contrasts the totalizing vision of the city to the "innumerable collection of singularities" that comprises the individual footsteps in the city (97). He describes going up to the top of the World Trade Center:

When one goes up there, he leaves behind the mass that carries off and mixes up in itself any identity of authors or spectators. An Icarus flying above these waters, he can ignore the devices of Daedalus in mobile and endless labyrinths far below. His elevation transfigures him into a voyeur. It puts him at a distance. It transforms the bewitching world by which one was "possessed" into a text that lies before one's eyes. It allows one to read it, to be a solar Eye, looking down like a god. The exaltation of a scopic and gnostic drive: the fiction of knowledge is related to this lust to be a viewpoint and nothing more. (92)

De Certeau notes that this removed vantage point creates a fiction of control and knowledge, which eventually crumbles before the messy particularity of moving through the city. But the network promises a space where there is no difference between map and territory. Dave Ciccoricco links the network to this change in mapping when he critiques the application of Fredric Jameson's theory of cognitive mapping to networks: "In a network text, if maps continually create and recreate a territory, then such representations do not displace or supplant an original territory—as in Baudrillard's model of the simulacrum. The concept of *territory* itself, in the strict sense of a spatially locatable area, region, or terrain, does not apply to the abstract spatiality of network typology (until, of course, we arbitrarily impose one, as with the spatial logic of the World Wide Web, where we are Internet Explorers™ traversing a Netscape™ . . .)" (n.p.). Such online spaces do not exist before they are mapped; consequently what allows us to move through them is also the organization that allows us to visualize them.

The blurry line between the material organization of the landscape and mental "maps" imposed upon it is carried over into the organization of Abish's story. This is particularly clear when he shifts his story from the Jane-centered narrative of the first half to the story of Bob's erotic pursuit of Jane in the second half. Bob's interest in Jane functions as the window through which we can observe her movements across Southern California. Near the end of the story, Bob opens the suitcase that Jane has apparently abandoned and rifles through her possessions. Jane has fallen out of the main narrative to become embodied in objects. Bob finds the map that Jane used in driving across the country, photographs of herself and others, and a "tiny yellow address book for the most part filled with names of people in the L.A. and San Diego area. He looked up his name and found that each new number he had left with the answering service had been entered in the book" (56). Here Jane's actions are narrated indirectly through other media that become part of the story by being represented as objects. The objects are ambiguous in much the same way as the network; they are both a map and a material condition of the landscape. The objects that Bob uses to understand Jane's movements are themselves the objects that she used to navigate this space. This is what makes Abish's story a network narrative: the protocols that organize the story are already implicit within the actions of the characters. This differentiates a network from a map—there is no preexisting territory to which the network refers. This is also part of what we mean when we say that communication is networked. It is not just that we are all connected by different communication methods, but also that we traverse a very different sense of space when we use these communication technologies.[10]

On some level, all fiction is like a network, since none of the spaces described exist before writing. There was a rather robust discussion about the nature of "spatial form" in literature during the 1970s and '80s that reflected the special role that spatial modeling has in verbal texts.[11] In the previous chapter I cited Paul Werth on the way that verbal narrative descriptions can project spaces that are incomplete and subject to increasingly specific mapping and remapping over the course of the story. Much more so than the spaces of filmic or other visual narratives, the spaces of written or oral stories are abstractions that we create over the course of the reading—all the while treating them as if they preexist the story that we are following. In this regard, networking is similar to encyclopedism in that both initially seem to be unique to new media but in fact exist in print culture as well. Usually we are encouraged to imagine that the space of a particular fictional work does exist and to treat it as real and model it cognitively in the same way that we do real-world spaces.[12] Abish, however, works against our ability to imagine the landscape as independent of its representation. He is not the only contemporary author to do so. A wonderful example of this same inquiry into the nature of fictional space is Paul Auster's novella *City of Glass*, where a map appears fairly late in the story (fig. 11). The map reflects the wanderings of Peter Stillman around New York and is recorded by Auster's writer-turned-detective, Daniel Quinn. At first the diagram seems meaningless, but after Quinn records the route of Stillman on subsequent days, it becomes clear that Stillman

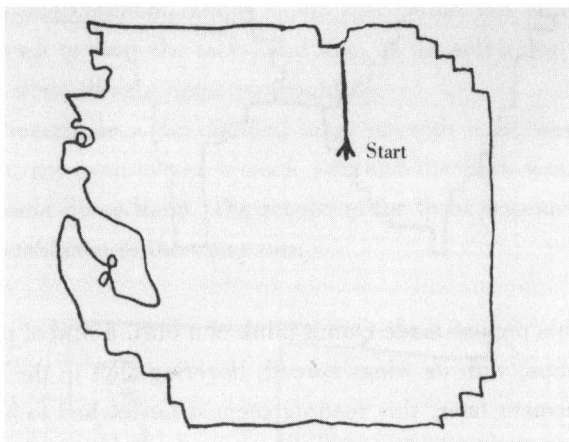

11. Map in *City of Glass* by Paul Auster. Courtesy of Paul Auster.

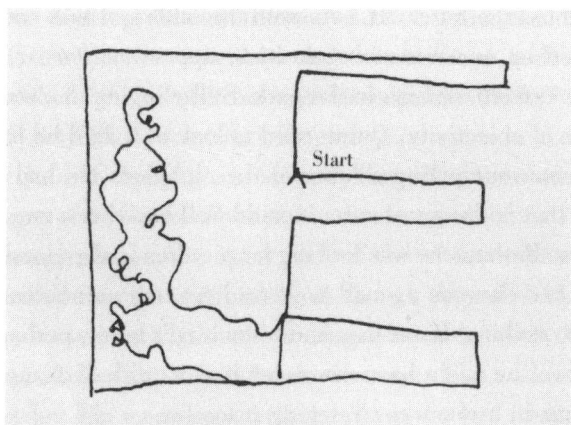

12. Map in *City of Glass* by Paul Auster. Courtesy of Paul Auster.

is literally writing letters onto the city (fig. 12). Quinn of course is immediately suspicious that he might be imagining patterns where there are none—after all, how likely is it that Stillman would be following such an elaborate path, especially since Quinn is pretty sure that Stillman is not aware he is being followed. The words scribbled on the city—as well as in Quinn's notebook and Auster's novel—reflect the metaphysical playfulness of the story. Auster has folded back his narrative in much the same way that "Ardor/Awe/Atrocity" does. The map should be a record of the movements of the characters through the story, and thus should be at or above the level of the "discourse" in the novel. But in fact the map that we are shown here may actually be a message from Stillman to Quinn, and thus very much a part of the "story" level of the narrative. Structure becomes message, map becomes network.[13]

Abish explores the network as a different way of organizing narrative, but in the process reveals that such an organization is already implicit, if frequently ignored, in the novel. Traditionally narrative depends on clear distinctions between narrative levels: we separate the author from the narrator, the narrator from the characters, and the settings of the narrative from whatever organization that the author imposes on the telling of the story. This distinction between levels is essential to conventional ways of thinking about narrative in terms of the "mediacy" that F. K. Stanzel describes—how a narrative reshapes the information that it conveys to the reader through the perspective of the narrator, author, or reflector character. Abish reminds us that these distinctions are not inevitable and offers in the network a metaleptic organizational principle that moves between the story world and how it is represented to the reader. We could see this focus on objects that move between the story and discourse levels as a corollary to the novels of media circulation discussed in this book. Both shift attention from mediacy to the *use* of media within a cultural context.

It should be no surprise that this kind of metaleptic mapping has particularly energized creators of new media—who, as we have seen, often turn to electronic media as a response to the perceived limits of print narratives. Many CD-ROM hypertext stories blur this line between the narrative and the artifacts and maps that readers use to explore that story. A nice example of this is M. D. Coverley's *Califia*, a kind of treasure hunt through an archive of maps, charts, and other documents. In some ways these items are simply navigational devices, as for example the chart that provides access to the four "journeys" that make up the spine of the story (fig. 13). Coverley also sees these maps and charts as objects with which we interact as readers. Thus, for example, we encounter a "Kit Bag" screen that is described as providing "gear for [the] journey" (fig. 14). This seems to be roughly equivalent to the highway network that Abish describes, in so far as it exists both at the level of our encounter with the text and within the world itself. What distinguishes a device like this from the map at the beginning of *The Lord of the Rings*, for example, or other inserted media like the photograph that provides the basis of Richard Powers's *Three*

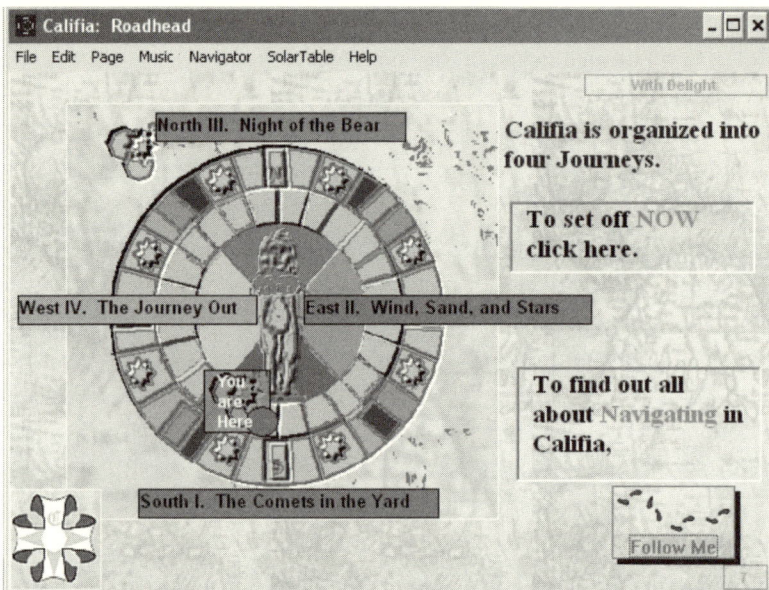

13. *Califia* organizing chart. Courtesy of Marjorie Luesebrink.

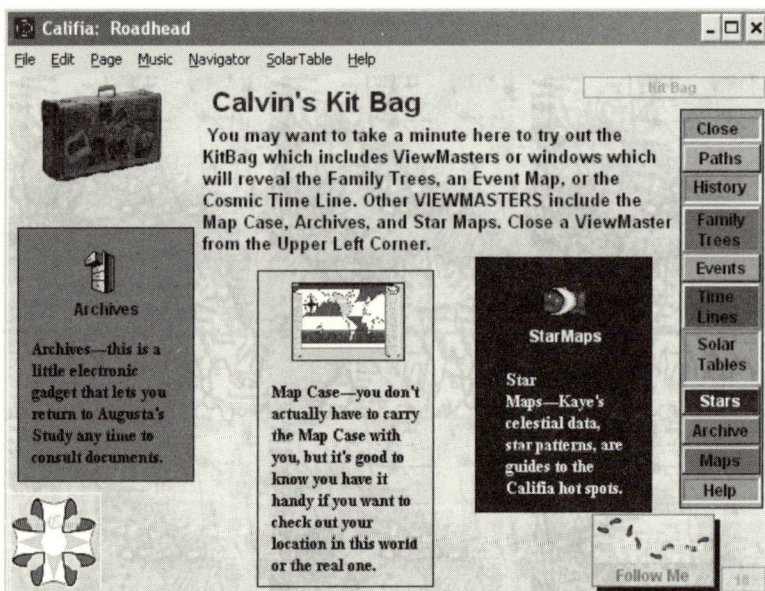

14. *Califia* "Kit Bag." Courtesy of Marjorie Luesebrink.

Farmers on Their Way to a Dance is that these network objects are much more ambiguous. Is the Solar Chart an object in the world or merely an organizational scheme? This ambiguity is precisely what gives the network its power and complexity as a narrative structure. It is an ambiguity with its roots in writing, even though we are usually encouraged to ignore it in traditional novels. Although new media theories often describe an ideal space of networked circulation in which specific objects dissolve into a stream of undifferentiated media, Coverley makes clear that individual new media authors *can* recognize and exploit the qualities of media just as much as the authors do in the media novels I have focused on in this book.

A networked narrative, then, is one in which the protocols of action within the story also organize the representation of that story to the reader; this duality exploits a tension implicit but usually ignored in print writing. I suggest that the shift toward such narratives is a common element of contemporary storytelling. In fact, the most distinctively new form of contemporary storytelling would almost certainly have to be role-playing and online games—forms of narrative that simply did not exist before the 1970s. Early commentary about online games usually tried to apply traditional literary models to these new forms. So, for example, descriptions of online avatars in early, text-based virtual spaces of the 1990s almost inevitably described play in this space as allowing individuals to be immersed in the electronic world. The fascination with the Eliza program, which mimics the psychiatric style of open-ended inquiry, arose from the possibility that individuals would be fooled and lose themselves in its fictional world. Early books like Sherry Turkle's *Life on the Screen* suggested something similar about how individuals could take on a new identity in cyberspace, noting that online, "people are able to build a self by cycling through many selves" (178). Turkle emphasizes how players learn to develop different aspects of their personalities, and that "the routine of playing them becomes part of their players' real lives" (188). Turkle's view of online activity leaves behind the medium and treats this online world as a kind of pure mimesis, in which virtual actions mimic real life. Similar, if less extreme, claims are made about pen-and-pencil role-playing games, which likewise were described as using dice and complex charts to prompt players to lose themselves in a fantasy world.[14] Each of these cases reasserts a fairly traditional model of narrative, in which the medium of the text (online communication, computer AI, or dice rolls) eventually disappear and individuals find themselves in a narrative world. This is once again an image of transcending the limits of older media, just as the multimedia encyclopedia promised to unify human knowledge by unifying previously separate media. In this case, Turkle promises a kind of immersion that becomes part of the "player's real lives" instead of some limited and temporary involvement in older media like the film or novel.

More recent work on these new forms of narrative recognizes that the relationship between narrative immersion and persistence of the medium is considerably more complex. Jesper Juul dismisses the idea that games can or should simply prompt stories that then leave behind the rules that generated them: "If games were simply storytelling media, this would be radically uninteresting. The interest of the rules themselves is the reason why games can be abstract and without points of identification and yet be interesting. In a game, the real-world player works to overcome challenges, and overcoming them is considered a positive experience" (161). What seems to be especially important is the way we imagine our social interaction in these spaces. In a recent study on massively multiplayer online games (MMOGs) like *World of Warcraft*, T. L. Taylor notes that although the fantasy settings of these games "seem to suggest a role-playing genre, players rarely employ any kind of formal RP [role-playing] orientation." Nonetheless, as Taylor notes, "The lack of role-playing in the game . . . does not mean that there is no interaction or social life among the players" (30). In fact, players in an online game like *World of Warcraft* seem no more likely to remember their time online as a matter of being lost in a fictional world than they are to frame the story they tell about themselves in terms of the mechanics of the game play. In a narrative published in the *New York Times* about an expansion to *World of Warcraft* early in 2007, which allowed players to achieve higher levels for their characters in the game world, Seth Schiesel describes the race to be the first player to the new level-limit of 70:

> I am proud to report that on my server, it was me. After racking up about 76 hours of playtime in a little more than 4.5 days of real time, shortly after 4 p.m. Saturday my warlock became the first charac-

ter to hit level 70 on my server. Unhealthy? Probably. Exhilarating? Definitely.

I'll report Tuesday about some of what I've seen in the game world and on Wednesday about the social dynamics of the race and about the hundreds of players I've heard from as a now-(in)famous citizen of my server. But today I'll share a bit about how I did it.

So the expansion opened for business at midnight last Tuesday (late Monday night). I was the first player on my server through the Dark Portal and into the new continent of Outland because I had received my game discs a couple of days early, but at that moment hundreds of stores opened their midnight madness events and thousands of gamers grabbed their copies and rushed home.

From inside the game it was fascinating to watch. At 12:02 a.m. Tuesday, and for 20 minutes, I had all of Hellfire Peninsula (the first region in Outland) to myself. By 1:02 there were 24 people in the expansion. By 1:30 I had maxed out my Hellfire list at 49 people and by the morning there appeared to be hundreds of players on the peninsula alone.

I played for almost 24 hours and went to bed the first time late Tuesday night after hitting level 63. I didn't get back to the game for about 15 hours, my longest break of the week.

I picked up early Wednesday afternoon in corrupted Terokkar Forest and hit 64 around 9:30 that night, second to a mage in my guild we'll call Goldie. I went out for a brief cocktail (for the muscle relaxation), played straight through Wednesday night and hit 65 around 7:15 Thursday morning, a server first. (n.p.)

In some ways, this narrative is atypical of the stories that players would tell about themselves, since it is clearly addressed to readers who are outsiders to the game and who want to learn about the culture of hardcore gamers. Nonetheless, the mixture of references in this story strikes me as revealing. Although some of the story takes place in the fictional world of the game (the Terokkar Forest, the Dark Portal), that space is mixed with the real world of eating and sleeping, and—especially—the awareness of encountering other characters who are being operated by other players. Even more importantly, the narrative of achievement constructed here is a mixture of fictional world accomplishments and awareness of the game mechanics that structure that fictional world—the language of levels, in particular. I would suggest that this is in fact actually quite common but largely ignored when we insist on seeing these games as examples of immersion rather than instances of the network's ambiguous materiality. Even players who enjoy immersing themselves in the fictional world usually describe their experiences there with reference to game mechanics—achieving levels, overcoming difficult, deliberately constructed challenges, and so on. This is not, in other words, a narrative world in which the game conditions fall away for the sake of immersion, but instead a story in which rules circulate between determining events and structuring narration. And in that regard, the narrative experience of these games is precisely the complex mixture of levels that I have associated with the network.

We may see this ambiguity as a failure of the medium—and, indeed, many early accounts of online play suggested that immersion was the ultimate goal of these games—but I suggest that it represents a direct expression of the logic of network narrative. To build a story out of objects that are already themselves shaped by narrative conditions produces a very different kind of story text—but one that still has its basis in the conditions of print. It was one of the scandals of postmodernism to insist that fiction is just words; as William Gass quips, "It seems a country-headed thing to say: that literature is language, that stories and the places and the people in them are merely made of words as chairs are made of smoothed sticks and sometimes cloth or metal tubes" (27). We suppress this awareness to immerse ourselves in plot and setting, but on some level we are always using the words of the story as both substance and map. This is why, I think, Abish playfully uses alphabetical entries as an organizing principle for his story, and ultimately why he turns back to insist on the utterly traditional nature of his networked narrative. When the narrator invokes his "latest book. The book is set in South California,[7] a place I've never visited" (57), Abish is returning to a simpler model of nested narratives. This conventional device—which goes back to the tradition of offering the novel as a "found" document that the author has merely edited for the reader—draws us back to familiar, novelistic territory. And in the process, it reasserts the role of writing in this story. If the highway system promises another form of story organization that moves us into hypertext, this turn back to the writing of novels reminds us that these ambiguities have always been there in print. As much as new media want to abstract writing and treat it as part of an idealized system of communication, these ambiguities remain in both electronic and printed texts.

Transparency

My focus here on the networked quality of new media has lead us to video games. As we have seen, the space of play in these new media works is actually indebted to ambiguities already implicit in print. Now let us take a closer look at video games, since they are certainly the most commercially successful and widely consumed form of new media, and thus are an important example of the storytelling appeal of new media. In particular, the frequently made claim that these games can achieve greater player engagement and more transparency of interaction than traditional print narrative arises from the belief that these new technologies allow us to transcend the limits of older media. In this promise of transparency, video games are like the other two new media dreams, encyclopedism and networking.

We might first note the continuities between this new media promise of transparency and the novel. One of the fundamental strengths of written fiction is its ability to convey the workings of the minds of others. In her influential book *Transparent Minds*, Dorrit Cohn cites Käte Hamburger as the first critic to articulate this principle: "Narrative fiction is the only literary genre, as well as the only kind of narrative, in which the unspoken thoughts, feelings, perceptions of a person other than the speaker can be portrayed" (7). Cohn makes clear that the representation of these thoughts is to a large extent a convention granted us by our understanding of fictionality; we allow novelists the (unrealistic) right to describe something that none of us really know in the real world (what others are thinking) in return for the enjoyment of a good story.[15] That fiction can show us things unknowable in real life has been a well-established appeal of the novel at least since E. M. Forster. Taking the example of historical figures like Queen Victoria, Forster writes that "it is the function of the novelist to reveal the hidden life at its source: to tell us more about Queen Victoria than could be known, and thus to produce a character who is not the Queen Victoria of history" (72).

Cohn also makes clear that the techniques novelists use once they are granted this right are inherent to the medium of writing. Much of the debate about the representation of character thoughts has focused on the nature of "free indirect discourse." In chapter 1, I briefly discussed criticism of this approach from Alan Palmer, who sees the focus on scenes of "self-communing" (9) as very limiting. Palmer rightly notes that much of our insight into character minds comes not from such self-communings, but instead from the "thought reports" that summarize the thinking of the characters without recourse to their own language: "Most characters' thought takes place in a social context of action and interaction with others. For this aspect of the novel, thought report is the most suitable mode of presentation" (77). Although Palmer is right that self-communings are a very narrow model for character thought, I argued earlier that critics have been so fascinated by free indirect discourse because this mixture of character and narrational voices is a particular capability of the novel. The representation of character thoughts through free indirect discourse seems to be a point at which the novel most fully exploits the potential of writing, and it should be no surprise that critics of the novel are strongly drawn to this essentially linguistic device.

Critics like Palmer who recognize the limitations of this focus on character language have responded by reintroducing character bodies and actions into this equation. Palmer argues that we need to see characters' thoughts as involved in "purposeful, engaged, social interaction" (59). An essential component of this shift is an appreciation of physical action. Palmer cites a passage from *Madame Bovary* discussed by both Auerbach and Poulet:

> But it was above all at mealtimes that she could bear it no longer, in that little room on the ground floor, with the smoking stove, the creaking door, the oozing walls, the damp floor-tiles; all the bitterness of life seemed to be served to her on her plate, and, with the steam from the boiled beef, there rose from the depths of her soul other exhalations as it were of disgust. Charles was a slow eater; she would nibble a few hazel-nuts; or else, leaning on her elbow, would amuse herself making marks on the oilcloth with the point of her table-knife.

Palmer argues that this passage is effective precisely because it combines the mental and the physical: "It is a complex mixture of thought report (the feelings rising from the depths of her soul), free indirect perception (her awareness of the room), and action (nibbling, making marks) that is highly informative about Emma's states of mind" (79). Of particular interest is the focus that Palmer puts on the last of these: "If . . . he had wanted to make her a purely subjective being, then nothing would have been left except the sensations and emotions caused in Emma by the surrounding objects. There would then have been no awareness on the part of the reader of Emma as a person standing against a background of things" (79). The tension between thought and physical action forms two poles of character representation (89) and marks the clearest point at which recent work on character minds departs from the earlier focus primarily on free indirect discourse and scenes of self-communing.

Surprisingly, then, analysis of character thought leads to an interest in the representation of character bodies. Palmer cites Wittgenstein: the "human body is the best picture of the human soul" (131). Cohn also suggests the importance of corporeality: "the special life-likeness of narrative fiction—as compared to dramatic and cinematic fictions—depends on what writers and readers know least in life: how another mind thinks, another body feels" (5–6). In a recent article on "embodied transparency," Lisa Zunshine has noted that our ability to interpret bodies is important to our belief that we can understand others' minds: the person I am speaking to "intuitively expects me to 'read' her body as indicative of her thoughts, desires, and intentions" ("Theory of Mind," 69). Zunshine concludes that our ability to read bodies is fundamental to our pleasure in reading fiction:

> Representations of embodied transparency regale us with something that we hold at a premium in our everyday lives and never get much of: perfect access to other people's minds via their observable behaviour. As such, they must be immensely flattering to our Theory of Mind adaptations, which evolved to read minds through bodies but have to constantly contend with the possibility of misreading and the resulting social failure. The pleasure derived from moments of embodied transparency is thus largely a social pleasure—a titillating illusion of superior social discernment and power. (72)

Thus, although the idea that fiction makes minds "transparent" seems to draw us away from the body, Zunshine shows that it is precisely through the body that we are provided with the tools to interpret character minds.

We can see, then, a dynamic between character mind and body, between transparency and physicality. Critics like Palmer and Zunshine invoke cognitive theories of the mind to move narrative theory away from purely linguistic models, but we can see this duality itself as a limit that helps to define the nature of novelistic discourse. The transparent minds that Cohn describes as a feature of written (fictional) narrative depend on looking at and through character bodies.

Let us turn to a print novel that anticipates and explores the hope of escaping these traditional novelistic tensions and limits through another medium. One novel with a great deal to say about the dynamic of reading character bodies is Paul Auster's *The Book of Illusions*, which I mentioned briefly at the end of chapter 3. This novel is told in the first person by David Zimmer, a professor of comparative literature at Hampton College, who loses his wife and children to an airplane crash before the opening of the novel. Zimmer is plunged into deep despair and only begins to emerge when he sees a silent comedy starring Hector Mann. Zimmer becomes fascinated with Mann, who disappeared mysteriously from the public eye at the end of the silent film era, and writes the first book-length study of his films, *The Silent World of Hector Mann*. In response to the book's publication, Zimmer receives a letter from Hector's wife and an invitation to come to New Mexico to meet Hector—who everyone had presumed to be long dead. Once in New Mexico, Zimmer discovers that Hector has continued making films in secret but has promised that they would be destroyed upon his death. Hector is already near death when he contacts Zimmer, and would like the films to be seen once by the sympathetic viewer he takes Zimmer to be. Hector's wife is less comfortable with having the films viewed, and when Hector dies shortly after Zimmer's arrival, she hastens to destroy the films. Zimmer manages to see only one film before all are destroyed.

Essential to the novel is the narrative tension between film and writing. After all, *The Book of Illusions* is about films on several levels. It is Auster's novel about a filmmaker, but it is also the story of several people writing books about films: Zimmer's initial scholarly book, a biography of Hector being written by his daughter Alma, and even Zimmer's first-person narrative about the experience and account of the one film he does get to see. In this regard, it is especially significant that Hector is a *silent* film star.

The narratives in which he engages are completely "other" in relation to written narrative, since they concern only the visual with little reference to language. This tension is brilliantly captured by Zimmer's summary of an important film from Hector's early (public) career: *Mr. Nobody.* With the possible exception of the one late-career film that Zimmer sees before it is destroyed, this is the longest and most complete summary of any of Hector's films in the book, signaling its importance. Zimmer notes that this film comes at the end of Hector's silent career, and marks an awareness of its end:

> Time was running out by then, and he must have known that once the contract [with Kaleidoscope Pictures] was fulfilled, his career would be over. Sound was coming. It was an inevitable fact of life, a certainty that would destroy everything that had come before it, and the art that Hector had worked so hard to master would no longer exist. Even if he could reconfigure his ideas to accommodate the new form, it wouldn't do him any good. Hector spoke with a heavy Spanish accent, and the moment he opened his mouth on-screen, American audiences would reject him. (38–39)

The film shows Hector as a rich and successful man, happily married with children and the president of a thriving soft drink corporation. To cover his gambling debts, Hector's vice president schemes to get rid of him and take over the company by turning him invisible using a potion disguised as a new flavor of beverage. The film cleverly plays on the nature of the medium, first showing Hector disappearing and then, after a cut, having him back in the scene. The audience concludes that the effects must have worn off, but soon we realize that we have simply adopted Hector's point of view; he remains invisible to everyone else. Hector's vice president fakes a note claiming that Hector is leaving the company to him and going off because of a terminal disease. Zimmer notes that Hector doesn't fight against his invisible condition—either by searching for an antidote or confronting his former friend—but instead accepts it as permanent and simply engages in the sorts of gags and rule-breaking that invisibility makes possible, such as tripping passersby and stealing jewelry. As he returns home, however, Hector comes to seem more and more of a ghost, cut off from his own family:

He sits down beside the girl [his daughter], studies her face for a few moments, and then lifts his hand to begin stroking her hair. Just as he is about to touch her, however, he stops himself, suddenly realizing that his hand could wake her, and if she woke up in the darkness and found no one there, she would be frightened. It's an affecting sequence, and Hector plays it with restraint and simplicity. He has lost the right to touch his own daughter, and as we watch him hesitate and then finally withdraw his hand, we experience the full impact of the curse that has been put on him. In that one small gesture—the hand hovering in the air, the open palm no more than an inch from the girl's head—we understand that Hector has been reduced to nothing. (50)

Although the film has a surprisingly happy ending—Hector awakes visible the next morning after sleeping in a chair—this ending doesn't do away with the fear implied, or void the questions raised. Zimmer claims that the film is ultimately "a meditation on his own disappearance" (53).

Noteworthy about this film is that it takes account of its condition as a silent film to emphasize the way the novel is able to read character bodies. As Zimmer implies, invisibility is an absolutely disabling condition in a silent film; to be invisible here is to be "reduced to nothing."[16] Initially, this film seems to be the antithesis of the description of character bodies, since Hector's initial disappearance promises a film with a missing central character. But of course the film cannot progress in this way, and must reintroduce the character body onto the screen. The film does this, paradoxically, by going inside Hector's mind and adopting his point of view. Immediately after Hector is reintroduced after the cut, the action of the film emphasizes the discovery that he is, in fact, still invisible—for instance, he stares into a mirror and makes faces at clerks in his office (43). If Hector were actually invisible, we might assume that he would be invisible to himself as well as to others. But treating his invisibility in this way would make his psychological realization impossible to represent; we would literally have no way to see his gradual understanding of his condition. Returning Hector's body to the screen becomes a way to represent his mind.

Just as important as the link between the representation of bodies and the representation of minds in this film is the way that *Mr. Nobody* essentially creates two parallel narratives that the audience follows. One involves the larger world, which cannot see Hector and is mystified by invisible actions like tripped pedestrians and disappearing baseballs (45–46). The other represents Hector's actions, and emphasizes his own inner turmoil and acceptance of his fate—as, for example, when he reaches out toward and then retracts his hand from his daughter's head. The film presents a double narrative that the audience must keep separate—understanding that Hector and others in a scene are seeing very different things. The same thing occurs in Zimmer's account, which likewise tells two stories: what is happening to Hector on screen and what the audience understands: "The effects of the drink must have worn off. We have just watched Hector disappear, and if we are able to see him now, it can only mean that the drink was less powerful than we thought" (43). Where Hector's film tells a double story of Hector's realizations and the larger world in which he lives, Zimmer's analysis describes both the physical Hector and the mind of the reader. In a way, Zimmer's account is actually closer to the techniques of the novel, since he contrasts the representation of a body with the narrating voice describing a mind. Nonetheless, both film and critical analysis depend on a kind of double reading that balances body and mind.

What seems to be especially important about this dual-channel narrative is that it embodies the duality of describing character bodies and minds that Palmer and Zunshine articulate as central to the novel. We understand Hector's despair most powerfully when he is invisible and off-screen precisely because we have a second narrative (Zimmer's or the film's switched perspective) describing this absent body. Like the transparent minds that Cohn describes, the image of Hector is surprisingly corporeal precisely because we have two channels of information—in this case, the film showing an empty room and its analysis that explains to us that Hector *is* there although invisible. In this regard, Zimmer's narrative of Hector's disappearance accomplishes the paradoxical task implicit in all written narrative: to make character bodies visible so that we can understand character minds. For all that Auster's novel seems to depend on film, its dynamics in the end are deeply entwined with the fundamental elements of writing.

It is in the context of this very complex relationship between character mind and body in the novel that we must understand new media's promise to provide us with transparent access to characters. Here is the well-known passage from William Gibson's novel *Neuromancer* that describes one character's connection to another through a yet-to-be-invented device for simulating physical stimulus (*simstim*): "The abrupt jolt into other flesh. Matrix gone, a wave of sound and color. . . . She [Molly] was moving through a crowded street, past stalls vending discount software, prices felt-penned on sheets of plastic, fragments of music from countless speakers. Smells of urine, free monomers, perfume, patties of frying krill. For a few frightened seconds he [Case] fought helplessly to control her body. Then he willed himself into passivity, became the passenger behind her eyes" (56). Virtual reality promises an experience that transcends the limits of language and its dependence on the body. Indeed, the mixture of mind and environment that this character experiences through the simstim link emphasizes the corporeal basis underlying character minds. We can see Gibson's description of this future technology simply as an extension of the dual-channel narration that is central to the novel in general. Gibson is *describing* this technology, and the way that he narrates both mind and body is completely consistent with the novelistic tradition that we see in Flaubert's *Madame Bovary*. It is for this reason that the attempt actually to create the technologies that Gibson describes is deeply problematic: the description of these technologies is rooted in the representational dynamics of the novel, and so any instantiation of this technology in the real world will need to confront the novelistic baggage that comes with it. Of course, the initial promises made in the early 1990s based on the sort of virtual reality technology that Gibson describes have to a large extent fallen through, but new media has indeed given us the ability to occupy another body in limited ways. Early installations of online chat conducted in virtual spaces using avatars initially struck critics as giving us the ability to try on other identities. I quoted above Sherry Turkle's celebration of the power of "life on the screen" to move beyond our own identities. More recently, critics have explored the potential for three-dimensional modeling to give us an experience of others' bodies. Moving a character through a virtual space would seem to be roughly equivalent to Case's experience of sharing Molly's perceptions through the simstim link. Rajani Sudan has suggested that the fantasy of moving beyond corporeality into a kind of transparency is part of contemporary technological culture: "Whether such invisibility happens on the drawing table or in the tabloids is not really important; the fact is that we *consume* the eradication of visibly corporeal markers as somehow legitimate, as part and parcel of technological evolution" (70).

The degree to which games can do this is at the heart of debates about the sexist or libratory potential of the popular *Tomb Raider* games of the mid-1990s, and these games provide a fascinating example of the way that the dual-channel description implicit in the novel's use of character bodies is carried over into this new media text. Debates over this game focused on whether playing the buxom character of Lara Croft encouraged players to think about female bodies differently, or if the obviously attractive avatar was merely one in a long series of objectifying representations of women. In reviewing the problems of deciding whether Lara Croft is sexist or feminist, Helen Kennedy focuses on the nature of "a games character who is simultaneously the hero (active) and the heroine (to be looked at)" (n.p.). Because of this duality, the nature of player identification is particularly complex and multilayered. Mary Flanagan has provided a more extensive and systematic description of players' engagement with these on-screen avatars. According to Flanagan, players relate to these avatars in five ways: (1) by using them in the game as a kind of puppet, (2) by watching the avatar act independently (through style of motion, breathing, and so on), (3) as acting with them as companions, (4) as objects to be watched as a spectator, and (5) as a point of identification (432). Flanagan's more detailed summary is particularly useful in reminding us how complex our relation is to such on-screen avatars—at times they are objects to be watched, at times mere tools for our own accomplishments, at times a point of identification.

Some critics have questioned whether "occupying" a body in this sense really has much in common with the traditional novelistic goal of representing another's consciousness. Flanagan describes this as a "double consciousness": "I would argue that the computer world user experience [*sic*] a kind of double consciousness: the class, race, and gender identity of the user's physical body, as well as the virtual body (bodies) of the character he or she 'becomes'" (438). Ken Perlin claims that when reading a novel, "the agency of a protagonist takes over, and we are swept up in observation of his struggle, more or less from his point of view, as though we were some invisible spirit or angel perched upon his shoulder, watching but never interfering." Video games ask us to interact with the protagonist in a very different way:

> By way of contrast, look at games. A game does not force us to relinquish our agency. In fact, the game depends on it.
>
> When you play *Tomb Raider* you don't actually think of Lara Croft as a person the same way, say, you think of Harry Potter as a person. . . . There is a fictional construct in the backstory of the game. But while you're actually playing the game, the very effectiveness of the experience depends on *you* becoming Lara Croft. The humanlike figure you see on your computer screen is really a game token, and every choice she makes, whether to shoot, to leap, to run, to change weapons, is your choice. (14)

Perlin suggests that the narrative goal embodied in reading depends on audience passivity, while new media objects generally equate immersion with activity.[17] In *Narrative as Virtual Reality*, Marie-Laure Ryan has suggested that these two views of the virtual—as the fake and as the potential—have corollary metaphors for the text: the text as a world that we lose ourselves in, and the text as a game that we play with (199). Having to express ourselves through our own actions works against the kind of immersion that Perlin and others associate with traditional literary experience. We could describe two different forms of immersion based on seeing and doing, which bring with them two different understandings of transparency. To return to the example of *Tomb Raider*, we could say the debate about Lara Croft turns on exactly which element of the character we emphasize—the object to be watched or the figure to be manipulated.

The new media hope of capturing the experience of human corporeality through audience involvement and manipulation is particularly complex, then, since transparency is of ambiguous value. Recalling the discussion of Cohn and Palmer, we can see that the game embodies a duality that is already implicit in writing—we are both outside the avatar and inside directing her. The debate over *Tomb Raider* helps us to clarify Palmer's observation about the importance of character bodies to reading character minds. Reading these characters means joining together two different messages being sent by the author: thought reports and physical description. This duality is particularly easy to see in *Tomb Raider*, where we use Laura's body in several independent, if not contradictory, ways: as a tool, as an object to be viewed, as a narrative agent, and so on. The same is true in the novel, where we both look at and through character bodies. Readers understand that they are being sent multiple messages when character corporeality is described alongside character minds. In this regard, *Tomb Raider* repeats a pattern that we have seen several times over the course of this chapter. Where initially new media seems to promise an escape from the limits of writing, in fact we find that it continues to depend on those same dynamics. In fact, one of the reasons that *Tomb Raider* emerged as a central example in the early discussion of video games is because of how strongly it depends on the dynamics of identification that we have inherited from print novels. The duality of Lara Croft as both object and agent repeats in a particularly strong way a dynamic of looking at and through character bodies which has always been implicit in print. Although her skimpy clothes and buxom figure may make Croft a natural figure for cultural analysis, games have routinely created such unrealistic female figures. What makes this game stand out is how strongly it connects to familiar ambiguities of voyeurism that are built into the novel.

Our relationship to video game characters like Lara Croft, then, is particularly complex and depends on descriptive dynamics that have been developed through other media like the novel, which has its own specific limits and contours. We could argue, in fact, that the multiplicity of our relationship to video game characters is a feature not just of such games, but of the computer interface in general. We might consider the ubiquitous language of "windows" in the personal computer. Although we routinely refer to different screens of information (often reflecting the operation of different programs) as separate "windows," the relationship between these screens and physical windows is very loose. As Anne Friedberg remarks, this metaphor "relies on the model of a window that we don't see through, windows that instead overlap and obscure, and are resizable and moveable" (229). Everyone has had the experience of having a window of one application hidden behind another, of having to close or move another window to get to the information we need. Such problems are, of course, impossible when dealing with the physical windows of a house, whose purpose is to allow us to *see through* rather than to block vision. In many ways, this contradiction is the same one that we see in *Tomb Raider*, where we are promised immersion in a character's actions while at the same time clearly being invited to look at her. We might ease this contradiction by instead referring to these windows as *screens*—which better reflects the idea of something that we look at and that might block our vision of other information. But the brilliance of the window metaphor is that it captures something that the concept of a screen does not: our sense that the window we are looking at is more than just an object to be observed; it is instead a means of accessing something beyond the objects that we can see. It is especially easy to see this in *Tomb Raider*, where the window through which we are looking is a means of exploring a three-dimensional world, but it is also evident in a simple word-processing program, where we recognize that the application window shows us only part of a larger document though which we can scroll.

The promise that new media will allow us to transcend the distinction between text and image, video, and sound disguises the continuing influence of these specific media limits. The novel's dual-channel description of character bodies may provide a template for our relationship to video game characters as well. Although *Tomb Raider* largely keeps its contradictory positioning of the audience implicit rather than explicit, there are many works that try to embrace rather than suppress the tension between the media that make up an electronic text. Take the example of a short electronic poem like J. R. Carpenter's "Entre Ville," whose primary interface screen plays on the relationship between two- and three-dimensional spaces (fig. 15). The text of the poem is placed within what appears to be a hand-drawn image of a notebook. The poem itself appears on the left side of the notebook; the rest of the space is taken up by drawings of apartment buildings. The windows and doors of these buildings each launch additional computer windows with images, video, and audio clips that help to describe this neighborhood. On top of the level of the hand-drawn notebook appear other, more photographic images (gloves, a flower, a postmark), which complicate our sense of what we are looking at, since they do not obey the spatial logic of the notebook but instead appear to sit *on top of* the title bar of the work itself. In many ways, this poem can be seen as an analysis of the contradictions of the window metaphor as it is applied to the computer interface, since the whole point of the poem is to question how we "enter" this space. The windows of the apartment

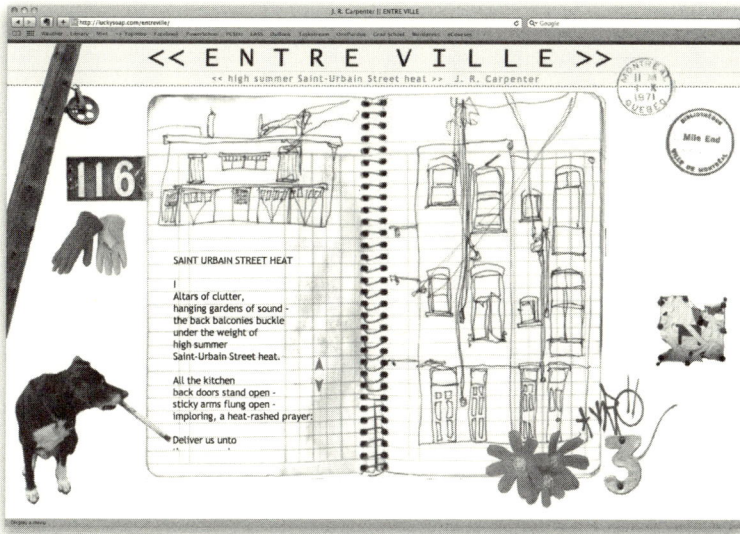

15. "Entre Ville" main window. Courtesy of J. R. Carpenter.

building allow this just as they would in the physical world, but they operate not by allowing us to see through them, but instead by performing the very distinct computer function of launching a new browser window and playing audio and video clips. This work embraces the multiplicity of media that make up the work—text, drawn image, photograph, video, sound—and emphasizes the tensions and contradictions between their understanding of space. Like Auster's media novel, Carpenter's poem embraces the tensions and limits of its constituent media.

New Media in the Print Age

My account of new media in this chapter has been fundamentally unfair. Many new media theorists have noted that it is a particular weakness of literary critics to emphasize those elements of new media that are the most similar to print narrative. Markku Eskelinen has argued recently:

> If there already is or soon will be a legitimate field for computer game studies, this field is also very open to intrusions and colonisations from the already organized scholarly tribes. Resisting and beating them is the goal of our first survival game in this paper, as

what these emerging studies need is independence, or at least relative independence.

It should be self-evident that we can't apply print narratology, hypertext theory, film or theater and drama studies directly to computer games, but it isn't. (26)

Eskelinen is a particularly strident and outspoken member of a group of critics who are often referred to as "ludologists," for whom the study of new media forms (especially computer games) must reject the tendency to treat them as versions of traditional narrative forms. And from one perspective, this is exactly right. Although storytelling games like *Tomb Raider* lead us into traditional novelistic questions about characters and bodies, it is hard to see how these problems would manifest themselves in a fundamentally abstract game like *Tetris*. Such works seem much more inherently independent of prior media than games that strive to tell stories, and it is very likely that if there is a genuinely *new* media on the horizon, it is in works like this that eschew the need to tell a story at all. These critics would bristle at the term *multimedia* that I have used so frequently in this chapter because it suggests that such electronic works are simply responding to and repackaging other forms of media, rather than developing a genuinely new form of representation.

My vision of new media is framed by an interest in print, and so I have emphasized those elements of new media that most directly promise to correct or improve limitations in traditional forms of written narrative. It seems to me that the difference between *Encarta* and *Wikipedia*, or between *Tomb Raider* and *Tetris*, is that the former are deeply connected to the goals and anxiety of print (the paper encyclopedia, the novel) while the latter represent a step toward exploiting the strengths and affordances inherent to its electronic medium. My emphasis on these more anxious and problematic transitional works is justified, I hope, by my interest in the fate of the print novel today. For all that new media may well be on its way to becoming a genuinely different kind of artistic object, at this moment in our culture it also functions as an *other* to print and especially to the novel. A new medium plays this role for critics—who often see in new media narratives challenges to our claims about the "universal" nature of certain narrative forms. And it functions this way for writers and artists as well, who often embrace the idea that a computer game can be a "version" of a movie or novel—no matter how little ludologists might like that way of defining the medium.[18] Many writers and theorists look to a new medium when they want to think about the degree to which stories could be told in different ways if they were not bound to the printed book. This is why, I think, we keep insisting on making books and films into games, and games in turn into books and films.[19] In this regard, and perhaps only for a short while, new media function as another way in which we explore writing at the media limit.

5 : Negotiating Public and Private Spaces

Contemporary media novels show us that authors are eager to understand what makes the traditional written novel distinctive among storytelling forms. Their eagerness is heightened by the lack of any consensus about what the novel *should* do today: what is its role within American public life? As I noted in chapter 3, writing, and thus the novel, is especially good at representing the absent, the potential, or the unrealized. By focusing on the absent, writers are able to discuss the community in which the story circulates. More broadly, contemporary media novels point to those elements of the story that are beyond its representational limits but which help to define its meaning, such as Reed's story about how Loop's revolutionary art is caught up in the dynamics of reception and dissemination. The novel's ability to represent the absent, potential, and unrealized allows it to gesture to what is beyond itself, and for this reason the media novel is particularly adept at discussing the media ecology. It is because the novel comes up against its limits that we see it as a bounded object hedged in by other media forms on all sides with different storytelling strengths and weaknesses. And once we recognize the novel as one choice among others, we see our participation in that form—either as an author or as a reader—as a matter of taking on a role within the larger media ecology. This is the most striking benefit of describing the relation between novels and other forms of storytelling as a media ecology: we see each as engaged in a series of interlocking actions. This is the way that Matthew Fuller, also quoted in the introduction, describes ecologies:"'Media ecology,' or more often 'information ecology,' is deployed as a euphemism for the allocation of informational roles in organizations and in computer-supported collaborative work" (3). It is for this reason that a focus on media *limits* dovetails with an interest in the media *ecology*: an interest in the boundaries of media forms is also an interest in the social connections between those forms. Writing's facility at addressing the absent, potential, or unrealized is especially important to the media novel, since it allows these writers more easily to address conditions that transcend an individual text. A good example of this is Susan Daitch's discussion of the economic conditions in which Electra operates; the novel's ability to describe the logic of Electra's fictional world makes it easier to recognize continuities and discontinuities between comics, writing, and photography.

This shift toward an interest in media limits helps to illuminate some of the paradoxes in debates about the place of the novel in contemporary culture. Despite its place within the very public contemporary media ecology, the novel is imagined as the most intimate of mass media forms. Unlike the communal space of the film theater, or the simultaneity of television broadcasts, the novel offers an individual experience of narrative. But this is not entirely because of qualities inherent to the printed page. In contrast to newer technologies like blogs and webcasts, the novel is a deeply commercial product, subject to advertising, mass production, and the involvement of many people in its creation. And yet the novel retains its traditional cultural identity as a private form marked by solitary reflection. That is why there has been so much angst among critics and reviewers about the novel's place within the new media ecology, which seems to take a private matter out of the hands of individual writers and readers. Certainly we have seen the importance of the tension between the public and the private throughout this book: *Jazz* is fundamentally concerned with how gossip makes private matters into public knowledge, the characters in "Duck Tape" are worried about how a story can get you sued, and the private sex lives of characters in "Ardor/Awe/Atrocity" are shaped by the production and distribution networks of Southern California. In this regard, the televisions that are members of the household in *Vineland* and *White Noise* are exemplary: they are emblems of the intrusion of the public into the domestic space of the home. Although chapter 3 was organized by formal terms (like plot, character, and setting), underlying the formal innovations of the contemporary novel is an embrace of the novel's place within systems of dissemination and circulation. The contemporary novel transforms the relationship between the private space of reading and the public object to be bought and sold, and in doing so claims a place within the contemporary media ecology.

There is, of course, a long tradition of connecting the origins of the novel to the rise of individualism, private property, and domestic space.

From Ian Watt's landmark *The Rise of the Novel* through more recent work like Michael McKeon's *The Origins of the English Novel, 1600–1740*, privacy is a fundamental reference point for the novel. Even histories that emphasize the social function of the novel, like John Bender's *Imagining the Penitentiary* or Nancy Armstrong's discussion of gender and contract law in *Desire and Domestic Fiction*, are framed by the way that novels deploy privacy as part of their political strategy. And yet at the same time, an equally strong and apparently complementary theory sees the novel as a means of creating national identity and "imagined communities." I have in mind, of course, Benedict Anderson's claim that the novel helps to define the relations between members of a nation even though "an American will never meet, or even know the names of more than a handful of his 240,000-odd fellow-Americans" (26). Anderson gives the example of how a novel establishes these relations, by describing three events concerning four characters (A, B, C, and D); in this example, A and D never meet:

> What then actually links A to D? Two complementary conceptions: First, that they are embedded in "societies" (Wessex, Lübeck, Los Angeles). These societies are sociological entities of such firm and stable reality that their members (A and D) can even be described as passing each other on the street, without ever becoming acquainted, and still be connected. Second, that A and D are embedded in the minds of the omniscient readers. Only they, like God, watch A telephoning C, B shopping, and D playing pool all *at once*. That all these acts are performed at the same clocked, calendrical time, but by actors who may be largely unaware of one another, shows the novelty of this imagined world conjured up by the author in his reader's minds. (25–26)

As this passage shows, Anderson sees the characters of a novel, like the members of a nation, linked by an imagined totality that is organized by calendar time, which makes possible a "conception of simultaneity" (24). The better example of this simultaneity is the daily newspaper, which includes an extremely heterogeneous mixture of material on any particular page: "What connects them to each other? Not sheer caprice. Yet obviously most of them happen independently, without the actors being aware of each other or of what the others are up to. The arbitrariness of their inclusion and juxtaposition . . . shows that the linkage between them is imagined" (33). Anderson makes clear that this conception of time is a radical departure from previous ways of imagining social continuity that supported dynastic and religious society, which were based on a very different understanding of simultaneity in which time itself seems to fall away: "Such an idea of *simultaneity* is wholly alien to our own. It views time as something close to what Benjamin calls Messianic time, a simultaneity of past and future in an instantaneous present. In such a view of things, the word 'meanwhile' cannot be of real significance" (24). Such a sacred time is fundamentally different than the modern vision of moments organized by the calendar and clock. The irony here is quite straightforward: imagining the novel as a private moment is itself a way of doing cultural work, of connecting individuals within a whole "imagined community." Privacy in this sense is always a fantasy that serves a social purpose.

The contemporary media novel clearly reconfigures the centrality of privacy to traditional accounts of the novel by placing far greater emphasis on the circulation of media objects within a community. In fact, many critics have questioned whether Anderson's theory, rooted as it is in the traditional novel of the nineteenth century, applies to contemporary global culture. Arjun Appadurai argues that contemporary media create communities with no sense of place: "The revolution of print capitalism and the cultural affinities and dialogues unleashed by it were only modest precursors to the world we live in now. For in the past century, there has been a technological explosion, largely in the domain of transportation and information, that makes the interactions of a print-dominated world seem as hard-won and as easily erased as the print revolution made earlier forms of cultural traffic appear" (28–29). Appadurai particularly emphasizes the way that globalization has undermined the sense of place that is the basis for Anderson's account of the nation, and instead substituted "deterritorialization, in which money, commodities, and persons are involved in ceaselessly chasing each other around the world" (38). As a result, Appadurai offers a revision of Anderson's theory, describing "five dimensions of global cultural flows that can be termed (a) *ethnoscapes*, (b) *mediascapes*, (c) *technoscapes*, (d) *financescapes*, and (e) *ideoscapes*" (33). These different *scapes* are "deeply perspectival constructs" that organize the different landscapes that a particular agent seems to be inhabiting.

Appadurai describes how these constructs change Anderson's model: "These landscapes thus are the building blocks of what (extending Benedict Anderson) I would like to call *imagined worlds*, that is, the multiple worlds that are constituted by the historically situated imaginations of persons and groups spread around the globe" (33). This framework implies that any particular location is actually a tissue of different landscapes that connect to other places—be it in terms of ethnic identity (ethnoscapes), technological training, production, and consumption (technoscapes), global currency markets and stock exchanges (financescapes), narratives and images (mediascapes), or political ideologies and counterideologies (ideoscapes) (33–36). According to Appadurai, instead of the coherent simultaneity that Anderson describes, the imagined worlds of globalization are marked by disjunction between these different "dimensions of cultural flows" and thus are "chimerical" (35).

Appadurai's central insight is that our participation within these flows means that we are always to different degrees and in different ways connected to the public world, and this has profound implications for how we understand the embrace of limits in the contemporary media novel. Appadurai notes that the specific, local sites that we often assume to be the bedrock of our social interaction are in fact very much produced rather than natural: "locality is an inherently fragile social achievement. Even in the most intimate, spatially confined, geographically isolated situations, locality must be maintained carefully against various kinds of odds" (179). In the contemporary, globalized environment these odds are quite high indeed: "It is in the fertile ground of deterritorialization, in which money, commodities, and persons are involved in ceaselessly chasing each other around the world, that the mediascapes and ideoscapes of the modern world find their fractured and fragmented counterpart" (38). Claiming that you simply *are* somewhere specific and precise—and thus, that there is a private space that you can then synchronize with the public world—is a way of ignoring all these global flows and complex involvements. Rather than assuming a tension between the private self and public rituals, Appadurai describes a world in which privacy itself is merely an effect of different forms of public involvement, a space of conflict between multiple *scapes*.

In this chapter, I will apply this theory to the media novel, which occupies a profoundly conflicted role within contemporary culture, since it strives to reconcile individual to social identity at a time when the nature of that identity is marked by fissures and deterritorialization. At such a moment it might be surprising to find so many writers and critics embracing a very traditional image of the novel as a bastion of privacy. A number of recent works directed to the general reader, like Alberto Manguel's *A History of Reading*, offer a history and analysis of the book while at the same time appealing to readers' nostalgic experience of coming to love reading as a child.[1] An even more explicit example is Sven Birkerts's *The Gutenberg Elegies*, which tries to reclaim the traditional purpose and privacy of reading: "For while it can be many things, serious reading is above all an agency of self-making. When undertaken freely, the effort of engaging a book shows a desire to actualize and augment certain inner powers. The reader assumes the possibility of deepened self-understanding, and therefore recognizes the self as malleable. Reading is the intimate, perhaps secret, part of a larger project, one that finally has little to do with the more societally oriented conceptions of the individual." (87) Birkerts's celebration of the "privacies of reading" is in many ways an exaggeration of the tradition linking the novel and individualism, since he sees little of the "extraordinary mass ceremony" that Anderson associates with the consumption of the novel, and instead emphasizes the intimate and personal. And yet, even such a conservative "elegy" still depends on some of the same dynamics that we can see in Appadurai. In particular, Birkerts emphasizes the physical book, which is surely part of Appadurai's technoscape. Turning to hypertext late in the book, Birkerts explains that he does not like encountering the text on the screen: "I was made so fidgety by the knowledge that I was positioned in a designed environment, with the freedom to rocket from one place to another with a keystroke, that I could scarcely hold still long enough to read what was there in front of me" (161). Birkerts admits that his way of thinking about the privacy of reading initially makes him discount the material shape of the word as he encounters it: "The shape of a word—its physical look—is only its outer garb. The impulse, the pulse of its meaning is the same whether that word is incised in marble, scratched into mud, inscribed onto papyrus, printed onto a page, or flickered forth on a screen" (155). But upon further reflection, Birkerts concludes, "The same word, when it appears on the screen, must be received with a sense of its weightlessness—the weightlessness of its presentation. The same sign, but not the same" (155). It is hard to imagine a better articulation of the way that the production of the physical reading object through a far-flung, global publishing industry shapes our experience of privacy.

Although Birkerts's elegy for the book is to some extent a simple response to the changing media environment, a conservative attempt to keep the novel in a space of privacy that it never really occupied without doing many other things at the same time, his articulation of this changing media environment repeats many of the same terms that Anderson and Appadurai use. All three locate the novel as the material site where cultural and technical changes can be studied. Like those other critics, Birkerts returns to the physical object of the book whose materiality runs against the "shadow life of reading" that he otherwise describes. Appadurai would characterize this as the intervention of the *mediascape* and would claim that it pulls us out of any simple location and subjects us to global flows that draw us into other relationships. If Birkerts wants to retain a belief in the privacy of reading, he does so only after admitting just the same structure of circulation of physical objects within the nation that we have seen throughout this study. In this final chapter, we need to recognize the importance of this paradox: our attempts to conceive of reading today negotiate this line between the public and the private, and in doing so create curious links through the physical book between those who embrace changes in media and those who seem to be resisting them. In the end, this emphasis on the physical book is part of an attempt to place the novel into our contemporary media ecology by defining how a public object takes on its meaning within our private lives. The contemporary media novel is at its most powerful, we will see, when it emphasizes these "middle spaces" between our private time of reading and the vast media networks to which we are inevitably connected.

Synchronized Time and Its Others

We begin our discussion of national identity and private reading with Sherman Alexie's *Reservation Blues*. Just as Reed's novel did for the issue of experience (see chapter 2), Alexie's story critiques the idea of a unitary imagined community upon which our ways of thinking about the novel are based. As a story concerned with the packaging of Native American identity for a broader U.S. market, Alexie's novel engages with the traditional, synchronizing function of the newspaper while at the same time raising questions about these representations—and introducing what Appadurai would call the flows of deterritorialization. Because the story begins in the very localized community of the reservation, and ends with its main characters leaving to make their way into the larger U.S. culture, Alexie's novel literally marks the tension between local and national identity. And as a novel about music, Alexie helps us to see that the way each medium negotiates the line between public and private defines its place in the media ecology.

Alexie's central character, Thomas-Builds-the-Fire, is given a guitar that has been made magical (and in some ways also cursed) by legendary blues musician Robert Johnson, who has wandered to the edge of the Spokane Indian reservation where Thomas lives. Thomas is described as a natural storyteller, but this gift has no place within the reservation community. In fact, as soon as he acquires the guitar, Thomas meets up with a couple of reservation trouble makers, Victor Joseph and Junior Polatkin, who threaten and tease him about his storytelling before settling on a bet: if he can play Victor's favorite Patsy Cline song, they will let him go, but "if you can't play the song, then you have to stop telling all your fucking stories" (15). Thomas's gift for storytelling is mocked and ignored, and it is only through music that he has any chance of expressing it. After this initial meeting, the magical guitar speaks to Thomas and convinces him to form a band (Coyote Springs) with Victor and Junior as guitarist and drummer: "Y'all need to play songs for your people. They need you. Those two boys need you" (23). Thomas gives up the guitar to become the band's lead singer and main songwriter.

From here the novel describes the early (hostile) audience reaction to the band, which gradually earns the distain of the tribe as a whole. An "open letter" about the band in a local newspaper summarizes the popular response: "Coyote Springs travels to a lot of places as a representative of the Spokane Tribe. Do we really want people to think we are like this band? Do we really want people to think that the Spokanes are a crazy storyteller, a couple of irresponsible drunks, a pair of Flathead Indians, and two white women? I don't think so" (175–76). This passage summarizes the problems that the band encounters in trying to be an "Indian" band. Initially a source of pride for the community, the band almost immediately encounters problems with its composition, that is, what is necessary for it to be authentic. The novel eventually builds toward an invitation by a major music label for the band to come to New York to record an album, but this opportunity is lost when the magical guitar refuses to cooperate during the recording session. Eventually the two white women are signed by the label as a kind of faux Indian band, replacing the apparent messy authenticity of Coyote Springs with a mass-marketed idea of Indianness for the general American public: "Can't you see the possibilities? We dress them up a little. Get them into the tanning booth. Darken them up a bit. Maybe a little plastic surgery on those cheekbones. Get them a little higher, you know? Dye their hair black. Then we'd have Indians. People want to hear Indians" (269). Coyote Springs disintegrates after their failed trip to New York: Junior commits suicide, Victor takes a responsible job on the reservation, and Thomas leaves the reservation.

It is clear that Alexie is interested in the distinction between national and local cultures, but at every turn he complicates any sense that the local is more authentic or should be isolated from larger communities. In this regard, he seems to agree with Appadurai that the self is caught between a variety of *scapes* that connect us to other people and institutions. This is especially clear in his handling of the newspaper, which represents not the national identity Anderson sees but distinctly local responses to the band. Alexie intersperses clippings from newspapers throughout his novel, usually in order to provide summary and transition from one section of the novel to the next. For example, after the band's first gig, at the Tipi Pole Tavern on the Flathead reservation, Alexie includes a review from the *Western Montana Alternative Bi-Weekly* that blasts them as drunk and talentless (59). When the band returns to the Spokane reservation, Alexie uses another newspaper clipping as a way to summarize community opinion about the band (censored to "They think they're hot [manure]") as well as to remind us of the rather narrow world in which they move: "They was going the speed limit" (83). In some ways these clippings simply do the same thing as Thomas's initial encounter with Victor and Junior: remind us how hostile the community is to Thomas's goals as a storyteller, which seem to articulate these lives in a more general context. But if the local community is conflicted and confused about its identity, the broader U.S. national context beyond the reservation is no better. As the focus moves to the national stage, Alexie is quite conscious that he is working against misinformation and stereotypes that readers will bring to his Spokane characters. Late in the novel, the band meets a man in the airport named Dakota who is part Cherokee; when they point out to him that Dakota and Cherokee are two very different tribes, he is confused—they're both Indian names, after all (259). Even band members are influenced by clichés about Native American identity. At the very outset of the novel we are told, "Junior always expected his visions to come true. Indians were *supposed* to have visions and receive messages from their dreams. All the Indians on television had visions that told them exactly what to do" (18). Another Spokane learning to play music insists on thinking about himself as "a warrior. I'm 'posed to fight" (208); "No, Michael," is the response, "you're a saxophone player and you need to work on your reed technique" (208). Throughout the novel, then, Alexie struggles to define the appropriate "imagined community" and finds neither the local nor the national perspective adequate.

Music, however, intervenes to supplement these choices and to insist that culture is actually a tissue of many communities. Alexie locates his band first and foremost in relation to American popular music—embodied in Robert Johnson—rather than to some distinctly Spokane or generally Native American musical tradition. As a narrative device, Johnson sutures Alexie's novel to American culture in general. When Thomas unveils his new guitar first to Victor and Junior, and then to the reservation community, he comes as a representative of a larger American culture as well as an expression of what seems to be a native storytelling tradition. In this regard, Alexie walks a very narrow line in his characterization of Thomas as a storyteller. On the one hand, Thomas represents an antidote to the provincialism embodied by the newspapers in the novel, which cannot transcend the most specific and local biases of the community. On the other hand, it is important that Thomas is not simply a representative of American mass media come to enlighten a backward Native population. This is why, I think, Alexie takes the initially strange step of having Thomas pass on the guitar to Victor so that he can concentrate on songwriting. If Thomas remained the guitar player, his song would come from a tradition outside the reservation; like Robert Johnson, the guitar must be passed to a secondary character in a supporting role so that Thomas's own storytelling skills, which we understand to be more organically connected to his Spokane life, can take center stage.

Alexie's careful handling of the relationship between Native American and general U.S. culture is especially evident in his creation of a mythical figure called Big Mom, who councils Robert Johnson and also helps to prepare the band for its big chance in New York. Big Mom is apparently natively Spokane even though many members of the tribe refuse to believe in her: "There were a million stories about Big Mom. But no matter how many stories were told, some Indians still refused to believe in her. Even though she lived on the reservation, some Spokanes still doubted her" (199). Alexie goes on to link Big Mom to the whole tradition of rock and roll: "Big Mom was a musical genius. She was the teacher of all those great musicians who shaped the twentieth century. There were photographs, they said, of Les Paul leaving Big Mom's house with the original blueprint for the electric guitar. There were home movies they said, of Big Mom choreographing the Andrews Sisters' latest dance steps. There were even cheap recordings, they said, of Big Mom teaching Paul McCartney how to sing 'Yesterday.'" (201). Big Mom puts the band's struggles to improve into the context of rock-and-roll history. As a narrative choice, creating the mythical Big Mom also negotiates the relation between Spokane and broader U.S. popular culture by suggesting a common but unrecognized source. She provides a context for cultural identity that is neither the provincial one encountered in the local newspaper nor the general national identity provided by television and record labels.

For both audiences, the Big Mom story offers an alternative to the synchronized time that Anderson associates with the novel. Instead, the time represented in this element of the novel seems to return to a pre-novelistic, pre-national sacred time. Big Mom solves the problem of discovering the commonality between apparently unlike events (which simply happen to have occurred on the same day) by claiming an underlying history. Indeed, Big Mom is defined by her ability to know things that others do not; if she has any "magical" powers at all, they come from understanding a wide history and being able to embody that history in a way that others can grasp. Shortly after being introduced to the band, Big Mom demonstrates what she has to teach by playing "the loneliest chord that the band had ever heard. It drifted out of her bedroom, floated across the room, and landed at the feet of Coyote Springs. It crawled up their clothes and into their ears" (206). This chord summarizes Native American history, played on "a guitar made from a 1965 Malibu and the blood of a child killed at Wounded Knee in 1890" (206) and "created especially for us" (207). Big Mom is thus magical only in the sense that she is able to recognize and articulate those elements of history and shared experience that others cannot. In this, she embodies Alexie's understanding of the blues. At the very outset of the novel the guitar tells Thomas that "the blues always make us remember" (22), and later Alexie is even more direct in describing how the audience refuses to accept the lesson of the blues: "Then the music stopped. The reservation exhaled. Those blues created memories for the Spokanes, but they refused to claim them. Those blues lit up a new road, but the Spokanes pulled out their old maps. Those blues churned up generations of anger and pain: car wrecks, suicides, murders. Those blues were ancient, aboriginal, indigenous" (174). Big Mom represents the attempt to articulate the feelings that result from that history, and embodying these in a mythical and trans-historical figure explains the need to escape narrow and mundane concerns.

What seems especially important in the context of contemporary negotiations of the public and the private is that Thomas's struggles are not between a private self and a public world but between multiple forms of public time: the modern synchronized time of the newspaper and the mythical time embodied in music. Where the newspaper emphasizes the smallest elements of identities, like the line between Flathead and Spokane, music emphasizes commonality, the links between Native American suffering and the blues in general. We can say that *Reservation Blues* as a whole is constructed in the space made possible between the newspaper and the song, between the narrow distinctions and boundaries that the community depends on and the broader historical sweep that gives those lives meaning. Alexie is careful to suggest that neither definition of his characters is accurate by itself. Narrow definitions of "Indian" identity are frequently hateful and usually debilitating, but Alexie clearly does not want to lose a sense of historical particularity; some chords are natural for Native Americans, he suggests, and it is always important to be able to distinguish a Dakota from a Cherokee. In a broad sense, we can say that these different media offer different ways of being engaged in public identities. This seems to me to be a fundamentally different way of framing individual stories than the account of isolated individuals (A, B, C) that Anderson describes. This focus on the conflict between times suggests that Alexie is implicitly aware of Appadurai's suggestion that we are caught within many different *scapes* and are subjected to different flows, rather than being defined by the comparatively simpler dynamic between a private and a public self that Anderson describes. In this novel, there is no moment when the characters are simply private and disconnected from the world; likewise, there are many different ways of being involved in the world.

Although Alexie's binding together of two different times through music seems quirky, this critique of unitary community is repeated in other novels concerned with media. Consider Gayle Jones's *Corregidora*, which also tells the story of a blues singer, Ursa Corregidora, who is struggling to come to terms with the history of her family under slavery. Ursa's grandmother and great-grandmother were owned by the particularly brutal "Old man Corregidora, the Portuguese slave breeder and whoremonger. (Is that what they call them?) He fucked his own whores and fathered his own breed. They did the fucking and had to bring him the money they made" (8–9). Ursa's family history is defined by shame and outrage, but this history is complicated because Old man Corregidora erases all records of his crimes: "My grandmother was his daughter, but he was fucking her too. She said when they did away with slavery down there they burned all the slavery papers so it would be like they never had it" (9). These experiences of shame and exploitation are carried on in stories told from one generation to the next; another character explains, "You know, they be some things that pass down. But they didn't just sit me down and talk about it. But they be stories" (77–78). Jones describes a world in which her characters are unable to synchronize the elements of their present and past precisely because some of those elements have been erased and thus rendered invisible to traditional novelistic representation. They are instead carried on unconsciously by the characters.[2] The paradox of the novel, then, is that memory is both a blessing and a curse, both a desire to testify to the cruelty of slavery and at the same time a pattern from which the characters struggle to extricate themselves: "*They burned all the documents, Ursa, but they didn't burn what they put in their minds. We got to burn out what they put in our minds, like you burn out a wound. Except we got to keep what we need to bear witness. That scar that's left to bear witness. We got to keep it as visible as our blood*" (72).

As Alexie does in *Reservation Blues*, Jones uses music to embody this other time that runs counter to the synchronicity of official documents. Music helps Ursa "explain what I can't explain" (56). A few pages later, Jones links blues singing with Ursa's more general corporeal movements through the novel:

"Yes, if you understood me, Mama, you'd see I was trying to explain it, in blues, without words, the explanation somewhere behind the words. To explain what will always be there. Soot crying out of my eyes." O Mister who come to my house You do not come to visit You do not come to see me to visit You come to hear me sing with my thighs You come to see me open my door and sing with my thighs. Perhaps you watch me when I am sleeping I don't know if you watch me when I am sleeping Who are you? I am the daughter of the daughter of the daughter of Ursa of currents, steel wool and electric wire for hair. (66–67)

This passage moves between the literal singing of the blues and a broader way of moving through her life, in which she "sing[s] with [her] thighs." It is clear here that Jones is aspiring to make her novel like the blues that Ursa sings. At the same time, however, Jones does not want to allow Ursa to disappear entirely into the collective memory that she articulates, just as Thomas's discovery of Big Mom does not simply dissolve his storytelling problems. In fact, the starting point for Jones's novel is a brutal attack that results in Ursa's hysterectomy, something that is especially important in the novel because memory has been associated with carrying on a legacy by producing "generations." Although procreation is "a slave-breeder's way of thinking," it is also a way of passing along the story: *The important thing is making generations. They can burn the papers but they can't burn conscious, Ursa*" (22). In this sense, Ursa is ripped from this ambiguous tradition against her will and isolated from the ability to carry on this form of testimony. Her blues singing naturally compensates for the loss, and we can see Ursa's struggles to articulate her experience as a response to her inability to carry on her past in the more direct, biological way of previous generations. Like Thomas, Ursa is separated from any tradition that would articulate the past, and thus she is forced to move between several ways of defining her identity.

Technoscapes and Circulating Books

Both *Reservation Blues* and *Corregidora* describe contemporary life not as an opposition between privacy and the public world but instead as a matter of moving between communities in a variety of ways. Thus, both critique the idea of a simple and stable imagined community. In fact, in neither of these novels is there a clear description of a private identity that is discovered or exposed over the course of the story. In this regard, these two novels can be seen as an indirect response to the fetishized privacy that Birkerts associates with the novel. It is helpful to recall a point that Appadurai makes: that our awareness of the deterritorialization of the national space emerges when other *scapes* intervene into the novel.[3] In thinking about community identity, both authors turn from the novel to music to provide a fresh perspective on the layered ways that characters are connected to the larger world. What seems especially important for thinking about the use of media in the contemporary novel is that these other *scapes* become visible when the *technical* and material conditions of the medium exert their influence.

Another novel that seems to show how such technical media issues can be used to transform the public role of the novel is Abraham Rodriguez's *The Buddha Book*. It tells the story of two Puerto Rican boys, Jose and Dinky, growing up in a poor section of New York City; with little hope for the future, they seem destined to a life of petty crime and drug dealing. Their time is spent resisting the lives of their parents, pursuing girls, and drawing an underground comic book distributed within their high school called *The Buddha Book*. Drawing this comic book raises practical problems for the two boys, since the self-important principal of Luis Muñoz Marín High School seems more concerned about how such a comic book makes the school and the community look than about truth, creativity, or even education. At the end of the novel, as they prepare what seems likely to be the final (fourth) issue of the comic book, they must keep the identity of the artists secret and hide all traces of their work to avoid being punished. Since the boys insist on drawing only actual events, the comic book also raises theoretical questions about the role of art within the community. This becomes especially important because *The Buddha Book* is framed by a murder that takes place at the very beginning of the novel. Jose's ex-girlfriend, Lucy, has taken up with a drug dealer named Angel, and Jose has gone to her apartment to confront her and kill Angel. Immediately, however, Jose gets into a fight with Lucy and (as the opening line of the novel explains), "The fight led them to the bathroom" where Lucy drowns in the tub, held down by Jose: "Jose couldn't say how it happened. All of a sudden Lucy was under the splash frantic rocking. He had been thinking about how it all had to end somewhere and here it was, no way out. Even mouthed the words as Lucy's moves went slow motion and bubbles streamed past her lips. Then, the sudden sinking down of everything. The eyes straight up, forever" (1). The remainder of the novel is spent in the shadow of this event. Jose is clearly guilty of murder, although he had not planned her death. Lucy continues to haunt Jose, popping up in dialogue with him at unlikely times; in fact, the fight between them seems typical of their relationship as a whole, which is marked by a cruel sexual teasing. And once Lucy is dead, her visits seem to Jose a continuation of his life with her: "*I'm talking to a ghost*, he thought. Couldn't take his eyes off of her. Alive or dead. Nothing had changed. She would always have the power to walk into every room every space and make him feel she was out of reach. The feeling that she was escaping him" (147). Jose's guilt is complex, then, since in part it is simply a way of continuing his relationship with her.

Events conspire to hide Jose's crime. As a high-profile drug dealer in the area, Angel has natural enemies who are much more likely to have murdered Lucy. Angel himself is unlikely to go to the police, nor does he want it known that rivals have (apparently) been able to murder his girlfriend. Despite his obsession with Lucy and Angel, Jose has the reputation for being a relatively clean-cut and serious student, and it is not until the very end of the novel when Lucy's death is announced at the school that even his friends accept the fact that he really did kill her. Even the authorities are relatively uninterested in solving the crime. Murders in this poor area of New York City are common, and are taken much less seriously than in areas like Manhattan; as another character remarks, "I can pop three guys in Manhattan, an' get headlines, did you see? . . . But lemme pop two dudes in the Bronx on the same day an' look, not even an inch of copy!" (144). Reyes, the school's principal, wants to keep scandal away from the school: "This student hadn't been coming to classes for quite a while. We pulled her records and, as far as I can see, this doesn't involve the school at all" (230). Among those who are uninterested in Lucy's death is Jose's stepfather, who is up for the job of assistant principal at the school and wants to avoid any scandal associated with himself and his family. For everyone involved, then, Lucy's death seems to be best ignored.

Working against the forces that try to hide Lucy's death is the comic book that Jose and Dinky draw. After doing earlier issues that involved fantasy scenes and rumors circulating within the school, the two boys promised to include only real events in this next issue: "They had already made that pact, that from now on everything in the comic would be real. No fake names, no rumor or fantasies" (48). Confronted by the realization of what he has done, Jose immediately represents the murder in the comic book: "Because last night, no sleep. The hot angry toss and turn. The instant replay. The way her words still burned. He kept taking it back. Chanting into the wet pillow. Falling in and out of vivid Lucy dreams until he woke for good. He started to draw." Soon he had twelve pages and "couldn't stop the story" (29). As the novel moves toward its conclusion, Jose understands that printing this edition of the comic book is essentially a confession, and one designed to break from the way that Lucy's death would normally be suppressed and written off as part of the gang culture in which they live. In response to the suggestion that "you can get away with it," Jose agrees but also claims, "My story begins when I get caught" (250–51). The decision to admit to the crime runs counter to all the conventional ways of thinking about the neighborhood and the cheapness of life among these kids. In fact, the previous edition of the *Buddha Book* told the story of Dinky's relationship with his brothers, and how they are pulled into dealing drugs: "The very last panel of the story showed Dinky yelling, 'What are we supposed to do?' Because, who's got a choice?" (63). Throughout the novel Jose and Dinky feel like they are trapped; asked by his mother what he wants, Dinky replies, "I want *out*" (182).

The issue of publicity and the representation of the community is sharpened by the story of Jose's stepsister Anita, who aspires to become "the first Puerto Rican female serial killer" (142). She kills for the first time to escape from domestic abuse but discovers that she enjoys the feeling of control and power. Over the course of the novel she continues to add to her murder total, hoping to set a new record: "America's number-one female serial killer is Aileen Wuornos. Seven confirmed kills" (142). She leaves clues with each of her victims and closely watches the news coverage of her crimes, "because like any star she had to check the reviews" (143). Anita's story parallels Jose's in that she, too, is fighting against preconceptions, since the news coverage assumes that the murderer will be male: "If a woman shoots a guy, it must be some accident. It's a man's profession. Guys at the posse house never believed me when I told them I planned my kill down to the last breath. They laugh" (140). In fact, Anita ends up fighting against exactly the same disinterest from the community and media about deaths in her neighborhood that Jose faces. Despite the clues that she keeps leaving behind, she decides in the end "I can't keep waiting for them to find me. . . . I'll get old" (295), and she joins Dinky in the last scene of the novel in walking into the police station to turn herself in.

Rodriguez's decision to turn to the comic book in many ways repeats a pattern we have seen throughout this study, that of using another medium to comment on the power and limitations of the novel. Rodriguez is more interested than Alexie and Jones are in the technical qualities of the medium, and he makes clear how the use of another medium within the novel draws our attention to Appadurai's technoscape. In fact, the comic book has some unique features that function as a useful foil to the novel that Rodriguez himself is writing. First, it is underground and subject to reproduction using very simple means. Jose and Dinky sneak into the school after hours using the key and alarm codes stolen from Jose's stepfather, and so are able to use the photocopiers to produce the very comic books that the school administration views as such a scourge. Second, the comic book itself clearly represents a popular and illegitimate form of storytelling. Principal Reyes articulates this bias against forms of writing that don't strive toward conventional literary qualities when he punishes a student who writes a sexually graphic story when assigned the topic of "a spring affair." In response to the complaint that "that stuff is true!" Reyes responds: "True doesn't make it art. This is a Puerto Rican school, no matter how many black kids the school board sends us! We tend to feel differently about such things. We are a highly moral people. We believe writing should edify the community. Otherwise, why read it? Don't the Americans think badly enough of us as it is? Why make us look worse? What's the purpose? I'm not trying to discourage you. But you should think of Gabriel Garcia Marquez when you write. Ask yourself: Would *he* write something like this?" (132). It is clear that Jose and Dinky's comic book takes this commitment to truth even further. Third, the comic book can be consumed nearly instantly. This means that distributing *Buddha Book 4* at the end of the novel produces an instant reaction that is closer to television or film. The publication of the comic book is a fundamentally *public* event: it is written about a shared reality referencing people the audience knows directly or indirectly; its reproduction depends on the appropriation of public facilities in the school, where it is stored until distributed on "splash" day; and it is consumed in public spaces, passed hand-to-hand and discussed immediately. Previously we saw the importance of time in thinking about national culture, but Rodriguez reminds us that the time of reading is also a reflection of the technical qualities of the medium. The novel takes a certain time to read, which is an inherent part of the ritual nature of novelistic consumption. This issue of reading time draws our attention back to the physical artifact, the technical substrate of the novelistic experience.

These technical qualities help the comic book to solve the problem of how individuals can place themselves within the American public sphere, a problem that especially troubles Anita. Of course, her aspiration to be a serial killer depends fundamentally on being recognized and having her discrete crimes linked together: "I wanna make this whole city, this whole country know who I am" (141). In particular, Anita is concerned about the way that she will enter into the American imagination: "Reading books on Amy Fisher, Carolyn Warmus, and Jennifer Reali dissuaded her. Killing in order to get the man just didn't work for females, though there were three Amy Fisher movies, and even Pamela Smart got played by Helen Hunt. Did you have to be white to get so much attention?" (168). Anita begins planning her crimes in terms of how they will get folded into America's way of thinking about murder and murderers: "She was thinking B-movies and Americana. Being a stripper was the perfect vocation for a female serial killer. Not only was it perfect for bagging victims, but it would make a movie deal more likely. (Being Puerto Rican was a hard sell—she was looking to add as many ready-made elements as possible)" (169). Anita understands that to be recognized as a serial killer at all, she needs to add the "elements" that will make her fit into the stories that the public has about her. The media that she focuses on are television and newspapers, and it seems clear that a large part of her difficulty in placing herself within American culture reflects the biases built into these media.

It is for this reason that her appearance in the *Buddha Book 4* is such a surprise and pleasure for her. Dinky becomes involved in a dangerous sexual relationship with Anita, and he adds her story to Jose's Lucy murder narrative to make up the issue. When she reads it, she is thrilled: "This is my story. . . . Dinky, do you see what you've done? You've immortalized me. It's like I can never die now. I've been in a comic book." She goes on to explain further how she sees the comic book helping her to fit into the American public imagination: "I can't believe how you did this. You really did something big for me. Imagine it, Dink. . . . After I get caught, I'm makin all the papers. People get wind there's a comic book. Some little guy goes an' finds a copy an' prints it up. Before you know it, it's on TV it's in magazines it's runnin around like an underground cult classic. I man, thass the joint. Thass Americana. Thass just what I want. To live forever" (248). Anita does not imagine that she will become famous *through* the comic book. Instead, the comic book works to negotiate the relationship between mass media and local culture, a way of filling out her story after she is caught and in "all the papers." This is what she means by referring to it as an underground cult classic. Such a classic bears the marks of having a very local origin—written at a certain time and read by people familiar with the story—but can be taken up and given new meaning by the national culture at large and become "Americana." In this sense, the comic book fundamentally reconfigures the relationship between the public and the private, which for her has been locked in a traditional opposition between the hidden personal actions and national exposure. Anita's comic-book story is not so much an articulation of her private acts but is instead an object that circulates within American culture, "Americana." It is the overlapping spaces of these different media that provide Anita with the feeling that the story of her life has finally been told. In this sense, Rodriguez ends with the mixture of heterogeneous spaces that we saw in *Reservation Blues*.

The way this object circulates (the speed of its consumption, specifically) draws attention back to the technical qualities of both media and reminds us of the limits of the novel, in particular of the time that traditional reading takes. Neither Alexie nor Jones emphasize these sorts of technical concerns in their use of music—instead, they are more interested in using music to embody a different understanding of community—but it is easy to see how these material issues shape the relationship between individual and larger national identities. What makes Rodriguez able to connect public and private life is finally a technical form that organizes the time of dissemination and consumption. In retrospect, we can see that the temporary gap between performance and reportage helped to create the community problems with which Alexie's characters struggle, since newspaper and music organized these retrospective times differently.

Rodriguez reminds us that these problems arise from the nature of the medium—comics, writing, music—and that the physical act of reading organizes our feelings of privacy and public space, and connects us to the different *scapes* in which we participate. The embrace of media limits becomes our way of being linked to the heterogeneous spaces that make up the media ecology.

Middle Spaces

The Buddha Book weaves together many of the uses to which media are put in the contemporary novel. Not only does it circulate books in order to raise questions about the use of narrative, but it does so in a way that paints a subtle portrait of our precarious place amid different sorts of public narratives and private spaces. What does it mean to read today, then, caught as we are between media and within these complex spaces? Many different authors have offered visions of reading—from Wittman's public performances in *Tripmaster Monkey* to Leigh-Cheri's extremely private dreaming over the Camel cigarette package in *Still Life with Woodpecker*. Again and again we have seen that the original, private story is less important to contemporary authors than the way it circulates in a community, and Rodriguez makes clear that ultimately these forms of circulation are made possible by the physical medium and its technical qualities. Indeed, throughout this book we have encountered stories about the threshold between private and public spaces. We might think of how DeLillo and Coover used television to embody those other spaces to which we are drawn, or Reed's description of a technological paradise that is "as far as you can see from where you're standing now" (170). To conclude this chapter, we will look at two novels that offer visions of what it means to read today—both as a corrective to the attempt to return to the past, and to show that reading in the new media ecology transforms the very traditional link between reading novels and flights of imagination.

Marianne Hauser's *The Talking Room* is a somewhat difficult and ambiguous novel narrated by a young girl of thirteen who is known simply as B. She is apparently the child of a lesbian couple, J and V. The drunk, restless, and unreliable J is her biological mother, who becomes pregnant at the insistence of the controlling V through anonymous sex at a local bar. After B's apparent birth, J continues to come and go from the household, drinking heavily and resisting V's attempt to tie her to the traditional domestic life that she imagines. Even this level of basic plot information may overstate the facts of the story, however, since B spends a great deal of time (especially early in the novel) discussing the ways that J has *failed* to get pregnant: "My nursery walls were in a blue swoon, waiting for me to arrive. But I never came" (5). B's interaction with J and V remains relatively indirect, and we are left to wonder through much of the novel whether B herself is merely a hypothetical child that is never really conceived. Indeed, the novel opens in this way:

> Again I can hear their voices coming nonstop from the talking room downstairs. I hear them through the rumble of the trucks in the night rain as I lie on my back between moist sheets, listening. And I know they are talking about me. But they call me an idea.
>   B? She was your idea and don't you deny it. (1)

B's narration mostly touches on J and V's life indirectly, although later B does seem to be a concrete part of the household—as for example when V urges her to lose weight (64) or when she is shunted off onto a family friend, D, who takes her to the zoo (104). Even here, elements of the story may be entirely in B's imagination—her belief that she is pregnant (96), that D has an S and M fetish (48), or that her long-lost mother slips back into her bedroom in the middle of the night to sleep on her floor (155). Overall, it is very difficult to draw a firm line between concrete events and those that are merely possible or imagined. As the title suggests, B emerges as the product of talking, a kind of self dependent on things said in the "talking room" below. Here is a very peculiar sort of privacy, dependent on outside information despite routine isolation.

The transistor radio that B listens to late at night is central to this quality of the novel. Specifically, the radio represents an unreliable source of information for B, and is usually associated with overhearing conversations. At the beginning of the novel B narrates, "The voices in the talking room go dead. I've smothered them with my pillow, and maybe I invented them in any case. How would I know?" (2). Later on, D challenges B about her belief that he has a "collection of bullwhips and cages" (48), asking her, "Where on earth did you hear that story!" (49). B explains: "I hug myself under his coat and say that I have heard it through a wall, though maybe I only dreamed it" (49). These possibly overheard, possibly imagined conversations largely define the style of the novel. B's transistor radio supplements the voices overheard in her own house, and it projects them onto a larger world. B's radio listening is composed primarily of news, advertisements, and talk shows. In particular, the sort of news that fills B's radio is mostly concerned with defining broad cultural trends rather than reporting hard political news: "Nine point nine of the national gross, my transistor says under the pillow. THE BABY BUST IS ON & THOUGH BIRTH STILL OUTNUMBERS DEATH TWO TO ONE THE TEENAGE INDUSTRY IS SERIOUSLY CONSIDERING A SWITCH TO SENIOR CITIZEN NECESSITIES" (47). Such reports encourage B to see herself in the news. So it should be no surprise when she comes across graffiti directly addressed to her: "B IS A TEST TUBE BABY, I read on the smeared wall of the women's toilet in Wash Sq. Park" (9). Such graffiti is like the radio broadcasts that B listens to, since they seem to make claims in the general public sphere that nonetheless apply to her very specifically. Hauser's image of B positioned by these public statements is an exaggeration of the kind of synchronization between private and public life that Anderson associates with the novel.

Although some novels do not distinguish between various forms of sound transmission, there is a fundamental difference between the radio and the record player in *The Talking Room*. Indeed, one of the sweetest images in the novel is that of V and J dancing at the very end, "their bodies melted together, their eyes shut," but this music is provided by a record player and not by the radio: "BONNE NUIT CHERIE. The needle has made it over the scratch and the old record is turning smoothly again around and around" (156). Although in some ways both media technologies—the radio and the record player—can deliver music, Hauser draws a sharp distinction between the two. The record player emphasizes repetition and familiar habit; the radio, conversely, is exclusively verbal and negotiates the complicated line between private space and public world. It brings information to B that she otherwise would have no access to—although B is never sure how accurate the information is, or whether she has heard it correctly. For this reason, the scrawled graffiti about B is ultimately much more like the radio broadcasts than the music that V and J dance to, since the information written on the wall is verbal and concerned with B's relation to the outside world. The radio, then, is the opposite of the record player, representing the public world in contrast to the private routines and romantic coupling that the music embodies.

The radio is especially important because it invokes the accidental, which appears to be the basis for dreaming and imagination in the novel, and draws our attention back to the technical nature of this transmission medium. Already we have seen that the radio conveys information of dubious value, since it is unclear whether B herself has merely imagined the things that she hears. Something similar happens late in the novel when V decides to print a classified ad to find J. Although the contact phone number is printed correctly, the advertisement itself is a mess of typos:

ANNI ONE WITH POSITIVE CLAWS AS TO
J'S WHIRABOOTS PLEASE TO COONTACT
V'S DEMON
CRASH REWARD FLESH (139)

Like most of the information from the outside world in this novel, this advertisement is accidental and unreliable. V is "swamped with calls, some of them so obscene Aunt V has passed them on to the FBI for decoding" (139–40). Nonetheless, V continues to take the calls: "She must answer each, must listen closely to every foul proposition, every four letter word, as there is always a chance that within the flood of obscenities she might detect one hint as to J's whereabouts" (140). V's dedication in answering these prank calls seems foolish, since we would assume that they are either honest attempts to convey information or obscene jokes about the mistaken advertisement. In the world of Hauser's novel, however, the outside world is considerably more mysterious and much harder to know, and information hides even where it is surrounded by the accidental and false. The same thing appears to be the case in the radio broadcasts that B listens to; despite the chance that they may be imagined, B must take each one seriously since she simply does not know where clues about herself hide. Hauser seems to have a particular fondness for radio reports and advertisements that are contradictory or in some way self-evidently wrong: "A COLOR TV FREE FOR EVERY BOWERY BRIDE, says my transistor. YOUR HONEYMOON CAN BE YOUR MONEYMOON. DEPOSIT BEFORE YOU EARN" (146). Such passages make little literal sense but do seem to tell B about how the world works—just as V has to listen to every obscene call in hopes of hearing some clue about J.

In *The Talking Room*, then, Hauser refuses to draw a firm line between the imagined and the real, and in fact suggests that dreaming comes out of just these technical accidents. Hauser equates the imagined and real because her characters are fundamentally cut off from direct knowledge of the public world. One of the main themes of *The Talking Room* is the mirror, which emphasizes the solipsism of Hauser's characters:

> Mom shrugs her shoulders in seven mirrors. They have missed other shows before, they both know that, and the only show they'll never be too late for is right here in this house with its countless echoes, mirrors: mirrors flecked and warped with age, or broken, or newly replaced, with the glazier's label still glued to them or pasted over with last year's Valentines, lipstick red hearts, V&J's. The house is a maze of mirrors. You run into yourself at every turn. There's no escape, and each time it is a different B I see because it is a different moment or mirror. (11–12)

This "maze of mirrors" seems to describe a world in which characters naturally turn inward, a world that only loosely and problematically matches up with the larger public space. This is why "the only show they'll never be too late for" is the one in their own home. In this world, all information from the outside is partially imagined, incomplete, accidental, or impossible. Thus, the radio is a perfect instrument to embody the nature of knowledge in *The Talking Room*. It is not merely mediated in the general sense that it reflects a certain filtering and shaping of information; it is mediated in the stronger sense that information is subject to all the vagaries of transmission, the traveling of information from outside to inside. This is why, too, the record player has a fundamentally different role in the novel—not as an example of an alternate medium but instead as a device that is firmly part of the *interior* life of the house. In figuring dreaming and the medium in this way, however, Hauser makes a striking claim that our dreams are always about outside spaces, about the worlds beyond ourselves. In this regard, the novel repeats a theme that we have already recognized in Alexie and Rodriguez: that the spaces of contemporary culture are multiple and varied, and that the technical qualities of the physical medium of our reading takes us through these spaces in complex and overlapping ways.

Dreaming in *The Talking Room* will remind us of the shadow life of reading that Birkerts describes. Indeed, against all likelihood, Hauser has given us a story that in many ways confirms the traditional power of this dreaming to connect us to the outside world. And yet, she also makes clear that this dream has always been based on an embrace of the technical limits of the medium—whether it is the print book or the radio transmission. The way in which these representations circulate as technical artifacts is inherent to how we use them, and how they negotiate between public and private world. It is for this reason that all of the books we encounter in *The Talking Room* are incomplete or ambiguous. In some cases, written messages simply reflect the same problems of transmission that we see in the radio. Late in the novel, for example, B finds a message that has been stuck up "with scotch tape so old it has turned the color of pure gold: WILL BE LATE/DON'T YOU WAIT UP FOR ME" (151). The message in this case seems relatively unambiguous, but (like all of the radio transmissions that B receives) the context is lost and the identities of sender and receiver are unclear. The same seems to be true of letters and notebooks that B encounters. She finds an "unfinished letter which reads, DEAR BR and then stops dead for all eternity" (83). Likewise, she finds a notebook that V gave to J: "I've opened it more than once to the first page, the one single line there in mom's ink-loaded hand which is as awkward as my own hand. JEDER ENGEL IST SCHRECKLICH [each angel is terrible]" (67). The notebooks that appear in *The Talking Room* are all the products of particular people at particular moments. More importantly, they are always on their way somewhere else. In a sense, these books are like the radio transmissions that B listens to—always intended for someone else and merely overheard by B. Ironically, we are able to dream while reading precisely because the means by which we receive this information is a technical object, whose physical nature opens up all these gaps and discontinuities in which our imagination can play. Hauser offers us an image of reading based not on imagining our place within a social whole, but on embracing writing's ability to connect us to something beyond its limits.

The remarkable image of dreaming that Hauser offers us in *The Talking Room* can be supplemented with one last example, this time drawn from Jonathan Lethem's *The Fortress of Solitude*—a novel whose title itself evokes (among other things) the privacy of reading that Birkerts celebrates. The novel is organized around an analysis of media and the way that it stages the relation between the public and the private. In this regard, it is an ideal capstone to this study. At the beginning of the novel, Dylan Ebdus's family moves to a predominantly black section of Brooklyn, mostly at the urging of Dylan's mother, Rachel, who idealistically embraces the fact that Dylan is "one of three white children in the whole school" (24). Rachel, however, soon abandons her husband (Abraham) and Dylan, and much of the drama of the novel arises from Dylan's feeling out of place in the rough, poor, and almost exclusively black public school that he attends. Fortunately, Dylan makes friends with Mingus Rude, the son of a once-famous rhythm and blues singer. The black and very cool Mingus provides some protection for Dylan, but as they progress into high school Dylan's grades earn him a place in the better, more racially mixed Stuyvesant (220) while Mingus and others from the neighborhood attend the "grim repository" of Sarah J. Hale (202). In time Dylan graduates and goes on to freelance writing about music. Mingus, conversely, gets drawn into a life of crime and drug dealing; Dylan finds him at the end of the novel in Watertown prison, incarcerated for life for a series of initially petty but increasingly serious crimes.

Lethem builds this novel around the line between public and private spaces and—as we have seen over and over in contemporary fiction—uses media to explore that line. Dylan's father is a painter who makes a living throughout Dylan's childhood by producing surrealistic covers for science fiction novels; his more serious work, however, is a hybrid form of painting and film, "an animated film painted by single brushstrokes directly onto celluloid" (9). Mingus's father, Barrett Rude Junior, is a singer; Dylan eventually goes on to write the liner notes for a collection of his songs. In addition to this work, Dylan later puts together an oddly hybrid project: *Liner Notes: The Boxed Set*. Dylan also tries to sell yet another cross-media project, a film based on the story of the Prisonaires, "one of the great unknown stories in pop-culture history," about a band formed in prison in the 1950s who are "victims of prejudice and economic injustice in the Jim Crow South" (327). *Fortress of Solitude* makes its most explicit media link to comic books; the title of the novel is a reference to Superman's secret retreat. Throughout elementary and then middle school, Dylan and Mingus collect comic books—a hobby first sparked by Rachel's interest in them (55). Each of these media reflects a different degree of private solitude or public involvement with others; as Alexie suggests, there is no simple privacy here but only different forms of public involvement. Abraham's private paintings in the "fortress" of his upstairs studio are one of the most private forms of representation in the novel; these works are not displayed publicly until the very end of the novel, when Abraham finds a new girlfriend who "organized my father, and she seemed, in a peculiar way, to make him happy. She made him visible to himself, by her contrast" (341). Ironically, film in its more traditional form seems to represent the exact opposite of Abraham's extreme privacy. Rachel is obsessed with film: "She had this routine, every time I tried to get her to do anything outdoors she'd say, 'I wonder what's playing at the Thalia.' Like I should know what she was missing, from her life before" (507). Rachel goes on, when pressed to explain why a particular film was so good, to narrate in full detail: "She told me the plot of that fucking movie for an hour. I mean, doing Peter Lorre's voice and everything, all the lines—she had the whole thing memorized" (507). In contrast to Abraham's inwardly turned, almost unwatchable film, the restless and political Rachel embraces the public display (at the Thalia) of a well-known film. These two ways of thinking about essentially the same medium define the extremes of the spectrum between the private and the public.

Between these two forms fall the other major media that the novel addresses: music, comic books, and writing itself. Music appears to be a largely public medium in *Fortress of Solitude*. Dylan's story of the Prisonaires, for example, is essentially about the way that public acceptance of discrimination determines the ability of musicians to perform. In contrast, comic books are not publicly displayed or performed the way that film and music is, making them a more ambiguous combination of the public and private. Comic books are public documents to be bought and sold, and at the same time they are fantasy works that often express very private desires and fears. This is particularly well exemplified in the novel by the activity of collecting comics, shared by Dylan and Mingus: "Two afternoons a week, sitting in the dimming light on Dylan's stoop, never discussing fifth or sixth grade, stuff too basic and mysterious to mention. Instead just paging through, shoulders hunched to protect the flimsy covers from the wind, puzzling out the last dram, the last square inch of information, the credits, the letters page, the copyright, the Sea-Monkeys ads, *the insult that made a man out of Mac*. Then, just when you thought you were alone, Dean street came back to life, Mingus Rude knowing everyone, saying

Yo to a million different kids" (66). This passage, where reading comic books is associated with sitting on the house stoop, nicely captures the threshold nature of the comic book, which is poised between the private and the public. Finally, although Lethem gives us few examples of writing in the novel, one important example is graffiti. Graffiti is represented in the novel in terms of tagging or marking with the name Dose, which Mingus and Dylan both use, creating an oddly hybrid identity attached to the name: "He's been allowed to merge his identity in this away with the black kid's, to lose his funkymusicwhiteboy geekdom in the illusion that he and his friend Mingus Rude are both Dose, no more and no less" (138). Tagging here is an expression of individual identity, the creation and then making public of a name that not everyone will recognize, a name that works like an almost secret identity: "At thirteen you'd begun to leave traces, occult names and signs proliferating" (191). This form of writing joins film and comic books in striking a balance point between the public and the private.

Lethem's novel embodies the dynamics that I have described throughout this book. Here a range of other media is deployed to help us to understand the limits and potentials of the novel and how it can help us to find a line between the public and the private, between representations of the world and the circulation of those representations between individuals. All these dynamics are brought together at the end of this novel, with an image that Lethem offers of an imaginative "middle space." Dylan has been kicked out of Camden College and drives home with his father through a snowstorm. Dylan puts on a Brian Eno tape and feels comforted by the sense of space that it invokes: "the middle space [it] conjured and dwelled in, a bohemian demimonde, a hippie dream" (509). The adult Dylan goes on to reflect on this space as a precarious construction halfway between the utopian and the tough real world that he grew up in, a space of potential that allows one foot to remain in a private dream world and one foot to rest in its historical moment: "We all pined for those middle spaces, those summer hours when Josephine Baker lay waste to Paris, when 'Bothered Blue' peaked on the charts, when a teenaged Elvis, still dreaming of his own first session, sat in the Sun Studios watching the Prisonaires, when a top-to-bottom burner blazed through a subway station, renovating the world for an instant, when schoolyard turntables were powered by a cord run from a streetlamp, when juice just *flowed*" (510).

This space between dream and flow, between imaging a relationship and being jacked into an electrical grid, strikes me as a rearticulation of the fragile location that Appadurai describes. This is an imaginative space of identification, where the outside world suddenly calls to you and offers a powerful representation of what reading is today. It involves not a fantasy of privacy, in which the reader is a passive respondent to the text cut off from the outside world, but an active participant caught up in something much larger. It is neither a matter of occupying some concrete, private location nor of subordinating identity to the synchronization of national culture. Instead, the middle space of reading embodies all those imaginative connections that become possible when we recognize the book as a fragile object poised between different technoscapes, subjected to a range of forces within the media ecology. Instead of simply undermining the traditional uses of the novel, this fragile position also makes possible a complex engagement in the world in which our dreaming is not just a matter of seclusion but instead an involvement in all of these flows.

Coda

*Connection through Limits
and the Myth of Media Fullness*

In this book, I have offered an unlikely image of the novel within the contemporary media ecology. We would expect that media would create a sense of connection to social and cultural forms by reaching out to describe larger media systems directly. Instead, what we have seen is that the contemporary media novel emphasizes quite the opposite: the limits of writing. Instead of isolating novelists, characters, and readers, those limits are precisely what allow them to be aware of the world beyond themselves. In emphasizing media limits, these writers are able to embrace an agency that comes from being an actor within a heterogeneous space in which media objects circulate among readers and authors, sellers and buyers, collectors and discarders.

This image of media limits stands in striking contrast to the way that the relation between various media is usually described today. The appeal to "multimedia" in popular culture, consumer electronics, and even some cultural criticism embodies a fantasy in which there are no limits that the addition of another medium cannot solve. If a song is good, then the addition of video is better, and links to the band's Web site, photographs, and lyrics are better still. The multipage advertisement in *Newsweek* that accompanied the launch of the Apple Macintosh in 1984 captures this spirit of endless media supplement: the capacity to integrate charts, illustrations, and text "makes Macintosh its very own form of communication. A new medium that allows you to supplement the power of the written word with the clarity of illustrations. In other words, if you can't make your point with a Macintosh, you may not have a point to make." In the years since, this appeal to the value of "supplementing" text has become an assumed part of our ways of thinking about media: the limits of one medium call for introducing another.

Equally striking about the appeal to media fullness is the anxious way that it promises to rejuvenate agency. This is already implicit in the Macintosh advertisement, where the specter of "not hav[ing] a point to make" haunts the promise of this new technology. Again and again the addition of another medium is described as suddenly making the reader active. This is certainly the case when hypertext narratives first emerged onto the scene of contemporary writing. Janet Murray celebrated such agency in her influential early study, *Hamlet on the Holodeck* (1997): "The more realized the immersive environment, the more active we want to be within it. When the things we do bring tangible results, we experience the second characteristic delight of electronic environments—the sense of agency. Agency is the satisfying power to take meaningful action and see the results of our decisions and choices" (126). It didn't take long for critics like Espen Aarseth to dispel these illusions: such electronic texts can actually limit reader activity, since we can no longer flip to the conclusion of a story if we are impatient to find out how it ends (*Cybertext*, 91). Reader agency is forestalled by electronic textuality in other ways as well. While we can do many things with an old copy of a novel—reread it, sell it, use the pages to start a fire—in many ways our choices with an electronic text are considerably more constrained. Currently, my original copy of Michael Joyce's influential early hypertext novel *Afternoon* sits on my bookshelf unused, since my computer no longer has the requisite floppy drive to read the diskette.

Our eagerness to find new and expanded forms of agency by adding other media is perhaps a natural response to the anxiety about the vocation of the novel. If we are no longer sure quite what the point of the novel is, then the broad assertion that electronic texts will allow us to do *more* in general seems like a natural consolation. Michael Joyce, for example, calls for "text-processing" tools: "If word processing may be thought of as a tool for thought (making any written text available for emendation, elaboration, and restructuring at any point along its length), text processing may be thought of as a thoughtful tool (making a master text and variations of it available to readers along a presentational path predetermined by the writer and selected or influenced by the reader). Text processing makes texts transparent, inviting readers to consider parallels, explore multiple alternate possibilities, and participate in the uncertain process of discovery and creation" (139). This is a common thread in early commentary on new media—the discovery of agency in unexpected places. This desire for agency also helps to explain the popularity among literary critics of Brenda Laurel's description of the computer interface as a kind of theatrical space. Even in simple games like the early *Spacewar*, we see the promise of the computer interface: "Its interesting potential lay not in its ability to perform calculations but in its capacity to *represent action in which humans could participate*" (1). The same desire to find and foster agency among readers and writers is evident in the participatory culture cited at the end of chapter 2: if the novel has lost its traditional vocation, then it seems natural to look to, for inspiration, the many uses to which fans can put the stories. Each of these instances seems to be the result of anxiety about agency and the novel: we aren't quite sure what we are supposed to do with it and why.

The description of media limits offered here is far less intuitive but at the same time far less dependent on fantasy. It offers a model of activity based on participation in a segmented space, in which our experience of a medium depends on awareness of where that medium ends. We have already seen a description of this space in theories of media ecologies, which Fuller described as the distribution of "informational roles in orga-nizations and in computer-supported collaborative work" (3). We might give this image of space the Deleuzian articulation on which Appadurai depends: "Multiplicities are defined by the outside: by the abstract line, the line of flight or deterritorialization according to which they change in nature and connect with other multiplicities" (9). This seems to me to be a powerful model for media today and one that the novel, with its facility at referencing the absent and the circulation of media artifacts through communities, is particularly well suited to describe. We saw that different periods construct models of media relations rhetorically—like appeals to synesthesia in the late nineteenth century and intermedia earlier in the twentieth century. In this model of segmented space organized by differ-ent media, in which actors working with these media—readers, writers, distributors—achieve agency through embrace of those media limits that also connect those media to "global flows," we have a media ecology ap-propriate to our present moment.

Notes

Introduction

1. I use the word "novel" to refer to printed stories, excluding hypertext narratives and all other forms of multimedia storytelling. I am not trying to devalue electronic texts or to ignore the likelihood that hybrid forms of storytelling may become important in the coming years. Retaining the word *novel* to refer to print, however, allows me a shorthand way to talk about the relationship between traditional book forms and these newer types of textuality.

2. The push-back against literary theory and experimentation in narrative has been a running element of contemporary literary culture at least since the 1970s. John Gardner's *On Moral Fiction* became a rallying point for writers and critics who felt that postmodernist experimentation lost touch with the pleasure of reading.

3. In her book of the same title, Phyllis Rose describes Proust's masterpiece as an object of almost pure reading, disconnected from any direct narrative imperative: "Unpropelled by narrative, caught in the spirals or circles of reference which generate his depth and amplitude, every reader of Proust has to find his or her own reason for moving ahead" (18).

4. As an example, see Janine Barchas's discussion of the complexity and diversity of book design in the eighteenth-century novel, which she argues made extensive use of layout, illustration, and punctuation for narrative purposes.

5. See Lennard Davis's discussion of this distinction as an "undifferentiated matrix" in *Factual Fictions*.

6. This story is explicitly offered to potential buyers, both in the prospectus for the book as well as in early reviews of the novel, which likewise emphasized the heroic nature of writer and publisher, and the future value of the novel (Rainey, 57–58).

7. Johanna Drucker notes how typography can work against the meaning of words and their "grammatical completion": "Spatial play, the hierarchy of size and color in the rendering, allows different groupings to occur—line by line sequence, and type by type. Not simply to restate the obvious. But to open it up. Smack against the popular plane, immodestly refusing a patent transparency" (140).

8. This emphasis on the spiritual value of synesthesia is echoed in Ogden, Richards, and Woods's 1922 *The Foundation of Aesthetics*, which argues that experiencing *together* is fundamental to beauty and to the kind of detached attitude that we take toward art: "As descriptive of an aesthetic state in which impulses are experienced *together*, the word *Synaethesis*, however, conveniently covers both equilibrium and harmony" (75–76).

9. Werner Wolf notes the distinction between the older concept of "interart studies" and the more modern notion of intermedia studies:"'Intermedial' is thus a flexible adjective that can be applied, in a broad sense, to any phenomenon involving more than one medium" rather than being restricted to the traditional "high arts" ("Musicalized Fiction," 40–41). Other critics have seen the focus on intermedia as a critique of aesthetic theories that separate media. Jürgen Müller claims that an "*intermedial* history of modern media . . . will bring an end to the idea and fiction of independent and 'pure' media or arts" (296). Katherine Hayles prefers the term *intermediation* (especially in contrast to *remediation*) both because it "is more faithful to the spirit of multiple causality in emphasizing interactions among media" and because it emphasizes the mediation between people and between people and machines (33).

10. See Marie-Laure Ryan's introduction and David Herman's "Toward a Transmedial Narratology" in *Narrative across Media*. See also Richard Walsh, *The Rhetoric of Fictionality*, 103–29.

11. It is worth noting that historians of composition studies frequently point to this time period—specifically, 1963—as marking a fundamental shift in the nature of writing instruction in the United States, away from traditional paradigms toward writing process and rhetorical concern for audience. For this history, see Stephen North, *The Making of Knowledge in Composition*, 9–17.

12. Didier Coste, *Narrative as Communication*; Adam Zachary Newton, *Narrative Ethics*; James Phelan, *Narrative as Rhetoric*; Marie-Laure Ryan, *Narrative as Virtual Reality*.

13. David Herman associates the rise of structuralist narratology with "an approach that likewise applied to narrative in general, not just the novel" (Introduction to *Cambridge Companion*, 16).

1. Multimedia Moments Old and New

1. Although this observation is commonsensical enough to need little theoretical justification, I would nonetheless invoke Darko Suvin's distinction between a narrative and a metaphor: "All texts are—by way of their paradigm, model, or macro-metaphor—based on a certain kind of metaphoricity, but . . . narrative texts add to metaphorical ones a concrete presentation in terms of space and time, the *chronotope*" (51). More recently, cognitive theorists like Mark Turner have argued that the parable that Suvin distinguishes from narrative depends

on a fundamental human capacity to project such miniature narratives onto a variety of different targets based on the situation of the utterance (5–6). Nonetheless, I think that Suvin's emphasis on concrete location remains essential for the extended literary narrative that defines the novel.

2. Stanzel makes clear that literary narrative in particular works to dramatize this process of mediation, while mediacy is "rendered only minimally in the popular novel" (6).

3. Michael Putnam explains: "The pride implicit in Aeneas' reaction complements the second way Aeneas views the murals, namely as evidence for the enormous sorrow such happenings engendered as they occurred and now arouse again at the moment of retrospection, and therefore of Dido's compassion in the face of human suffering and, in particular, of her understanding of Trojan hurt" (244).

4. Marie-Laure Ryan associates metalepsis in general with transgression. She distinguishes between merely rhetorical metalepsis (such as an author's comments about writing the story itself) and the more disruptive ontological metalepsis, in which narrative levels mix (*Avatars*, 206–7). She sees both, however, as "a grabbing gesture that reaches across levels and ignores boundaries" (206). Werner Wolf follows up Ryan's discussion by describing the latter as the only "genuine" form of metalepsis ("Metalepsis," 89) and suggesting that the intentional confusion of narrative levels is one of its primary characteristics (91).

5. In his well-known essay "Surfiction," Federman describes in these terms what the contemporary novel should be: "The kind of fiction I am interested in is that fiction which the leaders of the literary establishment (publishers, editors, agents, and reviewers alike) brush aside because it does not conform to *their* notions of what fiction should be; that fiction which supposedly has no value (commercial understood) for the common reader" (6–7). Thus we can say that Federman's use of literature is primarily a matter of overcoming convention, which he seems to believe that art and artistic convention transcend.

6. Warren F. Motte Jr. provides a good overview of Oulipo's commitment to formal restraint in his introduction to *Oulipo: A Primer of Potential Literature*. Coincidentally, Motte dates the formation of Oulipo to the same year (1960) that I have used as my starting point for the study of the contemporary media novel.

2. Story, Discourse, and Circulation

1. I discuss this issue of art reflecting experience in the Black Arts movement, to which Reed is responding in this novel, in "The Black Arts Movement and the Genealogy of Multimedia."

3. Defining the Vocation of the Novel

1. See Bruce Morrissette's discussion of the "cinema novel" in *Novel and Film* (28–39).

2. Other examples of this use of film include William Burroughs's *Blade Runner: A Movie* and Robert Coover's short story "After Lazarus."

3. David Herman notes that an understanding of space can be achieved indirectly through narrative action—as, for example, when we come to recognize the topography of a space through characters' actions within that space (*Story Logic*, 282). This kind of orientation nonetheless depends on the activity of description, since the writer must describe the action of the narrative that then implies this geography.

4. We should recognize that there are ways that objects get into the world of the story without explicit description on the part of the author. Later in this chapter, I discuss the principle of "minimal departure" advocated by some critics working in fictional world theory. According to this principle, fictional worlds conform as closely as possible to the actual world, and depart from it only when we are explicitly informed about it. I discuss some problems with this principle, but we should recognize that the choice of a setting or period for a novel implies elements of the world that need not be explicitly described. I would suggest, however, that invoking but not describing such settings (and thus leaving room for implied elements) is simply another way of limiting description, thus making room for reader evaluation and agency.

5. See Paul Werth's discussion of a Hemingway story, in which the text world "may be represented as a blank space which gradually gets filled in and defined as one reads through it" (53). An interesting corollary to this is the research that Richard Gerrig reports regarding when readers visualize details necessary to but unstated in scenes from a story. Taking the example of a scene in *Casino Royale* in which James Bond eats caviar but the instrument for doing so is not mentioned, Gerrig reports that "readers acquire information—say, about James Bond eating his caviar—without automatically imagining the instrument involved" (35).

6. We traditionally regard setting and plot as two distinct narrative elements (they are, after all, the basis for two separate sections in this chapter), but Coover's story makes clear that in writing in particular, settings imply plots. Herman notes that our standard distinction between narrative and description is problematic, and specifically focuses on the relationship between space and plot, "how stories encode entities moving or being moved along narratively salient paths—that is, how spaces and trajectories can have more or less saliency in a story depending on the way agents and objects are temporally distributed over regions linked by paths" (*Story Logic*, 298).

7. There is only one time in *The Colorist* when Eamonn's photographs have a more specific context, and that is the brief time when he makes a living taking wedding photographs (144). In contrast to the photographs described earlier,

these are all about relationships—both between members of the family who are photographed, and between one wedding party and the next, which locates Eamonn economically in a web of profitable jobs. In fact, at the end of the novel Eamonn gets a call from one of these families: "The wedding pictures were lousy. She wanted her money back. Perhaps she was getting divorced. The separation was acrimonious and she wanted to return the pictures to their source, as if the wedding had never taken place" (214). Here at the end Eamonn himself is integrated into the context of his job, and the status of the photographs that he took is made subject to a host of historical factors beyond his control—in particular, the possibility of a divorce that retroactively makes the pictures themselves "lousy."

8. See Richard Walsh's discussion of dreams in the graphic novel, focusing specifically on Neil Gaiman's *Sandman*. Walsh particularly notes that the medium combines image and text (112), and argues that the tension between these two channels is central to the success of the dream representation. This is a point that Scott McCloud makes as well, as he demonstrates how a visual scene is transformed by different kinds of scripting (157–60). It seems to me that graphic narratives frequently turn to scripts when they have particularly complex modal relations to articulate.

9. Gerald Prince would describe some of these passages as the "disnarrated": "All the events that *do not* happen though they could have and are nonetheless referred to (in a negative or hypothetical mode) by the narrative text" (30). He makes the interesting and important point that, unlike the merely "unnarrated" (things left unsaid in the story), "the disnarrated is clearly not essential to narrative" (34). We cannot tell a story without leaving some things out, but we can think of many stories in which the absent, potential, or unrealized are not explicitly described. I take this to be in part because such events are particularly important to writing, rather than to narrative in all media.

10. Edmund Husserl writes in *Ideas*: "As it is with the world in its ordered being as a spatial present—the aspect I have so far been considering—so likewise is it with the world in respect to its *ordered being in the succession of time*. This world now present to me, and in every waking 'now' obviously so, has its temporal horizon, infinite in both direction, its known and unknown, its intimately alive and its unalive past and future" (p. 92, sec. 27).

11. Murray is invited to teach a class called "Eating and Drinking: Basic Parameters." Jack initially thinks that the course is pointless, since it will only discuss things that "everybody knows," but Murray explains: "Knowledge changes every day. People like to have their beliefs reinforced" (171).

12. A number of critics have claimed that this rejection of unidirectional and inevitable plots is ethically necessary. David Herman associates the complication

through bidirectional influence with "narrative humility" (*Story Logic*, 230). Brian Richardson provides a nice summary of some of the ways that feminist critics have critiqued plot inevitability in *Narrative Dynamics* (68–69).

4. Writing Beyond the Media Limit?

1. This is not, of course, a precise definition; it does not address elements of contemporary media that are digital but not shackled to the computer screen. Is there, for example, a difference between an analog and digital picture that has been printed onto paper? Lev Manovich provides a much more powerful definition of new media as entailing numerical representation, modularity, automation, variability, and transcoding (27–48). Nonetheless, I think there is value in retaining this loose and imprecise definition of new media precisely because it captures the limited and sometimes contradictory hopes and beliefs out of which our cultural fascination with it emerged in the early 1990s.

2. Pynchon describes the creation of plastic molecules: "L. Jamf, among others, then proposed, logically, dialectically, taking the parental polyamide sections of the new chain, and looping *them* around into rings too, giant 'heterocyclic' rings, to alternate with the aromatic rings" (250).

3. On the role of music in the novel, see David Cowart, *Thomas Pynchon*.

4. In one of the first books on Pynchon's career up through the publication of this novel, Molly Hite linked this break from totalizing systems to the novel's comic style as a whole: its humor "always arises from violations of an apparent order: from liberating, if generally unnerving, surprises. And this observation may be the most compelling argument against a totalizing, Procrustean reading of *Gravity's Rainbow*. To take the arc of the rainbow seriously as a controlling metaphor is to betray a richly comic novel to the excessive gravity of its providential plot" (131).

5. Umberto Eco suggests that these lowered expectations are inherent to the encyclopedia, which has always been based on the idea that information is only loosely organized: "Knowledge cannot be recognized and organized as a global system; it provides only 'local' and transitory systems of knowledge, which can be contradicted by alternative and equally 'local' cultural organizations" (84).

6. This is quite in contrast to the hand-drawn images added to Kurt Vonnegut's *Breakfast of Champions* or Kathy Acker's *Blood and Guts in High School*. An even more striking contrast is *Still Life with Woodpecker*, which we will recall ends with the author abandoning the typewriter on which the novel has been written and handwriting the final two pages. In all of these cases, visual elements function as a much stronger contrast to print text than the images in *Gravity's Rainbow*.

7. See Lawrence Wolfley, "Repression's Rainbow."

8. Manovich contrasts narrative and database, which is a key "form of cultural

expression of the modern age." The database, according to Manovich, is "a structured collection of data. The data stored in a database is organized for fast search and retrieval by a computer" (218).

9. For a discussion of the implication of this claim for an understanding of the territory, see Gregory Bateson, *Steps to an Ecology of Mind*.

10. Mark Nunes notes in particular that the space of *electronic* networks departs rather strikingly from the simpler network exemplified by postal routes: "A[n email] message traveling from point A to point B would *not* follow a rigid, coordinated path, but would instead search for the route with the lightest traffic." As a result, "the enacted space of exchange articulated in material form by a distributed, redundant network suggests that in a space of flows, it is *traffic rather than distance* that holds spatial significance—and that social space itself occurs as an event rather than a thing. The distributed, fragmented material form of the enacted event-space of electronic transmissions allows for the production of a space that does not reduce to a networked 'space of places,' to use Manuel Castells's term" (93). The space of the network that Abish describes likewise cannot be reduced simply to a set of places; instead, it is a whole system that is frequently independent of the landscape.

11. See Joseph Frank's original essay and response to critics in *The Idea of Spatial Form*. Frank Kermode offers an influential critique of the concept in *The Sense of an Ending* and in his "Reply to Joseph Frank" in *Critical Inquiry*. For other broad attempts to address the topic, see Ricardo Gullón's "On Space in the Novel" and Gabriel Zoran's "Towards a Theory of Space in Narrative."

12. This is the underlying assumption in work on the cognitive response to the literary text. David Herman argues that we develop models of the story world in much the same way that we develop models of real space: "Reference assignment is made possible when narrative texts cue readers to activate contextual frames, that is, knowledge representations that store specific configurations of characters located at specific space-time coordinates in the storyworld. Referring expressions thus evoke not just fictional individuals but whole contextual frames" (*Story Logic*, 270).

13. As a parallel to this mixture of space and message, see Manovich's discussion of Jeffrey Shaw's *Legible City*, which likewise uses a physical space (Manhattan, Amsterdam, and Karlsruhe), onto which it maps letters (260–61).

14. For example, descriptions of role-playing games usually appeal to players' desire to lose themselves in the game world. In the first widely distributed role-playing game, *Dungeons and Dragons*, Gary Gygax describes the game (hyperbolically) as an immersive experience: "This game lets all your fantasies come true. This is a world where monsters, dragons, good and evil high priests, fierce demons, and even the gods themselves may enter your character's life. Enjoy, for this game is what dreams are made of!" (7).

15. In *The Distinction of Fiction*, Cohn notes a distinction, "obvious as it may appear, [that] has somehow gotten lost in the narratological shuffle: that the minds of imaginary figures can be known in ways that those of real persons can not" (118).

16. Naturally, we understand that Hector *can* speak in the world of the film, that he could simply announce his appearance to his family; indeed, we could imagine that in a sound film much might be made of the need for Hector to move silently in order to take full advantage of his invisibility. But in "the silent world of Hector Mann," sounds have a much more tenuous role—being reduced, really, to ideas or implications rather than something which is an important and concrete part of the story. Hector's medium is ultimately visual, and all other elements like sound merely tangential.

17. Of course, this blunt distinction ignores the work that readers do to make sense of the story they are reading. Richard Gerrig, for example, describes reading as a kind of performance akin to the work that an actor does when bringing a role to life (17). But even the most unsophisticated reader recognizes that how we read and interpret a story cannot change its outcome, and often our experience of plot depends on a sense of inevitability that we are powerless to stop. Perlin's distinction between this interpretive involvement in the story and the direct manipulation of characters for game-play goals strikes me as valid.

18. In the same collection in which Eskelinen's essay appears, Espen Aarseth dismisses the apparent success that video games have shown in combining stories and games: "However, sales figures are not a reliable measure of artistic success, or—dare we say—quality" ("Genre Trouble," 51). I discuss this essay and the general debate about narrativity in games that are based on movies in "From Synaesthesia to Multimedia."

19. There are many well-known examples of film-to-game translations, certainly the most extensive of which are the many games in the *Star Wars* franchise. Game-to-film adaptations have also become quite common, including two *Tomb Raider* movies. Somewhat less well known are game-to-novel translations. Probably the most extensive are the many books that supplement the *Myst* games, but even more recent action games like *Halo* have given rise to novels that tell the backstory of the game events.

5. Negotiating Public and Private Spaces

1. Manguel uses a common opening, citing the first remembered experience of reading: "I first discovered that I could read at the age of four. I had seen, over and over again, the letters that I knew (because I had been told) were the names of the pictures under which they sat" (5).

2. All of the female characters in the novel seem to be the victims of men who exploit them for sex, and all of the men seem to suffer from women who are

unable to fully accept them sexually. Central in this regard is Ursa herself, who is pushed down stairs at the beginning of the novel by her husband, Mutt Thomas, causing a miscarriage and requiring a hysterectomy. Once out of the hospital, separated from Mutt and remarried to Tadpole, Ursa remains sexually numb—which Tadpole uses as an excuse to take up with a younger girl. The pattern of violence, exploitation, and isolation repeats the condition that Old man Corregidora created during slavery.

3. In fact, the material conditions of the production and distribution of the book fall between two of these: they seem to be a matter of both *mediascape* and *technoscape*. Appadurai describes the mediascape as "the distribution of the electronic capabilities to produce and disseminate information" (35) but then defines the technoscape as equivalent to "technologies of production and information" (40).

Bibliography

Aarseth, Espen. *Cybertext: Perspectives on Ergodic Literature*. Baltimore: Johns Hopkins University Press, 1997.

———. "Genre Trouble: Narrativism and the Art of Simulation." In Wardrip-Fruin and Harrigan, *First Person*, 45–55.

Abish, Walter. *Alphabetical Africa*. New York: New Directions, 1974.

———. "Ardor/Awe/Atrocity." In *In the Future Perfect*, 42–57. New York: New Directions, 1977.

Acker, Kathy. *Blood and Guts in High School*. New York: Grove, 1978.

Adorno, Theodor W. *The Culture Industry: Selected Essays on Mass Culture*. Edited by J. M. Bernstein. London: Routledge, 1991.

Alber, Jan, and Fludernik, Monika. "Mediacy and Narrative Mediation." In *Handbook of Narratology*, edited by Peter Hühn, John Pier, Wolf Schmid, Jörg Schönert, 174–89. Berlin: Walter de Gruyter, 2009.

Alexie, Sherman. *Reservation Blues*. New York: Grove, 1995.

Amerika, Mark. *Meta/Data: A Digital Poetics*. Cambridge MA: MIT Press, 2007.

Anderson, Benedict. *Imagined Communities: Reflections on the Origin and Spread of Nationalism*. Rev. ed. London: Verso, 1991.

Anderson, Tim J. *Making Easy Listening: Material Culture and Postwar American Recording*. Minneapolis: University of Minnesota Press, 2006.

Appadurai, Arjun. *Modernity at Large: Cultural Dimensions of Globalization*. Minneapolis: University of Minnesota Press, 1996.

Armstrong, Nancy. *Desire and Domestic Fiction: A Political History of the Novel*. New York: Oxford University Press, 1987.

———. *Fiction in the Age of Photography: The Legacy of British Realism*. Cambridge MA: Harvard University Press, 1999.

Auster, Paul. *The Book of Illusions*. New York: Henry Holt, 2002.

———. *City of Glass*. In *The New York Trilogy*, 1–158. New York: Penguin, 1990.

Back, Maribeth. "The Reading Senses: Designing Texts for Multisensory Systems." In *Digital Media Revisited: Theoretical and Conceptual Innovation in Digital Domains*, edited by Gunnar Liestøl, Andrew Morrison, and Terje Rasmussen, 157–82. Cambridge MA: MIT Press, 2003.

Bakhtin, M. M. *The Dialogic Imagination: Four Essays*. Translated by Caryl Emerson and Michael Holquist. Austin: University of Texas Press, 1981.

Bal, Mieke. *Narratology: Introduction to the Theory of Narrative*. 2nd ed. Toronto: University of Toronto Press, 1997.

Ballard, J. G. *Crash*. New York: Noonday, 1994.

Bambara, Toni Cade. *The Salt Eaters*. New York: Vintage, 1992.

Banerjee, Mita. "The Asian American in a Turtleneck: Fusing the Aesthetic and the Didactic in Maxine Hong Kingston's *Tripmaster Monkey*." In *Literary Gestures: The Aesthetic in Asian American Writing*, edited by Rocío G. Davis and Sue-Im Lee, 55–69. Philadelphia: Temple University Press, 2006.

Barchas, Janine. *Graphic Design, Print Culture, and the Eighteenth-Century Novel*. Cambridge UK: Cambridge University Press, 2003.

Barth, John. "The Literature of Exhaustion." In *The Friday Book: Essays and Other Nonfiction*, 62–77. Baltimore: Johns Hopkins University Press, 1984.

Barthes, Roland. "Introduction to the Structural Analysis of Narratives." In *A Barthes Reader*, edited by Susan Sontag, 251–95. New York: Noonday, 1982.

———. *S/Z*. Translated by Richard Miller. New York: Hill and Wang, 1974.

Bateson, Gregory. *Steps to an Ecology of Mind: Collected Essays in Anthropology, Psychiatry, Evolution, and Epistemology*. San Francisco: Chandler, 1972.

Baudelaire, Charles. "Correspondances." In *French Symbolist Poetry*. Translated by C. F. MacIntyre, 12–13. Berkeley: University of California Press, 1958.

———. "New Notes on Edgar Poe." In *Baudelaire as a Literary Critic: Selected Essays*, translated and edited by Lois Boe Hyslop and Francis E. Hyslop, 114–35. University Park: Pennsylvania State University Press, 1964.

Baudrillard, Jean. "Simulacra and Simulations." In *Jean Baudrillard: Selected Writings*, edited by Mark Poster, 166–84. Stanford CA: Stanford University Press, 1988.

Beattie, Ann. "Janus." In *Where You'll Find Me and Other Stories*, 103–12. New York: Scribner, 2002.

Beaujour, Michel. "Some Paradoxes of Description." *Yale French Studies* 61 (1981): 27–59.

Beebe, Maurice. *Ivory Towers and Sacred Founts: The Artist as Hero in Fiction from Goethe to Joyce*. New York: New York University Press, 1964.

Bender, John. *Imagining the Penitentiary: Fiction and the Architecture of Mind in Eighteenth-Century England*. Chicago: University of Chicago Press, 1987.

Berressem, Hanjo. *Pynchon's Poetics: Interfacing Theory and Text*. Urbana: University of Illinois Press, 1993.

Binkley, Peter, ed. *Pre-Modern Encyclopaedic Texts: Proceedings of the Second Comers Congress, Groningen, 1–4 July 1996*. Leiden: Brill, 1997.

Birkerts, Sven. *The Gutenberg Elegies: The Fate of Reading in an Electronic Age*. New York: Fawcett Columbine, 1995.

Bloom, Allan. *The Closing of the American Mind: How Higher Education Has Failed Democracy and Impoverished the Souls of Today's Students.* New York: Simon & Schuster, 1987.

Bolter, Jay David, and Richard Grusin. *Remediation: Understanding New Media.* Cambridge MA: MIT Press, 1999.

Booth, Wayne C. *The Rhetoric of Fiction.* 2nd ed. Chicago: University of Chicago Press, 1983.

Borchardt, Frank L. "Towards an Aesthetics of Multimedia." *Computer Assisted Language Learning* 12, no. 1 (1999): 3–28.

Bordwell, David. *Narration in the Fiction Film.* Madison: University of Wisconsin Press, 1985.

Bourdieu, Pierre. *The Rules of Art: Genesis and Structure of the Literary Field.* Translated by Susan Emanuel. Stanford CA: Stanford University Press, 1995.

Brooks, Peter. *Reading for the Plot: Design and Intention in Narrative.* Cambridge MA: Harvard University Press, 1992.

Brown, Dan. *The Da Vinci Code.* New York: Anchor, 2006.

Browning, Robert. *The Complete Poetical Works of Browning.* Boston: Houghton Mifflin, 1895.

Buckley, Jerome Hamilton. *Season of Youth: The Bildungsroman from Dickens to Golding.* Cambridge MA: Harvard University Press, 1974.

Burney, Fanny. *Evelina: Or, the History of a Young Lady's Entrance into the World.* New York: W. W. Norton, 1965.

Burroughs, William S. *Blade Runner: A Movie.* Berkeley CA: Blue Wind Press, 1999.

Butler-Evans, Elliott. *Race, Gender, and Desire: Narrative Strategies in the Fiction of Toni Cade Bambara, Toni Morrison, and Alice Walker.* Philadelphia: Temple University Press, 1989.

Cantor, Jay. *Krazy Kat: A Novel in Five Panels.* New York: Vintage, 1987.

Carpenter, J. R. "Entre Ville." 2006. http://luckysoap.com/entreville.

Carver, Raymond. "Cathedral." In *Where I'm Calling From: New and Selected Stories,* 292–307. New York: Atlantic Monthly Press, 1988.

Chatman, Seymour. *Coming to Terms: The Rhetoric of Narrative in Fiction and Film.* Ithaca NY: Cornell University Press, 1990.

———. *Story and Discourse: Narrative Structure in Fiction and Film.* Ithaca NY: Cornell University Press, 1978.

Ciccoricco, Dave. "Network Vistas: Folding the Cognitive Map." *Image and Narrative* 8 (May 2004): n.p. http://www.imageandnarrative.be/issue08/dave ciccoricco.htm.

Clapp-Itnyre, Alisa. *Angelic Airs, Subversive Songs: Music as Social Discourse in the Victorian Novel.* Athens: Ohio University Press, 2002.

Cohn, Dorrit. *The Distinction of Fiction.* Baltimore: Johns Hopkins University Press, 1999.

———. *Transparent Minds: Narrative Modes for Presenting Consciousness in Fiction.*
Princeton NJ: Princeton University Press, 1978.

Compton's Interactive Encyclopedia. Version 1.01.VW. CD-ROM. Carlsbad CA: Compton's NewMedia, 1992.

———. Version 5.1M. CD-ROM. Cambridge MA: SoftKey Multimedia, 1997.

Coover, Robert. "After Lazarus." In *A Night at the Movies: Or, You Must Remember This*, 37–52. New York: Collier, 1988.

———. "The Babysitter." In *Pricksongs & Descants*, 206–39. New York: Plume, 1970.

———. "The End of Books." In Wardrip-Fruin and Montfort, *New Media Reader*, 706–9.

Coste, Didier. *Narrative as Communication.* Minneapolis: University of Minnesota Press, 1989.

Coverley, M. D. *Califia.* CD-ROM. Watertown MA: Eastgate Systems, 2000.

Cowart, David. *Thomas Pynchon: The Art of Allusion.* Carbondale: Southern Illinois University Press, 1980.

Crittenden, Charles. *Unreality: The Metaphysics of Fictional Objects.* Ithaca NY: Cornell University Press, 1991.

Culler, Jonathan. *The Pursuit of Signs: Semiotics, Literature, Deconstruction.* Ithaca NY: Cornell University Press, 1981.

Cytowic, Richard E. *Synesthesia: A Union of the Senses.* New York: Springer-Verlag, 1989.

Danielewski, Mark Z. *House of Leaves.* New York: Random House, 2000.

Daitch, Susan. *The Colorist.* London: Virago Press, 1989.

Davis, Lennard J. *Factual Fictions: The Origins of the English Novel.* Philadelphia: University of Pennsylvania Press, 1996.

de Certeau, Michel. *The Practice of Everyday Life.* Translated by Steven Rendall. Berkeley: University of California Press, 1984.

De Haven, Tom. *Dugan Under Ground.* New York: Metropolitan, 2001.

de Lafayette, Madame. *The Princesse De Clèves.* Translated by Nancy Mitford and Leonard Tancock. New York: Penguin, 1978.

DeLillo, Don. *White Noise.* New York: Penguin, 1985.

Doane, Mary Ann. *The Emergence of Cinematic Time: Modernity, Contingency, the Archive.* Cambridge MA: Harvard University Press, 2002.

Doležel, Lubomír. *Heterocosmica: Fiction and Possible Worlds.* Baltimore: Johns Hopkins University Press, 1998.

Dos Passos, John. *U.S.A.: The 42nd Parallel, 1919, The Big Money.* New York: Library of America, 1996.

Drucker, Johanna. *Figuring the Word: Essays on Books, Writing, and Visual Poetics.* New York: Granary Books, 1998.

Eco, Umberto. *Semiotics and the Philosophy of Language.* Bloomington: Indiana University Press, 1984.

Eliot, T. S. "Tradition and the Individual Talent." In *The Sacred Wood: Essays on Poetry and Criticism*, 47–59. London: Methuen, 1920.

Encarta 96 Encyclopedia. CD-ROM. Redmond WA: Microsoft, 1995.

Encarta Encyclopedia Deluxe 2002. CD-ROM. Redmond WA: Microsoft, 2001.

Eskelinen, Markku. "Towards Computer Game Studies." In Wardrip-Fruin and Harrigan, *First Person*, 36–44.

Ewert, Jeanne. "Art Spiegelman's *Maus* and the Graphic Narrative." In *Narrative across Media: The Languages of Storytelling*, edited by Marie-Laure Ryan, 178–93. Lincoln: University of Nebraska Press, 2004.

Federman, Raymond. "Surfiction—Four Propositions in Form of an Introduction." In *Surfiction: Fiction Now—And Tomorrow*, edited by Raymond Federman, 5–15. Chicago: Swallow, 1975.

———. *Take It or Leave It*. New York: Fiction Collective, 1976.

Fitzpatrick, Kathleen. *The Anxiety of Obsolescence: The American Novel in the Age of Television*. Nashville: Vanderbilt University Press, 2006.

Flanagan, Mary. "Hyperbodies Hyperknowledge: Women in Games, Women in Cyberpunk, and Strategies of Resistance." In *Reloaded: Rethinking Women + Cyberculture*, edited by Mary Flanagan and Austin Booth, 425–54. Cambridge MA: MIT Press, 2002.

Fludernik, Monika. *The Fictions of Language and the Languages of Fiction: The Linguistic Representation of Speech and Consciousness*. London: Routledge, 1993.

Foer, Jonathan Safran. *Extremely Loud and Incredibly Close*. Boston: Mariner, 2006.

Forster, E. M. *Aspects of the Novel*. New York: Harcourt, Brace and World, 1927.

Fowler, Robert L. "Encyclopaedias: Definitions and Theoretical Problems." In Binkley, *Pre-Modern Encyclopaedic Texts*, 3–29.

Frank, Joseph. *The Idea of Spatial Form*. New Brunswick NJ: Rutgers University Press, 1991.

Fried, Michael. *Art and Objecthood: Essays and Reviews*. Chicago: University of Chicago Press, 1998.

Friedberg, Anne. *The Virtual Window: From Alberti to Microsoft*. Cambridge MA: MIT Press, 2006.

Fuller, Matthew. *Media Ecologies: Materialist Energies in Art and Technoculture*. Cambridge MA: MIT Press, 2005.

Gage, John. *Colour and Culture: Practice and Meaning From Antiquity to Abstraction*. London: Thames and Hudson, 1993.

Galloway, Alexander R., and Eugene Thacker. *The Exploit: A Theory of Networks*. Minneapolis: University of Minnesota Press, 2007.

Gangemi, Kenneth. *The Interceptor Pilot*. London: Marion Boyars, 1980.

Gardner, John. *On Moral Fiction*. New York: Basic Books, 1978.

Gass, William H. *Fiction and the Figures of Life*. Boston: David R. Godine, 1979.

Gerrig, Richard J. *Experiencing Narrative Worlds: On the Psychological Activities of Reading*. New Haven CT: Yale University Press, 1993.

Gibson, William. *Neuromancer*. New York: Ace, 1984.

Goring, Paul. "The Shape of *To the Lighthouse*: Lily Briscoe's Painting and the Reader's Vision." *Word & Image* 10, no. 3 (July–September 1994): 222–29.

Greenberg, Clement. *Art and Culture: Critical Essays*. Boston: Beacon Press, 1961.

Gullón, Ricardo. "On Space in the Novel." *Critical Inquiry* 2 (1975): 11–28.

Gygax, Gary. *Advanced Dungeons & Dragons Players Handbook*. Lake Geneva WI: TSR Games, 1978.

Hamon, Philippe. "Rhetorical Status of the Descriptive." Translated by Patricia Baudoin. *Yale French Studies* 61 (1981): 1–26.

Harvey, W. J. *Character and the Novel*. Ithaca NY: Cornell University Press, 1965.

Hauser, Marianne. *The Talking Room*. New York: Fiction Collective, 1976.

Hayles, N. Katherine. *My Mother Was a Computer: Digital Subjects and Literary Texts*. Chicago: University of Chicago Press, 2005.

Heise, Ursula K. "Unnatural Ecologies: the Metaphor of the Environment in Media Theory." *Configurations* 10 (2003): 149–68.

Herman, David. Introduction to *The Cambridge Companion to Narrative*, edited by David Herman, 3–21. Cambridge UK: Cambridge University Press, 2007.

———. *Story Logic: Problems and Possibilities of Narrative*. Lincoln: University of Nebraska Press, 2004.

———. "Toward a Transmedial Narratology." In *Narrative across Media: The Languages of Storytelling*, edited by Marie-Laure Ryan, 47–75. Lincoln: University of Nebraska Press, 2004.

Higgins, Dick. *A Dialectic of Centuries: Notes Towards a Theory of the New Arts*. New York: Printed Editions, 1978.

Hijuelos, Oscar. *The Mambo Kings Play Songs of Love*. New York: Harper Perennial, 1992.

Hite, Molly. *Ideas of Order in the Novels of Thomas Pynchon*. Columbus: Ohio State University Pres, 1983.

Husserl, Edmund. *Ideas: General Introduction to Pure Phenomenology*. Translated by W. R. Boyce Gibson. New York: Collier Books, 1962.

James, Henry. "The Beast in the Jungle." In *The Tales of Henry James*, edited by Christof Wegelin, 277–312. Norton Critical Edition. New York: W. W. Norton, 1984.

Jenkins, Henry. *Textual Poachers: Television Fans and Participatory Culture*. New York: Routledge, 1992.

———. *Fans, Bloggers, and Gamers: Exploring Participatory Culture*. New York: New York University Press, 2006.

Johnson, John. *Information Multiplicity: American Fiction in the Age of Media Saturation*. Baltimore: Johns Hopkins University Press, 1998.

Jones, Gayl. *Corregidora.* Boston: Beacon, 1975.

Joyce, James. *Ulysses,* edited by Hans Walter Gabler. New York: Vintage, 1986.

Joyce, Michael. *Of Two Minds: Hypertext Pedagogy and Poetics.* Ann Arbor: University of Michigan Press, 1995.

Juul, Jesper. *Half-Real: Video Games Between Real Rules and Fictional Worlds.* Cambridge MA: MIT Press, 2005.

Kafalenos, Emma. "Effects of Sequence, Embedding, and Ekphrasis in Poe's 'The Oval Portrait.'" In *A Companion to Narrative Theory,* edited by James Phelan and Peter J. Rabinowitz, 253–68. Malden MA: Blackwell, 2005.

———. "Embedded Artworks: Who Sees Them and Why it Matters." Paper presented at the "Narrative and Image: New Theory for New Forms" session, MLA Convention, Chicago, December 29, 2007.

Kandinsky, Wassily. *Concerning the Spiritual in Art,* Translated by Michael T. H. Sadler. Boston: MFA Publications, 2006.

Kay, Alan, and Adele Goldberg. "Personal Dynamic Media." In Wardrip-Fruin and Montfort, *New Media Reader,* 393–404.

Kennedy, Helen W. "Lara Croft: Feminist Icon Or Cyberbimbo? On the Limits of Textual Analysis." *Game Studies* 2, no. 2 (December 2002): n.p. http://www .gamestudies.org/0202/kennedy/.

Kermode, Frank. "A Reply to Joseph Frank." *Critical Inquiry* 4 (1978): 579–88.

———. *The Sense of an Ending: Studies in the Theory of Fiction.* London: Oxford University Press, 1967.

Kernan, Alvin. *The Death of Literature.* New Haven CT: Yale University Press, 1990.

King, Stephen. *The Shining.* Garden City NY: Doubleday, 1977.

Kingston, Maxine Hong. *Tripmaster Monkey: His Fake Book.* New York: Alfred A. Knopf, 1989.

Kittler, Friedrich A. *Discourse Networks 1800/1900.* Translated by Michael Metteer. Stanford CA: Stanford University Press, 1990.

———. *Gramophone, Film, Typewriter.* Translated by Geoffrey Winthrop-Young and Michael Wutz. Stanford CA: Stanford University Press, 1999.

Krauss, Rosalind. *"A Voyage on the North Sea": Art in the Age of the Post-Medium Condition.* New York: Thames and Hudson, 1999.

Larsson, Donald F. "Every Picture Tells a Story: Agency and Narration in Film." Paper presented at the "Moves as Paradigmatic Narratives" session, MLA Convention, Washington DC, December 28, 2000. http://www.english2.mnsu.edu/ larsson/naragent.html.

Latour, Bruno. *We Have Never Been Modern.* Translated by Catherine Porter. Cambridge MA: Harvard University Press, 1993.

Lessing, Gotthold Ephraim. *Laocoön: An Essay on the Limits of Painting and Poetry.* Translated by Edward Allen McCormick. Baltimore: Johns Hopkins University Press, 1984.

Lethem, Jonathan. *The Fortress of Solitude*. New York: Doubleday, 2003.

Lukács, Georg. *The Theory of the Novel*. Translated by Anna Bostock. Cambridge MA: MIT Press, 1971.

Lunenfeld, Peter. "Screen Grabs: the Digital Dialectic and New Media Theory." In *The Digital Dialectic: New Essays on New Media*, edited by Peter Lunenfeld, xiv–xxi. Cambridge MA: MIT Press, 1999.

Manguel, Alberto. *A History of Reading*. New York: Penguin, 1996.

Manovich, Lev. *The Language of New Media*. Cambridge MA: MIT Press, 2001.

Martin, Wallace. *Recent Theories of Narrative*. Ithaca NY: Cornell University Press, 1986.

Maso, Carole. *The Art Lover*. New York: New Directions, 1995.

McCarthy, Mary. "The Fact in Fiction." *Partisan Review* 27, no. 3 (Summer 1960): 438–58.

McCloud, Scott. *Understanding Comics: The Invisible Art*. New York: HarperCollins, 1994.

McHale, Brian. *Constructing Postmodernism*. London: Routledge, 1992.

———. "En Abyme: Internal Models and Cognitive Mapping." In *A Sense of the World: Essays on Fiction, Narrative, and Knowledge*, edited by John Gibson, Wolfgang Huemer, and Luca Pocci, 189–205. New York: Routledge, 2007.

———. *Postmodernist Fiction*. New York: Methuen, 1987.

McKeon, Michael. *Origins of the English Novel, 1600–1740*. Baltimore: Johns Hopkins University Press, 1987.

McLuhan, Marshall. *The Gutenberg Galaxy: The Making of Typographic Man*. Toronto: University of Toronto Press, 1962.

Meltzer, Françoise. *Salome and the Dance of Writing: Portraits of Mimesis in Literature*. Chicago: University of Chicago Press, 1987.

Melville, Herman. *Moby-Dick: Or, the Whale*. Edited by Harold Beaver. New York: Penguin, 1972.

Mendelson, Edward. "Encyclopedic Narrative: From Dante to Pynchon." *MLN* 91 (1976): 1267–75.

Mittell, Jason. "Film and Television Narrative." In Herman, *Cambridge Companion to Narrative*, 156–71.

Morrison, Toni. *Jazz*. New York: Alfred A. Knopf, 1992.

Morrissette, Bruce. *Novel and Film: Essays in Two Genres*. Chicago: University of Chicago Press, 1985.

Morson, Gary Saul. *Narrative and Freedom: The Shadows of Time*. New Haven CT: Yale University Press, 1994.

Motte, Warren F. Jr. Introduction to *Oulipo: A Primer of Potential Literature*, edited by Warren F. Motte Jr., 1–22. Lincoln: University of Nebraska Press, 1986.

Müller, Jürgen E. "Intermediality: a Plea and Some Theses for a New Approach in Media Studies." *Interart Poetics: Essays on the Interrelations of the Arts and*

Media. Eds. Ulla-Britta Lagerroth, Hans Lund, and Erik Hedling. Amsterdam: Rodopi, 1997. 295–304.

Murray, Janet H. *Hamlet on the Holodeck: The Future of Narrative in Cyberspace.* Cambridge MA: MIT Press, 1997.

Nardi, Bonnie A. and Vicki L. O'Day. *Information Ecologies: Using Technology With Heart.* Cambridge MA: MIT Press, 1999.

Nell, Victor. *Lost in a Book: The Psychology of Reading for Pleasure.* New Haven CT: Yale University Press, 1988.

The New Grolier Multimedia Encyclopedia. Version 5.01. CD-ROM. Danbury CT: Grolier Electronic Publishing, 1992.

Newton, Adam Zachary. *Narrative Ethics.* Cambridge MA: Harvard University Press, 1995.

North, Stephen M. *The Making of Knowledge in Composition: Portrait of an Emerging Field.* Portsmouth: Boynton/Cook, 1987.

Nunes, Mark. *Cyberspaces of Everyday Life.* Minneapolis: University of Minnesota Press, 2006.

O'Neill, Patrick. *Fictions of Discourse: Reading Narrative Theory.* Toronto: University of Toronto Press, 1994.

Ogden, C. K., I. A. Richards, and James Woods. *The Foundations of Aesthetics.* London: George Allen & Unwin, 1922.

Palmer, Alan. *Fictional Minds.* Lincoln: University of Nebraska Press, 2004.

Pavel, Thomas G. *Fictional Worlds.* Cambridge MA: Harvard University Press, 1986.

Perlin, Ken. "Can There Be a Form Between a Game and a Story?" In Wardrip-Fruin and Harrigan, *First Person*, 12–18.

Phelan, James. *Experiencing Fiction: Judgments, Progression, and the Rhetorical Theory of Narrative.* Columbus: Ohio State University Press, 2007.

——. *Living to Tell About It: A Rhetoric and Ethics of Character Narration.* Ithaca NY: Cornell University Press, 2005.

——. *Narrative as Rhetoric: Technique, Audiences, Ethics, Ideology.* Columbus: Ohio State University Press, 1996.

——. *Reading People, Reading Plots: Character, Progression, and the Interpretation of Narrative.* Chicago: University of Chicago Press, 1989.

Postman, Neil. *Technopoly: The Surrender of Culture to Technology.* New York: Vintage, 1993.

Prince, Gerald. *Narrative as Theme: Studies in French Fiction.* Lincoln: University of Nebraska Press, 1992.

Punday, Daniel. "The Black Arts Movement and the Genealogy of Multimedia." *New Literary History* 37 (2007): 777–94.

——. "From Synesthesia to Multimedia: How to Talk about New Media Narrative." In *New Narratives: Theory and Practice*, edited by Ruth Page and Bronwen Thomas, 19–34. Lincoln: University of Nebraska Press, 2011.

Putnam, Michael C. J. "Dido's Murals and Virgilian Ekphrasis." *Harvard Studies in Classical Philology* 98 (1998): 243–75.

Pynchon, Thomas. *Gravity's Rainbow*. New York: Penguin, 1987.

——. *Vineland*. Boston: Little, Brown, 1990.

Rainey, Lawrence. *Institutions of Modernism: Literary Elites and Public Culture*. New Haven CT: Yale University Press, 1998.

Reed, Ishmael. *Yellow Back Radio Broke-Down*. Normal IL: Dalkey Archive, 2000.

Richardson, Brian. *Narrative Dynamics: Essays on Time, Plot, Closure, and Frames*. Columbus: Ohio State University Press, 2002.

Ricoeur, Paul. *Time and Narrative*. Translated by Kathleen McLaughlin and David Pellauer. Vol. 1. Chicago: University of Chicago Press, 1984.

Robbins, Tom. *Still Life With Woodpecker*. Toronto: Bantam, 1980.

Rodriguez, Abraham. *The Buddha Book*. New York: Picador, 2001.

——. "Space in Fiction." *Poetics Today* 7 (1986): 421–38.

Rose, Phyllis. *The Year of Reading Proust: a Memoir in Real Time*. Washington, DC: Counterpoint, 1997.

Rubin, Joan Shelley. *The Making of Middlebrow Culture*. Chapel Hill: University of North Carolina Press, 1992.

Rubin, Louis D. *The Curious Death of the Novel: Essays in American Literature*. Baton Rouge: Louisiana State University Press, 1967.

Rubincam, Catherine. "The Organisation of Material in Graeco-Roman World Histories." In Binkley, *Pre-Modern Encyclopedic Texts*, 127–36.

Ryan, Marie-Laure. *Avatars of Story*. Minneapolis: University of Minnesota Press, 2006.

——. Introduction to *Narrative across Media: the Languages of Storytelling*, edited by Marie-Laure Ryan, 1–40. Lincoln: University of Nebraska Press, 2004.

——, ed. *Narrative as Virtual Reality: Immersion and Interactivity in Literature and Electronic Media*. Baltimore: Johns Hopkins University Press, 2001.

——. *Possible Worlds, Artificial Intelligence, and Narrative Theory*. Bloomington: Indiana University Press, 1991.

Saper, Craig J. *Networked Art*. Minneapolis: University of Minnesota Press, 2001.

Schiesel, Seth. "Conquering the Burning Crusade." *New York Times*, January 31, 2007. http://nytimes.com/ref/arts/warcraft-journal.html.

Shaviro, Steven. *Connected: Or What it Means to Live in the Network Society*. Minneapolis: University of Minnesota Press, 2003.

Spiegel, Alan. *Fiction and the Camera Eye: Visual Consciousness in Film and the Modern Novel*. Charlottesville: University Press of Virginia, 1976.

Stanzel, F. K. *A Theory of Narrative*. Translated by Charlotte Goedsche. Cambridge UK: Cambridge University Press, 1984.

Steiner, Wendy. *The Colors of Rhetoric: Problems in the Relation Between Modern Literature and Painting*. Chicago: University of Chicago Press, 1982.

Sudan, Rajani. "Sexy SIMS, Racy SIMS." In *Race in Cyberspace*, ed. Beth E. Kolko, Lisa Nakamura, and Gilbert B. Rodman, 69–86. New York: Routledge, 2000.

Sukenick, Ronald. *Blown Away*. Los Angeles: Sun & Moon, 1986.

———. "Duck Tape." In *The Endless Short Story*, 68–87. New York: Fiction Collective, 1986.

———. *Long Talking Bad Conditions Blues*. New York: Fiction Collective, 1979.

Suvin, Darko. "On Metaphoricity and Narrativity in Fiction: The Chronotope as the *Differentia Generica*." *SubStance* 14, no. 3 (1986): 51–67.

Tabbi, Joseph. *Postmodern Sublime: Technology and American Writing from Mailer to Cyberpunk*. Ithaca NY: Cornell University Press, 1995.

Tabbi, Joseph, and Michael Wutz. Introduction to *Reading Matters: Narrative in the New Media Ecology*, ed. Joseph Tabbi and Michael Wutz, 1–25. Ithaca NY: Cornell University Press, 1997.

Taylor, T.L. *Play Between Worlds: Exploring Online Game Culture*. Cambridge MA: MIT Press, 2006.

Thackeray, William Makepeace. *Vanity Fair: A Novel Without a Hero*. Ed. John Carey. New York: Penguin, 2001.

Torgovnick, Marianna. *The Visual Arts, Pictorialism, and the Novel: James, Lawrence, and Woolf*. Princeton NJ: Princeton University Press, 1985.

Traylor, Eleanor W. "Music as Theme: The Jazz Mode in the Works of Toni Cade Bambara." In *Black Women Writers (1950–1980): A Critical Evaluation*, ed. Mari Evans, 58–70. New York: Anchor Books, 1984.

Turkle, Sherry. *Life on the Screen: Identity in the Age of the Internet*. New York: Simon & Schuster, 1995.

Turner, Mark. *The Literary Mind*. Oxford: Oxford University Press, 1996.

Tuten, Frederic. *Tintin in the New World: A Romance*. New York: Riverhead, 1993.

Virgil. *The Aeneid of Virgil*. Translated by Allen Mandelbaum. New York: Bantam, 1971.

Vonnegut, Kurt. *Breakfast of Champions*. New York: Dial, 2006.

Wagner, Richard. *The Art-Work of the Future and Other Works*. Translated by William Ashton Ellis. Lincoln: University of Nebraska Press, 1993.

Walsh, Richard. *The Rhetoric of Fictionality: Narrative Theory and the Idea of Fiction*. Columbus: Ohio State University Press, 2007.

Walton, Kendall L. *Mimesis as Make-Believe: On the Foundations of the Representational Arts*. Cambridge MA: Harvard University Press, 1990.

Wardrip-Fruin, Noah, and Pat Harrigan, eds. *First Person: New Media as Story, Performance, and Game*. Cambridge MA: MIT Press, 2004.

Wardrip-Fruin, Noah, and Nick Montfort, eds. *The New Media Reader*. Cambridge MA: MIT Press, 2003.

Warhol, Andy. *The Philosophy of Andy Warhol (From A to B and Back Again)*. San Diego: Harvest, 1977.

Warhol, Robyn R. *Having a Good Cry: Effeminate Feelings and Pop-Culture Forms.* Columbus: Ohio State University Press, 2003.

Watt, Ian. *The Rise of the Novel: Studies in Defoe, Richardson, and Fielding.* Berkeley: University of California Press, 1957.

Werth, Paul. *Text Worlds: Representing Conceptual Space in Discourse.* New York: Longman, 1999.

Williams, Raymond. *Culture and Society: 1780–1950.* New York: Columbia University Press, 1983.

———. *Television: Technology and Cultural Form.* Second ed. London: Routledge, 1990.

Wimsatt, W.K. *The Verbal Icon: Studies in the Meaning of Poetry.* Lexington: University Press of Kentucky, 1954.

Winthrop-Young, Geoffrey, and Michael Wutz. "Introduction: Media—Models, Memories, and Metaphors." *Configurations* 10 (2002): 1–10.

Wolf, Werner. "Metalepsis as a Transgeneric and Transmedial Phenomenon: A Case Study of the Possibilities of 'Exporting' Narratological Concepts." In *Narratology Beyond Literary Criticism: Mediality, Disciplinarity*, ed. Jan Christoph Meister, 83–107. Berlin: Walter de Gruyter, 2005.

———. "Musicalized Fiction and Intermediality: Theoretical Aspects of Word and Music Studies." In *Word and Music Studies: Defining the Field*, ed. Walter Bernhart, Steven Paul Scher, and Werner Wolf, 37–58. Amsterdam: Rodopi, 1999.

Wolfe, Tom. "The New Journalism." In *The New Journalism*, ed. Tom Wolfe and E. W. Johnson, 1–52. New York: Harper & Row, 1973.

Wolfley, Lawrence C. "Repression's Rainbow: The Presence of Norman O. Brown in Pynchon's Big Novel." *PMLA* 92 (1977): 873–89.

Woolf, Virginia. *To the Lighthouse.* San Diego: Harvest, 1981.

Yacobi, Tamar. "Pictorial Models and Narrative Ekphrasis." *Poetics Today* 16 (1995): 599–649.

Zoran, Gabriel. "Towards a Theory of Space in Narrative." *Poetics Today* 5 (1984): 309–35.

Zunshine, Lisa. "Theory of Mind and Fictions of Embodied Transparency." *Narrative* 16, no. 1 (2008): 65–92.

———. *Why We Read Fiction: Theory of Mind and of the Novel.* Columbus: Ohio State University Press, 2006.

Index

tellability of a story, 133
Tetris, 202
Thacker, Eugene, 178
theater, 24, 49, 61–63
thought. *See* character, and the representation of minds
Three Farmers on Their Way to a Dance (Powers), 151, 183–84
time, sacred vs. simultaneity, 206–7, 210, 213–17
Tintin in the New World (Tuten), 152
Tomb Raider, 197–200, 202, 246n19
Torgovnick, Marianna, 46–47
To the Lighthouse (Woolf), 53–54
transmedia, 113
transparency in narrative, 40, 185–86, 189–201
Traylor, Eleanor, 64, 67
Tripmaster Monkey (Kingston), 38, 61–63, 66–67, 69, 24
Turkle, Sherry, 185–86, 196
Turner, Mark, 240–41n1
typewriter, 96

Ulysses (Joyce), 17, 57, 60
U.S.A. (Dos Passos), 55–56

video games, 189, 197–201
Vineland (Pynchon), 38, 74–80, 81, 84, 98, 146, 205
visual design, 97–100

Wagner, Richard, 23, 163
Walsh, Richard, 240n10, 243n8

Walter Mitty, 125–26
Warhol, Andy, 83–84
Warhol, Robyn, 121–22
Watt, Ian, 206
Werth, Paul, 181, 242n5
White Noise (DeLillo), 3, 40, 143–52, 205, 224
Wikipedia, 160, 168–70, 173
Williams, Raymond, 8, 25
Wimsatt, W. K., 24
window (computer), 199–201
Wittgenstein, Ludwig, 191
Wolf, Werner, 114, 116, 240n9, 241n5
Wolfe, Tom, 32
Wolfley, Lawrence, 244n7
Woods, James, 240n8
world. *See* fictional world
World of Warcraft, 186–88
Worth, Sol, 134
writing, 40, 68–69, 73, 77, 232–33; associated with the absent, 114, 126, 136, 150; discovered manuscript topos in, 45–46; to reveal the logic of a fictional world, 134–35; under constraint, 74; and written narrative, 37–38. *See also* typewriter
Wutz, Michael, 12–13

Yacobi, Tamar, 51, 117
Yellow Back Radio Broke-Down (Reed), 33, 85–90, 94, 224

Zoran, Gabriel, 245n11
Zunshine, Lisa, 33, 191–92

To order or obtain more information on these or other University of Nebraska Press titles, visit www.nebraskapress.unl.edu.